D0457473

Also by Howard Blum

Nonfiction

WANTED! THE SEARCH FOR NAZIS IN AMERICA

I PLEDGE ALLEGIANCE . . . THE STORY OF THE WALKER SPY FAMILY

OUT THERE

GANGLAND

Fiction

WISHFUL THINKING

The Discovery of the True Mount Sinai

Howard Blum

Simon & Schuster

THE GOLD OF EXODUS

SIMON & SCHUSTER
Rockefeller Center
1230 Avenue of the Americas
New York, NY 10020

Designed by Karolina Harris
Manufactured in the United States of America

10 9 8 7 6 5 4 3 2

Library of Congress Cataloging-in-Publication Data
Blum, Howard, date
The gold of Exodus : the discovery of the most sacred place on earth /
Howard Blum.
p. cm.
Includes bibliographical references.
1. Middle East—Politics and government—1979– 2. Saudi Arabia—
Defenses. 3. Espionage—Israel. 4. Saudi Arabia—Antiquities.
I. Title.
DS63.1B59 1998 97-33296
956.05—dc21 CIP
ISBN 0-684-80918-4
A portion of this book was published in slightly altered form in
Vanity Fair.

In memory of

my parents,

Gertrude and Harold Blum,

and Dan Wolf,

my friend.

Contents

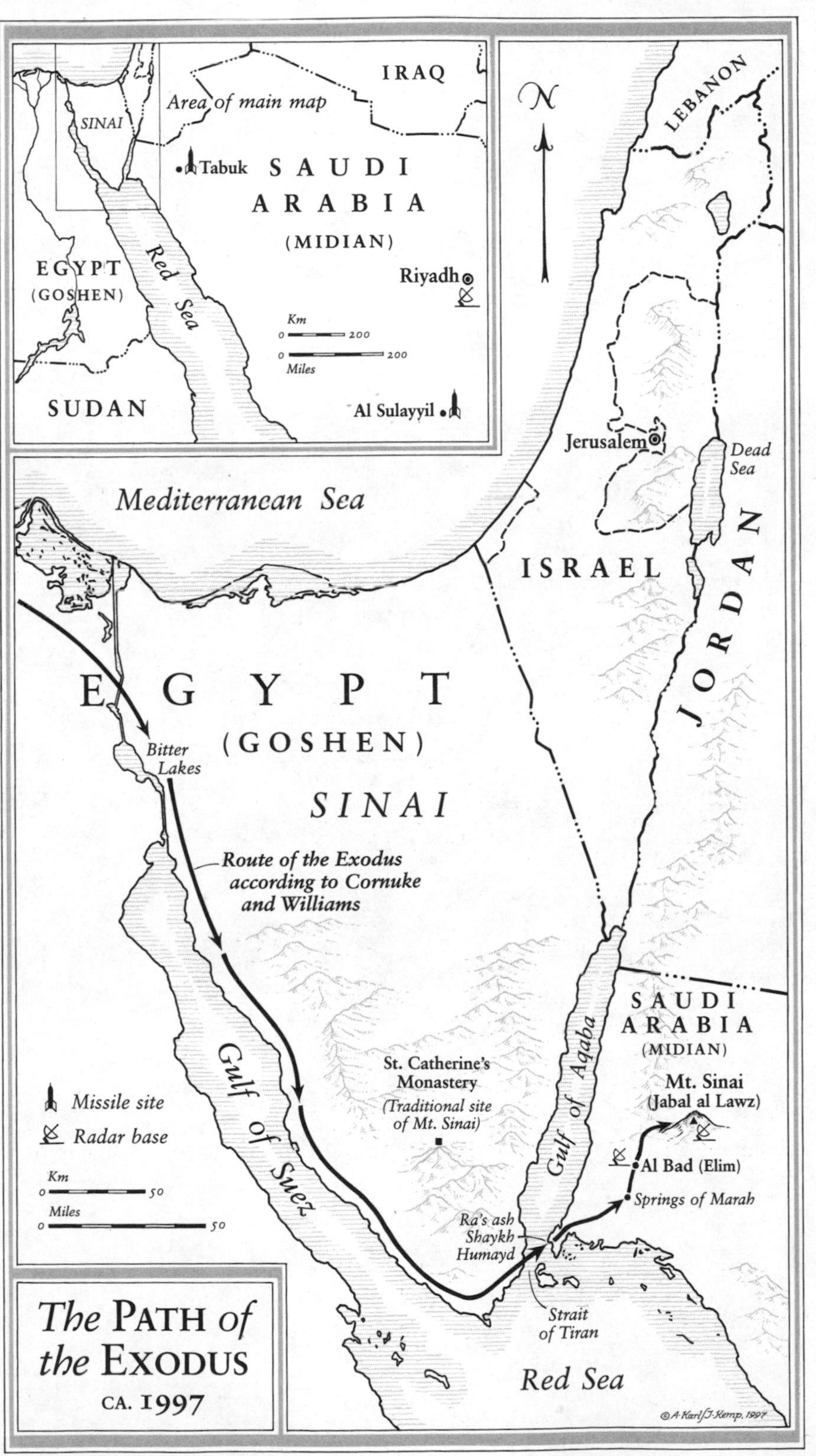

IRAQ
Area of main map
SINAI
Tabuk
SAUDI ARABIA
(MIDIAN)
EGYPT
(GOSHEN)
Red Sea
Riyadh
Km
0
200
0
200
Miles
SUDAN
Al Sulayyil
LEBANON
Jerusalem
Dead Sea
Mediterranean Sea
ISRAEL
JORDAN
EGYPT
(GOSHEN)
Bitter Lakes
SINAI
Route of the Exodus according to Cornuke and Williams
SAUDI ARABIA
(MIDIAN)
Gulf of Suez
Gulf of Aqaba
St. Catherine's Monastery
(Traditional site of Mt. Sinai)
Mt. Sinai
(Jabal al Lawz)
Missile site
Radar base
Km
0
50
Miles
0
50
Al Bad (Elim)
Springs of Marah
Ra's ash Shaykh Humayd
Strait of Tiran
Red Sea
©A·Karl/J·Kemp, 1997

The PATH of the EXODUS
CA. 1997

"Take heed that you do not go up into the mountain or touch the border of it; whoever touches the mountain shall be surely put to death."

THE BOOK OF EXODUS, *19:12*

"The thing about the ends of the earth is that someone somewhere—usually in Langley, Virginia—will imagine that they have strategic value."

Christopher Dickey, EXPATS

Prologue: The Descent

The Desert Southeast of Tabuk, Saudi Arabia: 1988

JUST before daybreak, Bob Cornuke decided they should leave the cave. The way he explained it to Larry Williams, if they headed down the mountain while it was still dark, at least they would have a couple of things working for them. First, they had a pair of night-vision binoculars to illuminate the narrow trail. And second, as best he could tell, things were still quiet in the concrete guardhouse at the base of the mountain; with a little luck the soldiers would not stir until after morning prayers. Cornuke tried to lay it all out in the same calm, reasonable voice his SWAT team lieutenant had used whenever he was sending them into something that had a large chance of going bad. And, another kindness, Cornuke decided there was no point in mentioning that even if down in the valley the soldiers were sleeping, that was no guarantee that night patrols were not combing the mountain. If there were soldiers out there, he figured, his friend would find out soon enough.

After only a moment's consideration, Williams agreed that the plan made sense, or at least as much sense as anything was making these days. A month ago his biggest worry was the dent his wife had put in the Rolls while backing into a tight space at Nordstrom's. Now he was about to crawl away from a musky cave to head down a treacherously steep mountain in the dark of night; and, one further complication, the mountain happened to be standing in the middle of a Saudi Arabian military base. "No problem," he assured Cornuke.

When they left, Williams led the way. He knew if he did not take that first step, he might never take one. He headed toward the ledge that led away from the cave, and all at once he heard the wind. It blew over the desert with a fierce, insistent, high-pitched whine. The noise was loud, but insufficient, Williams feared, to deaden the wild thumping of his heart.

They walked slowly, and since the path was narrow they went one behind the other like Indians. Footing was difficult; the mountain was mostly rock. But they made good progress, and after a while Williams was able to see with the night-vision binoculars down to the section of barbed-wire fence they had crawled under almost six hours ago. He was about to tell Cornuke when suddenly he was pushed to the ground from behind, the wind nearly knocked out of him. It was a moment before he realized that it was Cornuke's bulk on top of him, and his friend's hand wrapped tight across his mouth. "Quiet!" Cornuke commanded in a whisper.

There was a small hesitation, the overwhelming desire to do nothing; but then, moving carefully, Williams raised his head just inches from the ground and he saw it too: two silhouettes moving behind a boulder a hundred yards or so off, red-checkered *gutras* wrapped around their heads and Kalashnikovs strapped over their shoulders.

The two men lay there hugging the ground in the darkness until the figures moved noiselessly on. But even after the patrol had long disappeared down some unseen path, Cornuke and Williams couldn't find the will to go on. It wasn't until the sky was lightening, and they began to hear the first stirrings from the guardhouse, that they realized it was now or never. Besides, Williams reminded himself, there was still something else he needed to prove. It was the part of the mystery that, back in what now seemed like another lifetime, had first moved him to come to the mountain.

They both got to their feet. When they didn't hear a round of automatic fire come blasting at them, they silently gave thanks and continued the short distance down the mountain to the valley.

A FLAT, rocky plain without even a tree for cover stood between the base of the mountain and the barbed-wire fence. But there was no other way out, and so, on a count of three, they made a dash for it. There was no stealth, no pretense of quiet. All that mattered was getting to the fence and finding the spot by the dried-up creek bed where they had earlier dug a crawl space in the spongy sand. Williams was a marathoner, but after just a hundred yards he was huffing mightily since he had never before run for his life. Cornuke had not gone full out since he had blown his knee on a fullback sweep more than a decade earlier. But even if he had been years younger with a packed stadium cheering him on, he could not have imagined himself ever running faster than he did that morning across the desert sand. They hit the fence in a dead heat.

With both hands, Cornuke held up the fence and Williams crawled under on his belly. When he was on the other side, it was Cornuke's turn. He got down on all fours, ready to go, but all at once there was a noise as loud as the crack of a rifle. It was an unsteady instant that seemed like an eternity before they realized the door to the guardhouse had swung open. A soldier had come out to pee. Cornuke waited until the sound of urine hissing into the sand had subsided, and then he, too, crawled easily under the fence to safety.

The sun was now high, and the desert was beginning to bake. It was a mile or so walk from the fence to the wadi where they had hidden their truck, and, hot and completely exhausted, they took their time. Still, they felt good. It looked as if they had made it. And when they saw the truck sitting just as they had left it, their supplies still loaded in the rear, for the first time they congratulated one another. They had pulled it off! Done the impossible!

It was only as they were walking the final ten yards toward their campsite that the two Bedouins stepped out from behind a large bush. Where they had been waiting all along.

One of the Bedouins, the taller man, leveled a 12-gauge shotgun at them. Williams saw the weapon and, instead of coming to a stop, moved in closer. He had grown up in Montana and knew a bit about guns. A 12-gauge was only a single-shot, so he quickly calculated that maybe only one of them would have to die. He took another step toward the gunman. That was the other thing about shotguns: They need distance to be effective; up close the shooter has no room to maneuver.

The Bedouin waved the gun threateningly, motioning for Williams to stand still. But he took another small step forward. He wanted to get close enough at least to make a grab for the weapon. After all Williams had gone through, he was prepared to risk his life.

He caught Cornuke's eye. His friend understood. Now it was Cornuke's turn to take a small step toward the gunman. Simultaneously the two men inched slowly forward. The gunman was shouting, but they pretended not to understand. All that mattered was that at least one of them survive. One of them had to make it out of the desert to tell the world what they had seen on the mountain known as Jabal al Lawz.

Part One

PROJECT FALCON

1

Riyadh, Saudi Arabia: 1979

THE meeting was at midnight, and the king was the last to arrive. The members of the Saudi Higher Officers' Committee immediately jumped to attention when King Fahd, accompanied by his brother, Prince Sultan, who was the kingdom's minister of defense, entered. The windowless room was hidden two floors below the Air Force headquarters on Old Airport Road in Riyadh, and it was known as the "Black Hole." The name was grim but appropriate: The room was totally secure, a cave of secrets.

The king and Prince Sultan took seats at the head of the long table, but the officers continued to stand at attention. After a moment, the king began. On most occasions he spoke softly, people strained to listen, and his words often came slowly, a hesitancy that seemed more awkward than thoughtful. Tonight, however, his tone was a monarch's—firm and commanding. He did not speak for long, but what he said was spoken with such force that the words nearly echoed off the soundproofed walls.

The time has come, the king began according to a classified report that made its way years later to the CIA, for Saudi Arabia to become a power in the Middle East. There was a brief mention of Israel, how the defeat in the 1973 war had been "humiliating," but the king spoke mostly about his "sacred responsibility" to protect Islam's holy shrines at Mecca and Medina. "I am the Custodian of the Two Holy Mosques," he declared repeatedly. Saudi Arabia must be able to stand alone, proud and unafraid. His voice steady and emphatic, his words built to a declaration that was spoken with such intensity that it might as well have been a vow: We will pay any price. We will do whatever is necessary. But the kingdom must be able to defend itself. We must have a superweapon.

The king left immediately, but Prince Sultan and the members of the Higher Officers' Committee stayed past dawn. By the time the meeting ended on that spring morning in 1979, the preliminary plans had been made for what would become known as Project Falcon.

IT had been King Fahd's father, the visionary and decadent King Abd al-Aziz, who had introduced the brutal effectiveness of modern weaponry to the kingdom. Threatened by a revolt of his own private army of Bedouin warriors in 1929, the monarch sent emissaries off to England. When the expensive fruits of these hurried negotiations were delivered, he launched his counterattack at the Battle of Sabillah. Waves and waves of shrieking Bedouins, their cutlasses held high, came thundering across the sand on galloping horses and camels. It was a fearless, bloodcurdling charge—straight into a wadi where a long column of newly purchased armored cars mounted with British-made machine guns waited.

The automatic weapons opened fire as if at target practice. The desert warriors pushed on, too brave (or, truth be told, confused) to retreat. The guns spurted round after round, their overheated metal barrels glowing dangerously as if ready to combust. And still more rebels rushed toward the guns. As legend has it, Bedouins were slaughtered by the hundreds that day. With that bloody victory, the king, who by this juncture in his dissolute life was forced to use a long, hook-handled cane to support his bulk, became known forever to his intimidated subjects as "the Falcon of the Peninsula."

More than five decades later, as Prince Sultan and the Higher Officers' Committee began formulating their bold strategy to bring a superweapon to the kingdom, it was decided to pay wishful homage to this warrior heritage. Air Force General Khaled bin Sultan, who was the prince's son (and grandson of the old monarch) rather proudly came up with the idea. The general, a chunky, barrel-chested career soldier who commanded with the mirthless, officious demeanor of someone determined to prove himself worthy of the privileges birth had bestowed, recommended to his father that, as a matter of security, their activities needed a code name: Project Falcon—*al-Saqr* in Arabic—after the old "Falcon of the Peninsula," he suggested. The prince was impressed and delighted; the years he had served in the palace had left him with a genuine fondness for intrigue. He quickly summoned the Higher Officers' Committee. The battle of Sabillah, he told the officers, would seem like child's play when compared to the destruction Project Falcon would soon be able to inflict on Saudi Arabia's enemies.

YET while King Abd al-Aziz had to worry only about a few rebellious nomadic tribes, the modern kingdom was surrounded. Its 865,000 miles of mostly empty, barren land fronted on the Red Sea, the Persian Gulf, and a world of potential aggressors. To the north was Saddam Hussein's Iraq with its territorial ambitions and well-financed armed forces. To the east was a similarly hostile—and similarly unpredictable—Iran. On the southern flank was a newly unified Yemen. While to the west, just a stone's throw (or warship's barrage) across the Red Sea, was Jordanian and Iranian ally Sudan. Of course, there was also the threat posed by an increasingly unrestrained Israel; when it appeared possible that the Jewish forces would be overrun in the opening push of the Yom Kippur war, Moshe Dayan, the Israeli defense minister, had sent a warning to the Arab capitals that nuclear weapons would be launched if their armies did not withdraw. And not least, there was still one more simmering anxiety: the enemy within. The Muslim fundamentalists were becoming more organized and belligerent throughout the kingdom.

But as the 1980s began, the Higher Officers' Committee also had at its disposal a means, if not to solve, at least to assuage all these somber concerns—money, barrels and barrels of petro-billions. As luck—or Allah—would have it, the sandy, largely desolate kingdom was sitting on top of the largest oil reserve in the world. With the price of oil quadrupling over the last decade, a seemingly endless supply of money—as much as $30 billion annually by some estimates—began pouring into the kingdom. By the end of 1982, the country's central bank had an unprecedented $145 billion in foreign assets. "A shower of gold" was how an overwhelmed American ambassador accurately appraised the situation. And now, after a generation or so of energetically investigating the proposition of whether money could, indeed, buy a garish gold-plated happiness, the royal house of Saud decided it might be a more prudent investment to discover if money could buy security.

AND so on the king's orders, and with his coffers flung open wide, the Higher Officers' Committee began to move Project Falcon forward. The first tentative steps were taken in Washington in full view of the United States Congress.

On October 1, 1981, the Pentagon's Defense Security Assistance Agency passed on for approval to the Senate and House the tersely worded Transmittal Number 81-96. As required by the Arms Export Control Act, this brief document stated that the Air Force had found no strategic reason to refuse Saudi Arabia's request to purchase five Airborne Warning and Control System (AWACS) aircraft for $8.5 billion.

Congress, however, was more wary. There was a month of passionate, often shrill ("Hell no to the PLO!" was a frequent refrain) debate in both chambers. Yet at its conclusion, a majority of both the House and the Senate was persuaded that the radar-equipped planes were a defensive early warning system and not a threat to Israel or the fragile Middle East peace. Or, more pragmatically, that for $8.5 billion it was worth the risk. The purchase was approved.

But in all the fiery debate, there was never a thorough public analysis of *what* Transmittal No. 81-96 was allowing the Saudis to buy. If there had been, the senators and congressmen might have focused on paragraph iii of the single-page addendum. In addition to the five aircraft, the Saudis were also getting approval for the future "design, construction, and supply of required AWAC related ground base Command, Control, and Communications (C3) facilities and equipment, including an appropriate number of ground radar."

A C3 network is a coordinated nationwide air defense system that, like a high-tech trip wire, sets off alarms when an enemy plane intrudes into a country's airspace. But when certain strategic capabilities are added, a C3 network can become an offensive weapon—a means to launch a coordinated first strike. A ballistic missile is one "strategic capability" that immediately transforms the system.

IT took the Higher Officers' Committee four years to find its ballistic missiles. Actually, locating the weapons was easy; the roll call of nations possessing long-range surface-to-surface missiles is, as a matter of pride and military strategy, widely disseminated. The tricky part, however, was to find a government that was both willing to sell such advanced weaponry to Saudi Arabia and able to complete the complex transaction in total secrecy. The Higher Officers' Committee's constant fear was that Project Falcon would come to an abrupt end if either the United States or Israel learned of the purchase before the missiles were operational.

It was Prince Bandar bin Sultan, the Saudi ambassador to Washington famous for extravagant parties in both Aspen and the capital, where the champagne and caviar flowed as extravagantly as oil from the desert, who, in 1984, first carefully approached the Chinese. His secret mission to Beijing resulted in Lieutenant General Cao Gangchuan, deputy chief of the General Staff of the People's Liberation Army, coming to Saudi Arabia to discuss the possibility of a sale in more detail. The general flew directly to a remote desert air base and, one further security measure, emerged from his room only in the thick dark of the desert night for talks with members of the Higher Officers' Committee.

The negotiations continued for over a year with Prince Khaled bin Sultan, the air defense minister, now in charge. He hosted nearly a dozen tense, late-night sessions at a series of military bases hidden away in isolated patches of desert. He flew his own plane to China and at a secure facility in the northwest provinces was allowed to see a row of erect missiles on their launch pads, liquid fuel steaming from their engines, ready to be launched. And in a hotel room in Hong Kong, under an umbrella lined with metal foil to prevent electronic surveillance, the prince held whispered conversations with Chinese envoys. His mission, as ordered by the Higher Officers' Committee and his father, Prince Sultan, was not simply limited to negotiating a purchase price for the sale of missiles. He had to select a team of Saudi officers and men who would be trained both in China and in the kingdom as launch crews; arrange for the shipment of the weapons; and build secure operational and storage facilities for the missiles in a number of strategically chosen sites throughout Saudi Arabia. And, if Project Falcon ever were to succeed, it all had to be accomplished in complete secrecy.

Yet the prince did it. It cost a sum estimated to be in excess of $20 billion, and late in 1985, the first ships from China carrying 28 ballistic missiles began to arrive at the deliberately obscure Red Sea port of Al Qadhima. Known by the deceptively poetic name Dong

Feng, or "East Wind," the missiles were single-stage rockets fueled by liquid propellant. They had a maximum surface-to-surface range of about 2,500 miles. And they were able to carry a nuclear warhead.

It was that capability more than anything else that made the Higher Officers' Committee willing to pay any price to buy them.

THE Islamic bomb. A nuclear device that would transform the entire balance of power in the Middle East. A superweapon that would protect the House of Saud against its enemies. All along, from that first midnight meeting in the Black Hole, this had been the main operational thrust of Project Falcon. The C3 system, the ballistic missiles—these, however vital to the plan's ultimate success, were mere sideshows to the long-term secret push by the Higher Officers' Committee to acquire a nuclear weapon. An offensive missile delivery system, the officers understood, was of negligible strategic value without something to deliver.

Under the stern and urgent leadership of Prince Sultan, the Higher Officers' Committee worked simultaneously on several fronts to achieve nuclear capability. Nearly 350 miles southwest of Riyadh, on the edge of what was known as Empty Quarter, in the bleak oasis of Al Sulayyil, a nuclear weapons development program was started. At vast expense, a sprawling concrete-and-glass headquarters for this secret project was quickly built. A "nuclear library" containing unclassified papers (and, since money was no object, a few restricted ones) that detailed nuclear weapon technology in countries throughout the world was established in one wing. Foreign scientists, many of them Muslims from Western universities, were quietly recruited with promises of both fabulous salaries and, a rarer gift, citizenship. Yet even as these scientists settled in at their new laboratory in the middle of the desert and began their first, preliminary labors to build the Saudi bomb, the Higher Officers' Committee was also busy trying to buy one.

A deal was quickly struck with their fellow Muslims in Pakistan.

The Pakistani nuclear program, begun in 1969, had never tested an actual weapon, but its scientists had succeeded in manufacturing the components for several bombs. The Saudis agreed to fund further Pakistani nuclear research lavishly, and in return Pakistan signed a secret treaty. If the kingdom were attacked with nuclear weapons, Pakistan would unleash its primitive nuclear arsenal against the aggressor.

And in a tent erected on the outskirts of the dusty border town of Judeida, the desert for miles in each direction cordoned off by crack Saudi troops, members of the Higher Officers' Committee attended a clandestine two-day seminar with Iraqi nuclear officials. The Saudis listened as the Iraqis, full of militant optimism, insisted that their country's program to turn low-grade uranium into bomb-grade material had been only marginally set back by the Israeli destruction of its nuclear reactor at Osirak in 1981. It would not be long, one year, perhaps two, before their scientists would be able to manufacture a two-megaton bomb—if, the Iraqi officials pointedly suggested, they could only find sufficient funds to help bankroll this technology.

After consulting with the king, Prince Sultan struggled to ignore his misgivings and entered into one more covert treaty. He fully realized the mercurial, if not Faustian, dimensions of any deal with Saddam Hussein. Nevertheless, the king had reiterated his command: A superweapon must be had at any price. Saudi Arabia secretly agreed to invest billions in the Iraqi program, and in return the kingdom was promised a share of the weapons that would be produced.

Like extravagant gamblers, then, the Higher Officers' Committee had spread its high-stake nuclear bets lavishly around the table. One, the officers confidently believed, would be bound to come up a winner. It was only a matter of time.

UNLESS they ran out of time. Unless Project Falcon was discovered. Unless the Israelis or the Americans somehow stumbled upon the foreign construction teams working in the far reaches of the desert on the missile bases; or discovered the hidden training camps for the newly recruited launch crews; or noticed that the well-camouflaged command and control stations were now being configured to be part of a first-strike network.

So after many anxious discussions, the Higher Officers' Committee decided to add another element to the increasingly complex plot of Project Falcon. And once again, a prominent member of the royal family, on direct orders from King Fahd, threw himself personally into the intrigue.

With the approach each year of the King's Camel Race, the flat, gray stretch of desert beyond the air-conditioned terminals of the King Khalid International Airport was transformed into a vast Bedouin camp. From all over the kingdom, tribesmen draped in their soiled, gownlike *thobe*s, red-and-white-checkered *gutra*s wrapped about their heads and leather ammunition belts corseted across their chests, arrived with their veiled women and gaggles of children. Most of the tribesmen had traveled for days to this site outside Riyadh to participate in the annual eighteen-kilometer race. They had whipped their camels across the sweltering desert, or had crammed them into the back of their pickup trucks, the animal's long, spindly legs awkwardly folded like the limbs of a child's marionette for the journey. While they waited for the day of the race, the camels were tethered, spitting and baying, in one arid, sun-baked cauldron of sand.

Across from the corral, tents had been pitched as far as the eye could see. Some were boxy squares of striped sun-bleached canvas, others were dark and narrow as coffins and woven from goats' hair. Cooking fires blazed in front of each tent. Brass coffeepots filled with a pale brew the color of wet grass and spiced with cardamom had been put out to warm. Each afternoon dozens of lambs, their legs bound front and back, their heads pointing toward Mecca, were laid on their sides as daggers were plunged into their necks and blood spurted over the sand. By nightfall the lambs were roasting in makeshift oil drum ovens buried in the sand, the warm, rich aroma sweet in the first cool air of the evening. It was at that moment, as the evening meal was being prepared on the night before the otherwise uneventful 1984 race, that Crown Prince Abdullah, the king's half brother, entered the encampment and went from tent to tent, calling on the tribal sheiks to attend a meeting later that night.

Prince Abdullah, whose mother was a Bedouin, was head of the Saudi National Guard. There were 10,000 full-time soldiers in the Guard, nearly all descended from the desert tribesmen who had been defeated at the battle of Sabillah. In addition to this standing force, however, there were also units in each of the Bedouin villages throughout the kingdom that could be mobilized with the consent of the tribal sheiks for special assignments. These Liwa and Firqa troops, as the reserve battalions were called, were also willing to fight to the death in defense of Allah; they, too, were the direct heirs of that same fierce warrior blood. Yet unlike the regulars, they didn't trot out to duty in the Guard's starched dark green fatigues. Dressed in their *thobe*s, bandoliers crisscrossed over their chests, a bolt-action carbine or even the occasional AK-47 slung over their shoulders, they were, in appearance at least, no different than tribal shepherds.

Which, the Higher Officers' Committee had realized, was the perfect cover. And on that night before the Camel Race, as tribal leaders from throughout the kingdom gathered in Riyadh, Prince Abdullah tried to buy their services.

The meeting was held in a tent, and only after small cups of the pale coffee were served and sipped did Prince Abdullah begin. The tribal leaders listened to his request, and then, according to one account of the session, slowly, after much hesitation, came around to agreeing that there was a slight chance an arrangement could be made—for an outrageous price. It was their signal that the negotiations were to begin. But the crown prince, to the bewilderment of the sheiks who could not help but feel that they somehow had been outsmarted, simply agreed. In return for a hefty sum of gold paid directly to each tribe, men from the Liwa and Firqa units were to be mobilized as soon as they returned from the Camel Race.

Their mission: to guard specific locations deep in the desert. Their instructions: to keep all trespassers out of their assigned areas. And to arrest all foreigners on sight.

AND so, as the crates filled with missiles were unloaded from the freighters, as the convoys of bulldozers dug up acres of sand, and as the newly recruited nuclear scientists worked in a sprawling, air-conditioned glass-walled laboratory more than three hundred miles from the nearest city, Project Falcon moved forward in complete secrecy. The desert was so immense, a lost world of hidden places. It had protected so many mysteries for so many centuries. No one, the Higher Officers' Committee was convinced, would ever know what they were planning.

2

National Photographic Interpretation Center, Washington, D.C.: 1984

PATRICK Teague had great eyes. He was famous for them, at least among the other photo analysts at the National Photographic Interpretation Center. His desk was on one of the restricted, windowless floors in the NPIC's bright yellow cement building in the rear of the Navy Yard in Washington, D.C. It was in a room about the size of a football field and, like a newsroom, subdivided into an intricate maze of shoulder-high cubicles and constantly humming computer workstations. But Teague's space had a homey touch. A sign, the product of a dot matrix printer, was taped to the side of his computer screen. It read, one part challenge to an equal measure of irony, "God is in the details." And that was how Teague spent his days, a spy searching satellite photographs with almost religious devotion for hidden details. In his long career, he had helped determine that the Soviets were building submarines with titanium hulls, detected atmospheric plumes from secret North

Korean test launches, and, in an incident that earned him a still classified CIA citation, located a previously unknown poppy plantation that had been carved out of remote jungle in Belize.

Late in the winter of 1984, a rather indistinct photograph of a Chinese missile base was routed to his desk for further analysis. It was a routine procedure; a final visual check of a blurry image before cataloguing the picture as CONSTANT—the term used when there is "no significant change from previous images"—in NPIC's computer. But what Teague soon saw in that reconnaissance photo had office lights throughout Washington burning late into the night.

TWO days before the photograph had made its way to Teague, an Air Force Titan IIID rocket had been launched from the Eastern Test Range at Cape Canaveral, Florida. Its payload was a Lockheed Keyhole-9 satellite. Big Bird, as the launch crews called the satellite, was an orbiting spy station. It weighed 12 tons and was 55 feet long. Infrared scanners on board were capable of detecting underground missile silos, the silos' temperature being warmer than the surrounding earth. Its multispectral scanners were able to reveal camouflaged equipment. But the core of the satellite was a super-high-resolution camera that could distinguish objects 8 inches across from a height of 90 miles. Then again, Teague was fond of boasting, if the right pair of eyes were doing the looking, Big Bird might do even better.

For this mission, the satellite was launched into a north-south polar orbit. Its inclination was approximately 96.4 degrees, a route that took it directly over the People's Republic of China. No doubt it was programmed to maintain a longer "dwell time" above such strategic Chinese installations as the Shuan Cheng Missile Testing Center, where the country's incipient space program was being developed, as well as above the plutonium production facility at Yumen and the nuclear test sites at Lop Nur and Pao-tou.

At the completion of its ground track circuit, Big Bird jettisoned its canisters of film. Floating toward earth, the re-entry vehicles were recovered in midair by Lockheed C-130s stationed at Hickam Air Force Base in Hawaii. From Hickam, the film was transported by special Air Force jet across the country to Langley Air Force Base in Virginia. There, the package was transferred to the custody of an armed CIA courier. Even with Washington's frustrating traffic, it should not have taken the courier much more than forty-five minutes to deliver the film to the former heavy gun factory building in the rear of the Navy Yard.

The raw satellite photos had gone through a good deal of sophisticated image enhancement before they were sent on to Teague's cubicle. Computers had already dissembled the developed pictures into millions of electronic Morse code pulses. Using MAGISTIC, a software information extraction program developed by the government, each spot was manipulated. Intensity and color were programmed through hundreds of combinations. And according to all accounts, the computers had succeeded in sharpening the image to reveal a scene that, at first glance, was worrisome to the team of photo analysts.

A Chinese DF-3A missile, a weapon capable of landing in downtown Tokyo, could be seen standing erect on its launch pad at Shuang Cheng. Vapor fumes enveloped the missile's tail, evidence that its liquid-fuel rocket motor was engaged. And an analysis of the multispectral imagery showed the missile was "hot": It was armed with a nuclear warhead.

But this was not a launch. A closer look showed that the steel restraints gripping the rocket's body were still solidly in place. The mood in the room quickly dropped a notch as the analysts decided Big Bird had peeked in on a routine readiness test. The Chinese were making sure that if the moment ever arrived, all systems would be up and running. Case closed.

But not for Teague. His long career had been measured out in stubborn instances when, driven as much by instinct as certainty, he refused to move on. After only a quick study of the satellite photograph of this "hot" Chinese medium-range surface-to-surface missile, he preemptively decided it deserved more analysis. There were, he felt, more pieces to this puzzle. As his colleagues turned to other mysteries, he lingered. For a long while he just seemed to be staring at the photo with an intense, nearly trancelike gaze. (Or, as one impressed coworker described it, "When he's on a hunt, Teague gets this lost-to-the-world look, like my grandkids staring at Barney.") Later, Teague called up older, collateral photographs of the site for reference, and once again there was a long period of rock-hard concentration.

Then suddenly it was obvious to the handful of analysts who were discreetly following his investigation that Teague was onto something. There was no triumphant shout, no "Eureka!" echoing over the cubicles. But all at once there was activity. Teague was feverishly playing the computers, manipulating a grainy corner of the photograph pixel by pixel until, like the scattering of hazy, wafting smoke, a distant and still somewhat vague image was revealed: a row of stadium seats, a grandstand of sorts. And, no doubt about it, there were nearly a dozen spectators sitting in the seats.

Teague, however, did not stop there. A bit of a showman, it was not enough for him to announce to Langley that this was not a routine readiness test but rather an exhibition. He was determined to give the owls in the CIA's Directorate of Operations, the tweedy spies who puffed on their pipes and talked portentiously about the Big Picture, something truly valuable to mull over. He was going to tell them who was filling the seats, which Chinese generals, scientists, and party officials were of sufficient stature to be invited to such an auspicious and covert demonstration. His ambitious plan was to isolate each face and then cross-reference it with the agency's vast computer archive of Chinese officialdom. He was prepared to hunker down in his cubicle for days, weeks, whatever it took to get the job done.

But no sooner had Teague succeeded in magnifying the first randomly chosen face than he saw something totally unexpected. A beard! A carefully barbered and apparently black beard! He immediately abandoned his previous plan and, with mounting concern, began blowing up each of the remaining faces. When he was done, he had discovered two more beards.

The troubling thing was that Chinese officials don't wear beards. But Arabs do.

Before the day was over, the news of Teague's discovery had been announced to the CIA's director of operations. And soon the same worrisome question was being asked with increasing urgency throughout Langley: What were three Arabs doing at a top secret Chinese nuclear missile base?

It took another six months for the agency's intelligence specialists to get the final proof that confirmed their worst fears. And while it was the sighting of a beard that sparked their inquiries, it was, just as unexpectedly, some casual gossip about a missing ear that provided the conclusive evidence.

The source was a doctor's wife living in Saudi Arabia. Her husband, an American working at the King Faisal Specialist Hospital in Riyadh, had missed dinner with the kids one night because, he explained by way of apology, he had participated in a most amazing operation. A construction worker, unconscious and bleeding profusely, had been rushed to the hospital in Prince Khaled bin Sultan's private jet from somewhere deep in the desert. A steel beam had fallen and sliced off the unfortunate man's ear.

You must save him. He must be kept alive, begged the anxious prince. I would be eternally grateful.

The surgeons who examined the man knew the prince was not only the general who commanded Saudi Arabia's Air Defense Forces, but also King Fahd's favorite nephew. Was there a moment's reverie about the ways an oil-rich Saudi prince might prove his gratitude? If so, it was never shared. From the start, their manner was concerned and their diagnosis was succinct. We can save the man, they announced. No problem. We can even go one better. Find his ear and we'll sew it back on, good as new.

On Prince Sultan's orders, a convoy of cars, trucks, and military jeeps filled with soldiers was immediately dispatched to the remote desert site. It was a location nearly 350 miles southwest of the capital, on the outskirts of the oasis of Al Sulayyil. The vehicles were arranged into a wide circle around the approximate location of the accident, and with the glow from their headlights illuminating the desert, the soldiers began to sift through the grains of windblown sand. It took all night, but they found the ear. A film of dried blood had protected it, and by the next afternoon the ear was reattached and the patient was doing fine.

It was such a happy ending, such a tribute to American know-how, as well as the Saudi ruling family's thoughtful benevolence, that the doctor's wife couldn't help herself. She ignored her husband's admonition to keep the entire incident hush-hush. Conspiratorially, she shared the story over lunch the next day with her best friend, the mousy wife of a junior visa officer at the American embassy. The passport desk, however, was just a bit of diplomatic cover for this embassy underling. He worked for the CIA, not the State Department. And there was more to the secret: His wife was also on the payroll.

The report on the luncheon was filed jointly by the husband-and-wife team. It contained all the information the doctor's wife had whispered to her friend, including her bewildered assessment of Prince Sultan's charity: "He's gotta be one of the richest men in the world. And who does he worry about? Some grease monkey." But there was one small detail in her narrative, a piece of news she offered up without any apparent appreciation of its significance, that convinced the team of spies this was a story their superiors wanted to hear immediately—the construction worker was Chinese.

When the Flash cable arrived at Langley, the intelligence owls started quickly stringing the scraps of information together. Chinese workers were constructing a top secret site in the Saudi desert. The base was under the direct supervision of Prince Sultan, the general in charge of the kingdom's air defense forces. And months earlier, a bearded aide of the prince had been tentatively identified in the satellite photograph of the crowd at the Shuan Cheng Missile Testing Center.

There were no longer any doubts. The director of the Central Intelligence Agency was informed, and at a breakfast meeting the next morning he shared the news with the president and members of his cabinet. The balance of power in the Middle East had quietly, yet dramatically changed. The Saudis, with the help of the Chinese, were secretly building bases in the kingdom capable of launching nuclear missiles.

IT had been President Reagan, according to those familiar with that morning's anxious meeting, who, after taking a few moments to consider the news, first raised an immediate concern. "There's going to be hell to pay when the Israelis find out," he worried.

Three years earlier, in June 1981, fourteen Israeli fighter-bombers had attacked and destroyed the Iraqi nuclear reactor at Osirak. The U.S. government's official criticism of the raid had been only halfhearted. In fact, many military and intelligence officials were relieved that Iraq's nuclear program had been so forcefully set back. But this latest development in the Middle East, the men in the room understood, presented a much more complicated problem. Israel, the only democracy in the Middle East, was an ally. But so was Saudi Arabia. And no less a factor, the kingdom controlled approximately a quarter of the world's oil reserves. *Riyal politik*—a tribute to the riyal, the Saudi coin of the realm—had become a significant consideration in Washington's evolving Middle East *realpolitik*. Any Israeli military action in Saudi Arabia would force the Reagan administration to make a choice. And any choice would, by definition, be the wrong one.

That was when a shrewd solution was offhandedly proposed. "Who says," a cabinet officer wondered mischievously, "the Israelis have to find out? Suppose we don't tell them."

3

Anti-Terrorist Alert Center, Suitland, Maryland: 1985

A "courier card" is, arguably, the most coveted library card in the nation. It is certainly the most difficult to obtain. With the card, the bearer is "cleared for the world." He has access to warehouses of secrets. The archives of the CIA, the FBI, the State Department, the Defense Intelligence Agency, the Naval Intelligence Service, and even the National Security Agency will open its doors and computer links. And it is a virtually—it would be naive not to assume there is *always* something beyond one's grasp—unrestricted turf. The bearer's official clearance is a tantalizing notch above TOP SECRET. He can look into the dark vaults where the SPECIAL COMPARTMENTED INFORMATION is stored.

There is, however, one internal limitation on the information even a courier card can retrieve. This access is granted on a "need-to-know" basis. The holder, according to the classified agreement he signs when the card is issued, must *on his honor* confine his research and his curiosity to data that will facilitate the performance of his specific duties. A card-carrying Sinologist, for example, is prohibited from poking around to see who really shot President Kennedy. Knowledge is, after all, power; and, like any potent weapon, its use must be controlled.

But throughout the summer and fall of 1985, a spy held a courier card. Unknown—and perhaps even unimagined—by the intelligence mandarins who had wishfully relied on the holder's integrity to restrict his explorations, the traitor was very carefully, very deliberately using his card to plunder a specific corner of the nation's repository of secrets. His target was the Middle East.

THE spy was a balding, moonfaced 30-year-old analyst working at the U.S. Navy's newly created Anti-Terrorist Alert Center (ATAC) in suburban Maryland. He was assigned to the Caribbean Desk, and for each of his twelve-hour shifts his job, primarily, was to sit in his cubicle and read. Satellite photographs, phone intercepts, arms shipments, embassy communiqués—all, as long as they pertained to the Caribbean, were part of his required reading list, and all were accessed with his courier card. Classified information on the Middle East was not relevant to his job, but it was just as easy to get.

On the last Friday of every month, the spy would drive his Toyota through the main gate of the Naval Intelligence complex. He made a point of placing his briefcase on the gray bucket seat next to him. It was good tradecraft; a shout, he had been instructed, often attracts less attention than a whisper. If any of the armed guards looked—and, from time to time, no doubt they did—they would not have missed it. The briefcase, however, was never inspected.

From the gate, it was a tense twenty-minute drive to a car wash on upper Connecticut Avenue in Washington. Exhilarated by the danger yet always disciplined, he would wait until his car was being guided through the dark tunnel; and then, with volleys of water pounding and soap thickly curtaining the windows, he would act. From underneath his seat he would retrieve another briefcase—a present from his handler—and begin to transfer the contents of one case to the other. It was always a race. There were many handfuls of documents, but it did not take long—180 chaotic seconds—for the car to emerge, glistening and beaded, into the full light of the afternoon.

With the transfer successfully completed, the spy's edginess would ease. The mission, he would proudly congratulate himself as he made his way to a condominium apartment on nearby Van Ness Street, was near to being accomplished. A treasure chest of invaluable information—photographs taken by cameras silently orbiting in the sky, transcripts of conversations snatched from thin air by arrays of clandestine antennae, and the insights of secret agents working deep in enemy territory—had been snatched.

The apartment was on the eighth floor, and it was packed with sophisticated photocopying equipment. There were so many high-tech machines—huge satellite reconnaissance photos cannot be copied at the corner Kinko's—that an electronic blanketing system had been installed to ensure signals were not being radiated through the building. A neighbor wondering why his HBO was coming in fuzzy could have jeopardized the entire operation.

For nearly two years, everything went as the handlers had planned. The spy would give the briefcase to his postman, a doe-eyed, dark-haired woman who always greeted him with an enthusiastic smile. She would spend a busy weekend making copies of the documents. On Monday morning, as the spy dutifully returned the originals to the various intelligence libraries, the copies would be on their way to Tel Aviv.

And that was how, despite the elaborate precautions taken by the Higher Officers' Committee and the careful silence of the Reagan administration, Israel managed to learn what was happening in the Saudi desert. After studying satellite photographs and intelligence reports stolen in the fall of 1985 by its agent Jonathan Pollard, Israel knew that bases were being secretly built throughout the kingdom for 28 Chinese DF-3A missiles capable of delivering nuclear warheads anywhere in their small country within minutes.

THE Israeli cabinet, after only cursory debate, authorized an attack. A formation of aircraft took off across the Red Sea, turned right, and, hugging the desert to avoid Saudi radar, headed toward the military city of Tabuk in the northwest corner of the kingdom.

The planes flew over the sprawling base precisely at dawn. They came in from the east with the rising sun behind them so that the Saudi gunners would have the light in their eyes and the Israelis' target would be illuminated. Their IP—Initial Point, the start of the bomb run—was a control tower a mile north of the base's main jet runway. The runway was their target. They caught the Saudis by complete surprise. One after another, the planes dropped their payload.

The sound of live pigs hitting the concrete from a height of one hundred feet was sickening. The noise of the C-130 engines drowned out their squeals, but there was a sharp, hard thud, like a car's door being firmly shut, each time an animal slammed into the tarmac and its internal organs splattered. The oozing remains of twelve pigs lay scattered in an impressively neatly spaced row by the time the planes had completed their run and were heading back toward the Red Sea.

It had been an odd bombing mission. But the message sent was as succinct and effective as if the planes had dropped 1,000-pound laser-guided smart bombs. The Saudis were being told: Spend your barrels of petro-dollars on all the missiles you want. It does not matter. The Israeli Air Force owns the sky. Whenever we want, we can penetrate your airspace. We can destroy your missiles. We can destroy your country. So don't get any aggressive ideas.

There was a goading streak of mischievousness packed into the message too. Pigs were *haram;* Islamic law, like the Torah, prohibited the eating of their flesh. The gift of a dozen splattered pigs was a gesture that was calculated to be rude, vulgar, and totally infuriating.

And no less an inspiration, the attack shrewdly acknowledged the realities of international politics. The Saudis were too embarrassed to make a fuss. More important, the Americans did not have to choose sides, which, the Israelis realized, was just as well. If a line were drawn in the sand, oil and all it could buy on one side, and Zionism and all its baggage on the other, it would be a real worry waiting for the Americans to take their giant step.

Yet even as the Israeli Air Force high command was congratulating itself on the successful return of the planes to their base outside Eilat, a meeting of the Israeli cabinet was being convened. The mood that morning in Jerusalem was more anxious than celebratory. Soldiers, after all, fight battles; politicians wage wars. The ministers understood that if the Saudis could buy missiles, then it was possible—even likely—that their petro-dollars could in time buy a nuclear bomb. Prime Minister Shimon Peres ordered that all intelligence operations aimed at Saudi Arabia be intensified. It was of the highest priority, he decided, for Israel to discover what the House of Saud was planning.

It was not long after receiving this order from the prime minister that Amnon Shahak, the commander of military intelligence, met with the officers of Unit 269 of the Israeli Defense Forces. The existence of Unit 269 was a state secret. It was an elite *sayeret,* or reconnaissance force, whose members were recruited from all branches of the military. The *sayeret* commandos were trained to work behind enemy lines in groups of three or four men and to set up observation posts for long periods of time. On Shahak's orders, three Unit 269 teams were sent into the Saudi desert.

4

Dogubayazit, Turkey: 1986

So much, then, for Kipling's notion that "the desert is the loneliest of all places." Satellites with high-intensity infrared cameras were now zipping overhead, peering down on the Arabian nights. Chinese construction crews were busy excavating bunkers for ballistic missiles. Command and control centers with vast radar arrays were being raised. Bedouin militiamen roamed about on constant patrol. Israeli commandos were hunkering down in covert observation posts. And if all that weren't enough, straight into the heart of this activity came Dave Fasold with his machine that could find gold.

It was a matter of chance, and a fair amount of greed, that brought Fasold to Saudi Arabia. He had just spent a melancholic month trekking through the oozing spring mud of the little Turkish town of Dogubayazit as part of an expedition that had set out to find the remains of Noah's Ark. A deep-sea salvager by trade and adventurer by inclination, Fasold was, he quickly realized, the odd man out in the clubby group of born-again Christian amateur archaeologists he had hooked up with for the trip to Turkey. It wasn't just that the wiry, compact former merchant seaman, with his tattoos and next-round's-on-me grin, saw himself as, he was fond of saying, "a born-again pagan." What really gnawed at him, a sore no doubt exacerbated by the steady gloom and mud of Turkey, was the incredible gullibility of the true believers he was traveling with. "They wanted, hell, they *needed* to believe the Bible was true," he complained. "They were always whirling like dervishes and praying to God, thanking him for all the incredible discoveries they were making." "Lies for God" was how Fasold dismissed the certainty with which some of his fellow travelers insisted they had found proof that the remains of the Ark were perched on Mount Ararat.

Still, the born-again crowd had little choice but to put up with Fasold's grumblings. They had brought him along because of his uncanny ability to coax results out of an ingeniously modified Simpson Frequency Generator model 420-D. Fasold, now in his early fifties, had become a salvager after his years as a seaman, and over time he had learned to play the machine like a virtuoso. If there was buried metal near the spot where Fasold was pointing the rods of his remote sensing device, he would find it. Even better, by reading the precise frequencies the buried objects generated, he was able to determine conclusively if the hidden source was tin, aluminum, lead, or even silver or gold. It was no wonder the others were willing to ignore his peevish skepticism. Fasold, however, put up with them for another reason—he was always up for adventure. But after a month in Turkey, he had had enough. Or so he thought until Ron Wyatt, an anesthesia nurse from Nashville with a proudly biblical white beard who had helped arrange the expedition, came up to him in the lobby of the Kent Hotel in Ankara, coaxed him into a dark corner, and then, with a conspiratorial whisper, made a proposition.

Wyatt was just the sort Fasold was looking forward to escaping. He had a habit of saying he was on a mission from God to find the

Ark, and—an even greater insult to Fasold's well-honed sense of irony—truly believing it. But now sitting a cozy arm's length across from each other in two threadbare chairs in a seedy hotel in Ankara, the sliver of midday sun that managed to penetrate the tightly drawn curtains the only apparent light in the room, Wyatt, as provocative as any temptress, played to Fasold's passion: *treasure.* He knew about a fabulous treasure buried in the plain surrounding a mountain in Saudi Arabia. With your machine guiding us, it will be easy pickings, Wyatt promised.

"Ron! I don't have time to go to Arabia," Fasold can still remember growling. "I have to get home. You can't get a tourist visa for Saudi in any case. They don't grant tourist visas."

"Want to bet, Pilgrim?" challenged Wyatt.

THE night flight from Jeddah north to Tabuk was just a short hop, but to an excited Fasold it was an exotic sampling of what in another era had so attracted T. E. Lawrence and St. John Philby to Araby. Taking up an entire row was a quartet of chunky salesmen, their dozen or so valises ballooning with copper pots and pans, each of the men stuffed into Western suits and vests, and each with a stained *gutra* wrapped around his head. By a window a jet-black African in a brilliant rainbow print dashiki was sitting next to a regal-looking East Indian woman in a pastel sari adorned with an intricate gold frieze. The other passengers were Arabs dressed in sheetlike white *thobe*s, and their wives in long, black *abaaya*s, their faces hidden by black veils that, both provocative and ominous, left only their eyes exposed. Children sat on their laps, and more children squatted in the aisles. As the engines started to race, over the speaker a flight attendant recited *salah,* a traveler's prayer from the Koran, as tenderly as a mother singing a lullaby. And then, after a moment's struggle, the overloaded plane seemed to defy gravity and was suddenly coasting over the minarets of Jeddah as it headed into the total darkness of the desert.

Sitting next to Fasold, sleeping thickly from the aftereffects of a liberal dose of Dewar's and honey elixir administered as a head cold remedy before they left Ankara, was Samran el-Mutainy. It was Samran who over the last whirlwind twenty-four hours had become Fasold's partner, benefactor, and host. Just as Wyatt had planned. Only a couple of days earlier he had shown up unexpectedly at the Ark dig and introduced himself with a big, self-deprecating grin as an old friend of Wyatt's. With a mixture of respect and fascination, Fasold had watched Samran march into the Saudi consulate in Ankara, and a few hours later a Saudi official had personally delivered (!) their three visas to the hotel.

Next thing Fasold knew, Samran was explaining he had bought the airline tickets to Tabuk. "Do not think of repaying me" was how the Arab graciously put it, and Fasold restrained himself from blurting out that it was the farthest thing from his mind. "Of course you will be my guests in my country. You will stay in my house," Samran continued. Of course, agreed Fasold amicably. And there was one last piece of quick business to get out of the way before they rushed to the airport. It seemed Samran and Wyatt had worked out a contract they wanted Fasold to sign. He read:

> Mr. Fasold and Mr. Wyatt will provide special mineral detection equipment, and will examine sites to be designated by Mr. Samran el-Mutainy. . . . Should commercial minerals be located by these surveys . . . Mr. Samran el-Mutainy is to receive 75 percent of the . . . profits. Mr. David Fasold and Mr. Ronald Wyatt are to receive the remaining 25 percent. . . .

Fasold couldn't help feeling he was being set up, everything being so rushed while clearly Samran and Wyatt had been cooking up this little scheme for some time. Still, a free trip to Saudi was too good to turn down. Not to mention the prospect of a treasure hunt. Besides, if these guys were so hot to trot, then maybe. . . . He signed just below the line where they had already conveniently typed in his name. And before he knew it, the plane was landing in Tabuk.

• • •

A six-foot wall surrounded Samran's house and grounds, and by his third day in the compound, Fasold was beginning to wonder if the wall was to keep strangers out or to keep the servants in. A small, industrious army tended the estate. As an exercise, something to share with his wife when he got back to Florida, Fasold filled part of an aimless morning trying to take inventory of the staff.

There was the grim and incredibly gaunt Egyptian cook who always seemed to be either roasting beans in a skillet or grinding them with fresh cardamom in a mortar so he could brew his continuous supply of noxiously bitter green coffee. Then there was the handful of young, lithe, and giggling women from Sri Lanka who went scurrying after the children from Samran's three households, all living in apparently peaceful coexistence on the estate. The gardens seemed to require the constant care of a half-dozen or so intensely focused Filipinos. Same for the cars. Parked in a long line of parallel bays were three Mercedes sedans, a Cadillac, at least two Land Rovers, a Toyota Scout, and a custom-made black Mercedes four-wheel-drive jeep complete with car phone. And all the vehicles were kept showroom clean, which was quite a trick, Fasold realized, in the middle of the desert. He almost overlooked the houseboys, unobtrusive but forever clipping roses or sweeping and polishing. Still, there were enough of them, Fasold decided, to man a football team, with separate squads for offensive and defensive. And he didn't want to forget the maids. Samran's three wives prowled around the estate trailed by a flock of young girls who seemed to have no other purpose but to keep a deferential distance. The bottom line, Fasold finally calculated: maybe a hundred or so on staff.

But the meals left him most impressed. Dinner was his favorite. It was held in the *majlis,* the central area of the tent erected in the middle of the estate. Of course, one man's tent, Fasold was learning, was another man's palace. Samran's was air-conditioned, seemed about the size of the Astrodome, and even had a wall of glass that offered a view onto the acre or so of gardens. Each night it was filled with Samran's wives, their relatives, and assorted guests. But no matter how many plopped themselves onto the overstuffed pillows, Samran's kitchens were prepared. A parade of somber kitchen girls who, despite their gravity, seemed not much older than grade-schoolers kept lugging five-foot brass platters weighed down with mountains of rice or esoteric parts of sheep or orchards of polished fruit to the long tables.

It was during dinner on Fasold's third incredulous evening in Arabia, just as he was beginning to wonder if his host had forgotten why he had brought him and his machine to the desert, that Samran made his announcement. It was all done very casually, Samran first grabbing a handful of rice from a tray and rolling it into a smooth ball with his fingers before dropping it absently into the middle of Fasold's brass dinner plate. As Fasold studied this little gift, Samran spoke with a sudden yet succinct authority. "We leave tomorrow morning at sunrise. We'll take three vehicles. A caravan. Any luck, we should reach the mountain by midday." Then, flashing a nasty smile at Wyatt, he added as if in an afterthought, "And this time, I assure you, as long as I'm around you won't have to spend seventy-eight days in jail for trying to get there."

SEVENTY-EIGHT days in jail! And a *Saudi* jail, to boot! Even years later, Fasold, usually the calmest of men, had to rein in his fury as he recalled how all at once he had realized he had been led with indulgent smiles and ready promises down the proverbial garden path—the free trip, the fancy house, even a share of the mythical treasure. No doubt about it, he suddenly understood with infuriating clarity, Samran and Wyatt had set him up. And nothing they had given or were promising was worth 78 days—or maybe longer—in the dank hellhole that was sure to be a Saudi jail.

"I'm not going," Fasold finally spoke out, his anger solidifying. "I'm not going unless you level with me. Just what is this treasure? And what did you do to wind up in jail? It's true confession time. Now—or I'm out of here."

Samran and Wyatt exchanged defeated glances; and then Wyatt told a little more of the tale they had been keeping from their partner.

The arrest, he began with an amused smile that seemed to suggest that doing time in a Saudi jail was really the most normal of occurrences, had actually been the result of a stupid mistake on his part. You see, he explained, upping the wattage of his grin in the process, he had foolishly entered the kingdom without a visa. Accompanied by his two sons, he had walked across the Jordanian border into Saudi Arabia. No one would notice, he had figured, or, worst case, he'd get a slap on the wrist and a one-way ticket back to Amman. "I guessed wrong," he admitted with a nervous shrug. "They caught us. And they weren't too happy about it. End of story, Pilgrim."

Like hell it is, thought Fasold. If Wyatt wanted him to pull the rest out, in his current mood he was prepared to tug tooth and nail. "Why the big rush? Couldn't you simply wait, get a visa, and enter legally?" he challenged.

"Well," Wyatt began, "we tried. Oh, *how* we tried. The Saudis are kind of reluctant to let in tourists. Or archaeologists. They're very private people." He looked to Samran for confirmation and the Arab nodded vigorously.

But Fasold pressed on. "I still don't get it. What was so important? What were you after? What was worth the risk of getting caught sneaking into this country?"

Wyatt fixed him with the sort of weary look a parent saves for a particularly slow child. "Why, the treasure of course. Don't tell me you forgot about that?"

"Maybe you should tell me a little more about this treasure," Fasold demanded evenly.

All at once Wyatt was genuinely excited. "Waiting out in the desert," he said, "are riches beyond imagination. Gold. Rubies. Sapphires." He spoke with certainty, as if he could already feel the heft of the gold in his hand, see the sparkle of the gems with his eyes. "Waiting for us," he went on, "ripe for the taking, is the colossal treasure the ancient Hebrews took with them when they fled from Egypt. The gold of Exodus."

"Whoa, now. Slow down," Fasold interrupted. "The gold of what? Just what are you telling me?"

Only now did Wyatt hesitate; but whether that was because he was afraid he wouldn't be believed, or he was reluctant to divulge the whole story to someone he didn't quite trust, was a matter Fasold would consider in the years to come. At that moment, however, he simply watched as Samran gave Wyatt a small, consenting nod; and at last unrestrained, a man proud to be sharing his long-guarded secret, Wyatt plunged into his fantastic story.

"Tomorrow we're going to nothing less than the holiest site on earth. It's the real Mount Sinai. The mountain on which God descended and gave Moses the Ten Commandments. Sure, a lot of people think the mountain is in the Sinai Peninsula. Malarkey! Pure myth! A tourist trap! Check your Bible. Mount Sinai is in ancient Midian. And Midian is Saudi Arabia. That's a fact. Heck, the Bedouins have known the true location of Moses' mountain for centuries. With ol' Samran's help, we should get there lickety-split. Then you and your machine are going to point us to the treasure the six hundred thousand Israelites took with them when they left Egypt. The loot they left behind at the foot of Mount Sinai as penance for building the Golden Calf. The gold of Exodus."

Fasold didn't say another word. It was all too absurd, he realized with exasperation. Loony, even. He blamed himself. It was his own fault for letting born-again Wyatt talk him into coming to Saudi Arabia in the first place. With the perfect calm of resigned anger, he carefully washed his hands in the bowl of rose-scented water that was in front of his plate, stood, and then, striding quickly, left the *majlis*.

But that night he had trouble sleeping. His head, resting on a camel saddle, looked heavenward, and his eyes followed the gentle swaying of the brass-studded, red-lacquered tent poles in the desert breeze. And soon he began to rethink his predicament. He had come this far. What if there was treasure? What if he could walk on Moses' mountain?

5

THEY left at dawn, but the day was already uncomfortably hot. It was, as Samran had promised, a caravan. Two Land Cruisers were packed with diggers and even a cook, while leading the way was the impressive black Mercedes jeep. Samran was at the wheel, Wyatt next to him, and in the rear, full of energy, free of his previous misgivings, was an eager Fasold. In the course of a long night, he had climbed his own mountain, and when he reached the summit, he had decided that at the very least this was going to be an adventure: *I'm in.* He stared out the window as Samran sped like a race car driver through the empty early-morning streets of Tabuk. Soon the jeep was out of the city, turning north toward Hagl.

Samran continued at this reckless pace for over an hour, going deeper into the desert. Fasold kept his watch, but there was little to see, only an occasional black tent or a stray camel. Finally Samran took one more sharp turn, went a few yards, and all at once the jeep began to sink slowly into the soft sand. Samran motioned to the diggers in the Land Cruiser with the sort of casual gesture another man might use to summon a waiter, while at the same time he turned to Wyatt and quietly admitted, "I'm lost."

They might have remained lost if a rusted, ancient Datsun pickup, kicking up a wake of sand, hadn't appeared. The driver was a wizened Bedouin, and he seemed to Fasold's eye only slightly less rusty than the truck and certainly a lot older. Still, after an intense conference with Samran in the air-conditioned jeep, the Bedouin appeared eager to help. "Jabal Musa," he announced happily to Wyatt and Fasold. Moses' mountain! And he pointed with his staff out into the desert. Fasold looked and tried to convince himself that, despite the haze, he saw out in the distance a dark peak rising against the sky. With the pickup now leading the way, it wasn't long before they were once again racing across the desert, a caravan of speeding cars throwing off comets of sand.

HOW should he feel standing in front of the holiest spot on the planet? Awed? Overwhelmed? Reverential? Fasold asked himself these questions as he stared up from the flat, rocky plain at the black peak of Jabal al Lawz. Truth was, he felt exhausted. It had been late in the afternoon of what had stretched into a very long day by the time the Bedouin had led them into a wide valley that ended with the mountain rising like an unexpected wall in front of them. In this frayed state, after all he been through in the past hectic month, Fasold's thoughts were too crowded to make room for the divine. His only concern, he realized, was to take a few sample readings before the sun sank even lower in the sky.

He set up the frequency generator about fifty feet from the edge of a wadi. It took a little effort to shove the probes into the rocky ground. Then, in a final ritual, he sprinkled a handful of water from his canteen on the probes for good contact and began playing with the machine, adjusting the range and the frequency controls as he walked his course. Immediately a dozen signal lines spreading out like spokes from a wheel began to register. It didn't seem probable. He was suspicious when things were too easy. Besides, the pattern was odd; he had never before run into one like it. Still, he decided to walk out each of the signal lines. The first went thirty feet, and he followed it very carefully. He was busy methodically tracing these initial readings, one long line after another to its source, when Samran and Wyatt appeared.

If we want to get back to Hagl before it's dark, we'd better get going, Samran said. He had been off exploring the base of the mountain with an excited Wyatt. As Fasold had expected, Wyatt had already found solid proofs to shore up his many speculations. We'll return first thing tomorrow, Samran promised.

When they were walking to the cars, Samran, as though it was just suddenly crossing his mind, asked, "How'd you do? Come up with anything?"

"We'll see," said Fasold vaguely.

THE police were coming for them at dawn. That's the time executioners come, Fasold thought the moment he heard the news. Perhaps it was just as well, then, that he was the last to know. Samran was the first, awakened by the excited servants sometime after 4 A.M. They were spending the night in a large, rambling house in the old port town of Hagl, a home that belonged to one of Samran's friends who was conveniently out of the country. As soon as he dressed, Samran peered cautiously out the window and was immediately heartened to find the street empty of any activity. In fact, he had calmed down considerably by the time he went to get Wyatt. The two huddled for a while, and after a heated discussion—hightail it north to the safety of Tabuk or try to lose them in the desert?—an escape plan, of sorts, was agreed on.

It was ominously closer to dawn by the time Wyatt shuffled into Fasold's room. "Time to get out of Dodge, partner," he said with unseemly cheer as he shook a deeply sleeping Fasold. As soon as Fasold heard the part about the police, however, he was up. And if he needed any more encouragement to get moving, Wyatt, once again trying to put the best possible face on things, pointed out that "Samran's already heading for the barn door."

Samran had pulled the black Mercedes jeep into the courtyard in front of the house. He was sitting hunched at the wheel, engine running, when Wyatt, once again choosing to ride shotgun, and Fasold climbed in.

The plan was to race, literally, out of the city. Samran decided that if they could just make it out of Hagl and onto the highway, then in only another hour or so they would be back in Tabuk, where at least he would know whom to bribe. And it looked as if the strategy was going to work. Samran, delighted to have an opportunity to push his beloved Mercedes to the limit, was speeding contentedly along. With a nonchalance that struck Fasold as dangerous if not a bit mad, the Arab zoomed through intersections and shot into dauntingly narrow cross streets.

The sun was just coming up, and Fasold could hear the muezzin crying for the faithful to come to prayers. *"Hayya 'alas-Salah . . . Hayya 'alal-falah. . . ."* At that moment, sitting in the backseat of the wildly racing Mercedes and with the prospect of a Saudi jail threatening, prayer, Fasold decided, was certainly at least worth a try. The highway to Tabuk, after all, couldn't be more than ten minutes off. With a little luck, they could make it. And so he prayed. To God. To Allah. To anyone who would listen. But his silent appeals were suddenly interrupted by Samran's anxious voice.

"Think we got company," he nearly moaned.

Fasold looked out the back window and saw a big black car that might have been a hearse, except it was bristling with antennae.

"What should we do?" Wyatt worried. Despite the grim circumstances, Fasold enjoyed a small, unexpected moment of satisfaction. At least Wyatt had been scared out of his annoying cowpoke routine.

Samran answered by putting his foot straight down on the pedal. The Mercedes responded with a guttural roar of its own and took off.

"Can we lose 'em?" Wyatt asked.

"Certainly," said Samran coolly. But looking out the rear window, Fasold saw that the hearse was right on their tail. Samran tried a sudden right turn. The hearse turned right. Samran now went left. So did the hearse. By now Samran was actively cursing his Mercedes. And when they came to a wide patch of road, the hearse without any apparent effort glided past them, flashing a host of lights.

Now it was the hearse's turn to lead. It played this game for a few miles, until, as if suddenly bored, its driver began flicking his directionals. Pull over, the flashing lights ordered. Samran had no choice but to obey.

The hearse had come to a stop by the side of the road, and Samran's car was parked behind it. No one in the Mercedes spoke. They just waited for something to happen. When nothing did, Samran, with a small, defeated sigh, jumped out and went to the hearse. A back door flew open and Samran, after a moment's weary pause, disappeared inside.

When he returned to the Mercedes, his face was masked in a halfhearted smile. He tried to give one of his customary confident performances, but it was obviously a struggle. "It's a mere formality," he began obscurely. "It's early. We'll still have plenty of time to head back out to the mountain today. It shouldn't be long."

"What's up, Samran? Just tell us," Fasold ordered.

At last Samran spoke. "They want us to follow them to the police station."

THE guard was dressed in black and stood at attention like one of death's sentinels. He wore a black cloak, a black head scarf, and high black riding boots. Across his chest was a leather munitions belt. And in his shoulder holster was a chrome revolver with a long barrel. For the past hour, Fasold had been studying the guard, and he was convinced the man had not once moved a muscle. Still, he was better company than Wyatt, who, his head in his hands, sat across the room on the floor, mute and depressed.

Fasold didn't know where Samran was or what had happened to him. As soon as they had been led into the police station, Samran had been taken away. Fasold had begun to convince himself that

Samran had been beheaded. He knew it was a common enough practice in the kingdom. And with each uncertain moment Fasold couldn't help thinking that it would be his turn next. It certainly wasn't hard to imagine the man in black wielding the sword. Being kept under guard in a Saudi police station, Fasold was learning, was a catalyst for all kinds of grim thoughts.

Suddenly Samran, head firmly attached to his shoulders, walked into the room followed by three stocky Saudis. The heaviest one did the talking. "You are to come with us," he ordered.

They were led to three separate cars, which seemed like possibly a reprieve; or then again, maybe a death sentence. Fasold was shoved into the backseat next to an Arab who reeked of mutton. When the Arab volunteered a smile, Fasold was encouraged. For the second time that day, he said a small prayer, and then, struggling to keep his voice somewhat steady, asked where they were taking him.

"Why, back to the mountain, of course," said the Arab cheerfully.

In the course of the next two hours in the car, Fasold learned that the Arab's name was Memet and that Samran had told the authorities everything. Now it was Memet's turn to try to get all that he could out of Fasold.

"Tell us, Mr. Da'oud," Memet demanded in his amicable but relentless fashion, "how does your metal-detecting instrument work? Have you found gold at the site?"

"Wait a minute, Memet, I'm not here to find gold. My interest is to find anything of historic value—"

Memet cut him off. "But your contract with Samran states you share twenty-five percent in the value of recoveries. A division of the spoils is implied, is it not?"

After that Fasold realized there was no point in lying. It would be better not to say too much. He didn't want to get caught trying to pull a fast one, but at the same time he was reluctant to tell all he knew.

Fasold continued to play things out in this careful, controlled way when they arrived at Jabal al Lawz. He cooperated, but only up to a point. Therefore, he made a big production of showing them how he worked his Simpson 420-D, but at the same time he tried to muddy the waters with a barrage of technical mumbo jumbo, some real and a lot invented right on the spot. But the Arabs were smart. Like all interrogators who know their business, they kept the partners separated. So while Fasold was leading Memet and a group of diggers toward a rocky part of the plain that was, he confided with what he hoped was convincing sincerity, emitting promising frequencies, Samran already had a team in another sector. Under Samran's encouragement and direction, they were digging in a wadi. The very one that only a day ago Fasold had staked out with such care and attention.

And that was when it happened.

A digger working with Samran let loose with a piercing, triumphant yell; and then everyone at the site saw him holding high above his head a bracelet that glittered for all the world like the purest of gold.

It wasn't long after the uproar caused by the bracelet that Memet ordered Fasold to turn off his machine and return to the car. When he tried to argue, Memet cut him short. "Mr. Da'oud, I can only say that a major discovery has been made. You and Mr. Ron are under arrest."

THE trial was before the sharif of Tabuk, and he held court, such as it was, in his house. The defendants sat on velour cushions and drank weak tea served in porcelain cups as the king's prosecutor made his case. His name was Abu Colet, and he was fat, imperious, and nasty. He did not speak as much as shout violently, and as a result a thin trail of spittle was often dripping from his lower lip. Like a camel, Fasold cruelly observed, and the nickname stuck. The charge, according to the translator, was that they had come to Saudi Arabia to rob an archaeological site. What bothered Fasold most about The Camel's accusation was that it was true.

When the trial dragged on into its seventh day, Wyatt complained that it had taken God only six days to create the heavens and the earth. Fasold quickly silenced him by pointing out it was still 71 days less than his last incarceration in Saudi Arabia. And then on the ninth day, there was a verdict. It was announced by the sharif.

All photographs taken at the site were to be confiscated, he began. All notes, diaries, and letters that Wyatt or Fasold had in their possession were now property of Saudi Arabia. They were forbidden to publish or even talk about their findings. And if they returned to Saudi Arabia, Abu Colet was empowered to execute them without further hearing. If they agreed to those terms, they could leave immediately for Jeddah and the flight back to Istanbul.

Without an instant's hesitation, Fasold and Wyatt solemnly agreed.

Yet on the flight to Istanbul, while Wyatt slept, Fasold busily worked. He was drawing a map while his memory was still fresh. A treasure map. A map showing the precise route to Jabal al Lawz. For there was one secret he still had not shared with anyone. Not with Wyatt or Samran or the sharif. His frequency generator had shown that the plains surrounding the mountain were definitely loaded with buried gold—the gold of Exodus. And even if he couldn't risk returning to face the certain vengeance of Abu Colet, he was pretty sure he knew just the man who would jump at the chance.

IT must not have been long after Fasold returned to the United States, certainly by the winter of 1986 at the latest, that the Higher Officers' Committee meeting in Riyadh finished the work on its own secret map. After much consideration, Project Falcon site N-4 was chosen. It was the mountain known as Jabal al Lawz.

Part Two

THE CALL

6

Grants, New Mexico: 1986

LARRY Williams was nearly twenty-five feet below ground, sorting through the sand and clay that had been scattered about the hole by the dynamite blast, when he heard the lookout over the walkie-talkie: "We got company coming."

"How far off?" Williams asked.

"Hard to tell. But there are three sets of headlights. I don't know, ten, fifteen minutes or so before they get here."

Williams looked straight up. The shaft was not much wider than a door well and painted with a thick, black darkness. When he aimed his flashlight, hoping to get a reassuring glimpse of the night sky, the cone of light stretched up for what seemed like miles.

"Give me a minute," he said at last.

"Larry, come on, man!"

But Williams had made up his mind. Quickly, he was back on his knees and picking carefully through the dirt and debris.

"They're getting closer, Larry. Coming right this way. And kicking up a shitload of dust."

Williams continued to ignore the warnings. He did, however, decide to use his shovel. He was shoveling rapidly, like an engineer stoking a fire on a speeding train, when he heard a distinct thud. It was only a small noise, but with the eerie silence in the shaft it boomed in his ears like thunder. Another shovelful and he saw that it was a piece of wood. With racing excitement, he immediately realized nature could not have put it there, not at this depth.

Suddenly the lookout was back on the walkie-talkie. "This ain't a game, man. Another minute, I'm out of here."

Williams pulled a piece of wood not much larger than a football from the dirt. The carving was crude, primitive even, but it definitely was man-made. It was, he wanted to believe, a cross. Clutching the object in his hand, he jumped into the basket.

"What're you waiting for? Get me out of here," he ordered into the radio.

The two men pulling the winch put their backs into it. The basket moved jerkily up the dark shaft, but Williams was oblivious. His mind focused on the wooden cross in his hand. It had to be a "tell," an object left—by the Indians? by the Spaniards?—to announce that this was the right spot. Just keep on digging. The treasure was buried somewhere farther down below. But that discovery, he told himself, would have to wait until the next time.

Only all at once he realized there wouldn't be a next time. He was climbing out of the basket and back onto the ground when he was suddenly bathed in a red glow as three cars, their emergency lights flashing, pulled into the camp.

"Run for it!" Williams yelled. The instruction was unnecessary. His crew was already heading for their cars as an amplified voice was announcing, "This is the Ancoma Indian Police. Stay where you are. You are under arrest."

He heard an engine start, and at the same time the sound of someone chasing on foot across the dirt in pursuit of other footsteps. There were more angry shouts, and in the confusion he somehow made it to his pickup. The engine caught on the first try, and, more luck, he was able to use the stars for illumination so he could pull away without hitting his lights. Then his luck ran out.

A glance at his rearview mirror and he saw the flashing lights. There was only one car, but it was right on his tail. He cursed, flicked on his brights, and stepped on the accelerator.

His pickup took off, bouncing over the rough terrain, and for a while the car, its headlights jumping in his rearview mirror, stuck with him. But after he had gone a few more miles, Williams looked back and all he saw was the night sky. Whether his pursuer had broken an axle or simply lost the will was a puzzle he had no interest in solving. He was glad to have made it off the reservation and to be heading down the highway, an all-night talk show coming in over the radio as a scarlet New Mexico dawn was breaking.

Williams left the pickup in the long-term lot at the Albuquerque airport with the keys under the seat; one of the guys from the dig would retrieve it, he figured. Unless they all were in jail by now for trespassing on an Indian reservation. The flight from Albuquerque took him to Las Vegas, and he hung around the Vegas airport, cradling the cross against his chest as he tried to sleep until the next flight to San Diego was announced.

It was only after he was seated in the first-class cabin and the plane had lifted off over the desert that Williams noticed the curious looks some of his fellow passengers were shooting his way. He must be quite a sight, it suddenly occurred to him. Five days ago, just after he had received the call that his crew had found five sandbags and then a layer of adobe bricks at nineteen feet below the surface, he had ordered them to hold off shooting any more sticks of dynamite in the hole until he got there. Then he had caught a plane and hurried to the dig.

Since his arrival he had lived out of his bedroll, not bothering to shave or, for that matter, shower. His jeans and T-shirt looked as if he had been crawling around in a pile of dirt, which was, of course, exactly the case. His face, baked by the desert sun, had taken on the tarnished mahogany patina of an old saddle. Despite all his self-conscious efforts, it was going to take something more efficient than his fingers to rein in his curly brown hair. And the finishing touch to an already bizarre picture, he admitted with a small smile, there he was protectively clutching a wooden cross to his sweat-stained chest. Williams decided there was no point in trying to explain or even apologize to the chunky matron in the seat next to him, so he simply closed his eyes. In a moment he was fast asleep, and he remained that way until the plane touched down for a landing in San Diego.

It was a clear, perfect southern California day, and the first thing he did after he found his silver blue Rolls-Royce Corniche in the parking lot was to put down the top. He drove the big car up into the green hills past the city. Framed by an arc of tall trees, he had a view of the Pacific shimmering in the midday sun and seemingly stretching on forever. The wooden cross rested on the tan cowhide seat across from him.

When he pulled up to the gatehouse, the guard eyed him suspiciously. The car was familiar, but it took him a moment to recognize the scraggly, unshaven driver. There was a long pause before the guard announced, "Good to see you, Mr. Williams," and then the gate was raised. Williams waved cheerfully and drove the car up the hill.

The house was new, sprawling, and, with its red tile roof, vaguely Spanish. It was spread across the crest of a hill so that from its acres of wide windows the view extended past the pool and over shaved green lawns toward the Pacific. Williams pressed the device on his visor, and the iron gates swung open on his command. He left the Rolls in the courtyard and found, as usual, the back door unlocked. He walked in and carefully placed the wooden cross on the marble island a decorator had floated in the middle of the kitchen. It was good to be home.

His wife and daughters weren't around, still at school or tennis or something. He should have called and said he was on his way. His plan was to take a shower or maybe two to get rid of all the layers of New Mexico dirt, and then, clean and shaved, head over to the club to find his wife. Over an icy dry martini, he would tell her how his latest adventure had panned out. On his way to the bathroom, he passed through the windowed crow's nest that served as his study. His laptop was on the desk, and he couldn't resist the temptation to check the markets. Copper was doing just what he had predicted, and, as always, he did not hesitate. It took Larry Williams only one phone call to sell his pile of futures and to lock in a profit that was just short of $300,000.

Buoyed, he began to call up the rest of his portfolio on the computer. He made a few more trades, diving out of coffee with a loss that stung, and rather matter-of-factly went long on platinum with the money he had made in copper. When his concentration started to slip, Williams, still in his muddy jeans and T-shirt, turned off his computer and got up from his desk.

He was, at last, about to disappear into the shower when he noticed the five-day stack of mail his wife had piled carefully on the lamp table next to his favorite reading chair. He skimmed through the envelopes containing bills, glanced at the covers of the magazines, until near the bottom of the pile he came to a handwritten envelope. The return address said it had been sent by Dave Fasold. It took Williams an instant to remember that Fasold was the guy who was trying to get him to invest in a documentary about the search for Noah's Ark.

He opened the envelope and pulled out two pages of lined, spiral notebook paper. Each sheet, front and back, was completely filled, the words running across the page in a tight, confident script. He read Fasold's opening sentence: "Larry, I have an unbelievable story to tell you." Intrigued, he settled down in the high-backed chair, turned on the lamp, and read on. His shower and martini would have to wait.

7

North of Billings, Montana: 1952

LARRY Williams found his first hidden "treasure" at the age of ten. He had to wait another nineteen years to make his first million. In an odd way, the two events were not unrelated.

He had grown up outside Billings, Montana, the son of a laborer for Continental Oil, and it had been a rural, hardscrabble sort of childhood. Making ends meet was always a concern, but, no small trade-off the way his father figured it, the boy had wide, open spaces and the great outdoors as his playground. Williams was off stalking deer and antelope as soon as he could hold a rifle, and by the time he was 11, he had taken down his first buck. He had been even younger when he landed his first trout. But for the Williams family, hunting and fishing weren't merely a sportsman's pastime. It was the way they put food on the table. From an early age, Larry, without ever really thinking too much about it, became comfortable with the notion that nature's bounty was his for the taking, a provider of sustenance and, a larger gift perhaps, adventure.

Adventure! That yearning, too, was definitely deeply rooted in the young boy. He was raised in a part of the country where intrepid pioneers, daring cattle drives, galloping cavalry, and rampaging Indians were still fresh legends, where the spirits of the Old West seemed to hover over the plains and snowcapped mountains. These hair-raising tales were his birthright, and his heritage.

Yet it took a small event, as Williams tells it, to focus these subtle boyhood influences into the stronger magic of grown-up ambition. He was off playing with some friends, General Custer charging up a foothill in pursuit of Geronimo and his renegades, when his eyes happened to catch the opening to what looked like a cave. It was hidden by a veil of overhanging leafy branches, and his first thought was that it was just the sort of place where a bear might make his den. But even as a child Williams was dismissive of any instinct for caution; fear, his daddy had lectured him, was something to be overcome. So he pulled back the branches and, ever so slowly, entered the cave.

He had to crouch, but once he was farther inside the ceiling rose unexpectedly. It was as if he had walked into a secret room. He was scared, but now that the branches had been pried apart, shafts of daylight illuminated the cave. He went on.

The first thing he found was an arrowhead. It was, to his delight, just lying there. Encouraged, he kept his eyes fixed on the ground, searching. It didn't take him long to spot something else. It was a bead about the size of a quarter. When he brushed off the dirt, he saw it was as blue as a Montana summer sky. He put it carefully into his pocket and, excited, went deeper into the cave. With each new step he kicked at the dirt, hoping to uncover something. That was how he found the moccasin. It was just lying there, in his path, under some loose dirt. The hide had turned a jaundiced yellow, but it was intact. In the world of a ten-year-old, it was an incredible treasure. Wildly proud of his discovery, he ran from the cave to show his friends.

After that, Larry and his buddies returned to the cave nearly every afternoon that summer. It became their clubhouse, hideout, and, not least, their treasure chest. When Williams was older he realized he had stumbled into an Indian burial cave, but that summer, as he and his friends explored and plundered the cave, their happy greed couldn't have been surpassed even if old man Palmer had given them the key to his general store in Billings. All this wonderful, authentic Indian loot—a drum, mountains of beads, even a tomahawk—and it was theirs for the taking. Sure, they had to hunt around, sometimes digging for days with a big tin shovel Larry had sneaked out of his daddy's shed, before they found a single bead, but that only heightened the drama. A storehouse of exotic gifts, treasures from the past, an intoxicated Larry was beginning to understand, was waiting out there for anyone daring, adventurous, and shrewd enough to go off and find them.

Before the summer was over, Larry and his friends started an Explorers' Club. He was elected president by a unanimous show of hands, and as his first order of business he shared a plan he had been secretly mulling for weeks. His dad had once told him about a cliff not too far away that, legend had it, the Indians had used as a buffalo jump. The way his father had explained it, the Indians would stampede a herd, driving the animals to the edge of a cliff where, blindly charging on, they fell to their deaths. Maybe if we poked around, Larry eagerly suggested to his buddies, we could find some buffalo horns, or even something better. Like what? one of the kids challenged. "Could be anything," Larry recalls himself confidently answering back. "We won't know until we start digging. But I bet we find something. Something terrific. I just bet." He was only ten, and he was hooked.

COLLEGE nearly ruined him. At least that's how Williams looks back on the experience and, even more sullenly, its consequences. He was an All-State center out of Billings Senior High, and Brigham Young University recruited him with a scholarship. It was the first time he saw a ten-story building, and it was also the first time he saw up close the size of the pumped-up linemen on a big-time college varsity. At a lean 170, he knew he was going to take a real pounding. No less depressing, the coeds flashed promising smiles when he asked them out, but by the end of the evening it was clear their eagerness was animated by a more spiritual sort of seduction than he had hoped. "You positive you don't want to become a Mormon, Larry?" they would plead constantly. After he found himself being hauled before the honor council for a variety of minor but un-Mormon-like infractions, such as drinking and cardplaying, Williams, his battered body and his agnosticism still intact, transferred to the University of Oregon.

Glad to be liberated from the stern Mormons, Williams devoted himself to having a good time. He was a journalism major but, he would remember with an unembarrassed grin, a lot more of his energy went into Sigma Chi than his studies. He was a handsome, easygoing frat brother with soft brown eyes and the bright, automatic smile of a talk-show host. He wore white bucks, madras shirts, V-neck sweaters, and chinos. There were parties all week, and on the weekend the festivities got really serious. After graduation he found himself living in New York City and working for J. Walter Thompson. He was on his way to becoming, he realized, "the man in the gray flannel suit," and he hated it. A transfer to the San Francisco office, and then to Portland, just delayed the inevitable. He was getting ready to quit when they fired him.

By now his new marriage was pretty rocky, and he was playing with the idea of heading off to Australia and starting life from scratch. Then, just when he thought he had run out of options, a friend happened to mention that he had made a little money lately playing the commodities market. It was, his friend said, "real easy money."

Intrigued, Williams scraped together $6,000. It would make the most sense, he decided, to zero in on a commodity where a guy from Montana might have an edge. So he put it all into cattle futures. Within three months, his nest egg was cut in half. Failure, however, only seemed to energize him. He was, as he later put it, "more determined than ever to figure this one out." "Pure greed," to use his own candid appraisal of his motives, pushed him on. He was confident there was, as his friend had assured him, "easy money" out there. He began reading books, studying the market, but he soon decided these were unnecessary, even counterproductive exercises. He developed his own strategy and, in part, it grew out of a very personal metaphor. Everything he knew about success, he came to realize, he had learned as a ten-year-old in an Indian burial cave. "The world was ripe for the picking," he truly believed, "if you're curious enough to go where other people hesitate. Be bold. Be adventurous. Life is not for the meek. Boldness always defeats brilliance."

After just three more months, Williams boldly lost everything he had. Still, he never considered walking away from the game. Success would, he confidently insisted to himself, simply take a bit longer than he had anticipated. He just needed to go farther into the cave. He needed to keep on digging. And as things worked out, he was right.

Two years later, at 29, he made his first million. He celebrated the event in his book, *How I Made One Million Dollars Last Year Trading Commodities,* and then made another killing from the royalties. And as the volume of his trading increased, so did the good years. In fact, his runs were often spectacular and far outnumbered what he referred to, talking in a newly adopted breezy market-speak, as "the corrections." When his picture appeared in *Forbes*—a bush of curly hair, an open, wide-collared shirt, and a necklace of love beads around his neck—his iconoclastic, whiz-kid success was official. Friends and even friends of friends began pestering him for tips. Picking up on something that had been drilled into him by the gray flannel suits at J. Walter Thompson, he decided there was "no point in giving anything away for free." He started the "Williams Report" and quickly had so many subscribers at an annual fee of $100 that, hunting for more treasure, he went on the lecture circuit. For a fee of $1,500, he promised to share a system that would teach investors to recognize market trends and lock in profits.

It was a grandiose promise, and it attracted the somewhat incredulous attention of *The Wall Street Journal,* which reported:

> The first seminar was held . . . and 63 seekers of the Holy Grail arrived at the Barbizon Plaza Hotel in New York. They were photographed, they signed checks for $1,500. . . .
>
> "Why would you want to share something like this?" a student asked. "What kind of man are you?"
>
> "Mercenary," Mr. Williams answered. "Very mercenary." The audience laughed.

In the first six days, the lecture tour grossed $780,000, and now investors and the press weren't the only people paying attention. The Securities and Exchange Commission, contending that the seminar's money-back guarantee made it an investment contract, ordered that it should be registered as a security. Williams stubbornly dug in his heels and his legal battles with the government began. When the dust cleared—and the mountain of bills were paid off—he had won three successive cases (including their appcals) and kept his SEC license. But after a fourth case was filed, he threw up his hands and, without admitting any guilt, settled by agreeing to sell his newsletter.

So, at 32 and feeling a little frayed around the edges from both his recent divorcc and the hassles with the government, he hit the road. He traveled to the Mideast, then to all the postcard spots in Europe, and after that he just followed the sun. One afternoon, lying on a stretch of velvet beach in Hawaii, trying to recover from another night spent rejuvenating his spirits, he had, as he would describe it, "a breakthrough." "This is so damn pasteurized. So damn shallow," he told himself. His money, he decided, wasn't buying anything worthwhile. And then in a flash, just as sudden and unexpected as the round of self-criticism that preceded it, he knew what he craved—adventure! His "spirit"—with all his laid-back beachcombing a bit of the New Age had crept into his vocabulary—required the vitalizing energy that he had experienced as a boy. He needed, he told himself as he fixed on the metaphor that had served him so well in the past, to go deeper into the cave. He left the next day for Montana.

Back home, his adventures began to unfold rapidly. He moved into a tiny backwoods cabin perched above a fishing lake. On a trip down from his hilltop to what was undoubtedly Montana's only organic restaurant, he met Carla, the dark-haired, big-eyed owner, and they were soon blissfully married. Next thing he knew, he had two daughters and was building a redwood mansion as big as Mount Butte. By the time it was completed and the locals were all talking about the hot tub and the "environmental room," where at the push of a button the sounds of the seasons could be electronically mimicked, Williams had bought into a small bank that was on its way to becoming a bigger one. Of course, all the while he was keeping his eye on the market and systematically trading his personal accounts. After six fast-paced years, he was the first to admit that returning to Montana had worked out pretty well. He was a very happy and prosperous man, when, emboldened by a self-made man's conceit, he decided the time had come to try a new adventure—politics.

THERE was no hesitation, no pretense of paying dues or accumulating markers. Instead, he plunged headfirst into the sea of candidates who were seeking the Republican nomination to represent Montana in the 1978 U.S. Senate race. As in so many of his life's determining challenges, Larry Williams emerged a natural. He was telegenic—although the modish, whiz-kid look had given way to aviator glasses, suits and ties, and a plastered-down Kennedyesque pompadour—and his time on the lecture circuit had made him comfortable on a podium or with a sound bite. His philosophy was a fierce and individualistic conservatism, and that these were truly held beliefs, not ideology cut and pasted together from the latest polls, gave him an advantage in any debate. Without previously having held or even sought office, Williams, to quote an impressed Havre (Montana) *Daily News,* "demolished" his two rivals.

He was now the Republican candidate for a U.S. Senate seat. Bob Dole, Gerald Ford, and Ronald Reagan trekked to Montana to campaign with him. And still the Democrats didn't take him seriously. Williams was portrayed as a novice, a bored millionaire looking for a new game to play. Which, however true, was of little consequence to the voters in a blue-collar state where a self-made fortune was many a workingman's dream. Statewide polls had Williams trailing by only a few percentage points. Yet it was only after he went one-on-one against his Democratic opponent, Congressman Max Baucus, in a 60-minute televised debate near the end of the campaign, that the Democrats started to reevaluate whom they were up against. It was a "massacre," according to one newspaper, which went on to mix a few more combative images into its stunned report: "Baucus found himself on the ropes, groping for words to counter Williams' arrows." So now things got down and dirty. The Democrats brought up the SEC's suits against Williams. And in an inspired bit of meanness, they plastered flyers all over the state with his turned-on, tuned-in picture from the *Forbes* article. How many votes did that string of love beads cost him? No polling was done, but when the votes were counted, first-time candidate Larry Williams had lost a seat in the U.S. Senate by about 10 percentage points.

The bruised morning after, he vowed to his family that he would stay out of politics. But it was an oath that was firmly held only until the next election. "I loved the action," he would explain, punctuating the revelation with a small shrug that seemed to acknowledge that he knew this was not the best of reasons for wanting to represent the good people of Montana. In 1982, after winning the Republican nomination by the largest margin in the state's history, he ran against John Melcher for the Senate seat. And this time the Democrats, realizing they had just squeaked by last time out, targeted Williams from the opening days of the campaign. They hurled all the SEC stuff at him again, and for good measure they threw in some gossip about his divorce a decade earlier.

Williams got trounced. Now when he repeated his morning-after vow to walk away from politics, he meant it. He also decided to leave Montana. In his angry mind, he had a hard time dealing with the reality that he and Carla, as well as the two girls, were no longer private people. They would go shopping or sit down at a restaurant, and Williams could feel the curious stares burning into him and his family. After all the notoriety that two no-holds-barred Senate campaigns had kicked up, he was certain people were whispering about his money or his divorce or his battles with the government. He wanted to retreat into a comfortable anonymity while he figured out what to do next.

He sold the big redwood house to a lottery winner (in his mind, a poetic gesture that was enormously satisfying) and, like so many dreamers looking to reinvent their lives, relocated to southern California. He moved to the outskirts of San Diego, into a gated compound of sprawling fantasy homes, a sunlit, manicured world designed, it seemed, for first-generation fortunes (the widow of the man who had created the McDonald's empire lived in the colossal house down the block). And as Williams put one more life behind him, as he settled into the uncomplicated easiness of southern California, buying the requisite Rolls, playing with his computers, swallowing the vitamins, mixing the yogurt shakes, a new scheme was taking hold.

It moved forward in stages. First, he hooked up with a guy who was working on a new technology for metal detectors. Convinced of the machine's powers, he threw some cash into a deep-sea dive off the coast of Florida to hunt for pirate strongboxes. When word of that investment got around, wild-eyed treasure hunters started lining up—some days quite literally—at his front door. He listened to tall tales about Emperor Maximilian's treasure, Confederate gold, and Doc Noss's hidden mine. Most of these he dismissed with an exaggerated roll of his eyes. But when he heard about the dig at the Ancoma reservation, he was intrigued.

After a month of due diligence, he bought in. And when former astronaut James Irwin—a man who had walked on the moon, he told his wife with genuine awe—tried to get him involved in the search for Noah's Ark, Williams decided that, as he put it, "Irwin was onto something." He promptly wrote out a check for $200,000.

If pressed about his participation in these and a handful of other expeditions, Williams would find his authoritative banker's voice and do his best to end the discussion with an easy, sober-sounding logic. "There's more wealth buried under the ocean and under the ground than there is in circulation. A man could get seriously rich if he got his hands on some of that loot."

Of course it was a windfall that, Williams understood, was predicated upon a gigantic "if." A speculator but not a gambler, he would be quick to acknowledge the overwhelming odds. That admission usually ended the conversation. But when his interrogator was persistent, he would finally surrender. "Look, the money is part of what I'm searching for," he would say, his candor laced with exasperation. "No doubt about it. But it's not the whole nine yards. I want to live all my lives before I run out of them. I want adventure. When the time comes to dive into the sea or go down into the hole, I'm right there leading the way. Maybe that's treasure enough. Anything I actually find is gravy. How can I lose?"

He couldn't. Halfway through his forties, he was still the boy in the cave, still pressing deeper and deeper into the beckoning mystery. He was still hooked.

How do people dream up these things? The real Mount Sinai? The gold of Exodus? By the time Williams had come to the end of Dave Fasold's letter, he was thinking that now he had heard everything. No doubt about it, he told himself, Davey must have headed up to the surface a bit too quickly after his last dive. If you don't take the time to decompress, it can really screw up your brain.

Williams crumbled the pages into a ball and concentrated on gauging the distance to the wicker wastebasket across the room. But then, even as he took aim, his mind abruptly shifted back to Fasold's letter. Maybe, he would later suggest, it was something in the tone. It wasn't a wild man's letter. There was none of the feverish, gushing excitement that raced through most of the tall tales he had been hearing. It was as if, Williams decided, Fasold was genuinely awed by the significance of the expedition he was suggesting.

But then again, Williams also would readily admit, it just might have been something else that drew him back to the letter—the gold of Exodus. The glittering prospect of the bounty the Hebrews had taken with them out of Egypt and into the desert. Fasold had written that for a moment he had seen the glimmer of this gold with his own eyes. The readings from his machine promised more. An ancient treasure whose value could not be measured simply in the weight of its gold, in the sparkle of its gems—it was truly priceless—was buried near the foot of the mountain. Or maybe, Williams would suggest as he searched for another reason, it was simply too good a story to dismiss without savoring its possibilities for a little while longer.

Whatever the reason, whatever his motivation, he found himself taking an atlas down from the bookshelf catty-corner to his desk. He hunted for a map of the Middle East, and when he found it he looked down the length of the Sinai Peninsula until his eyes settled on a black dot the size of a pinhead. Above the dot were the words "Mt. Sinai." And directly below it, to his total amazement, he saw a tiny, but nevertheless unmistakable question mark.

It was true, he suddenly realized. *No one knew where Mount Sinai was located.*

8

Pikes Peak: 1986

OVER the next busy few weeks, as a bright spring eased into the full bloom of a southern California summer, Williams found himself returning to Fasold's letter. Part of him—"my Republican banker mind-set," he called it without a touch of irony—was distrustful, and lectured that dismissing Fasold's story as fanciful, a wild-goose chase to end all wild-goose chases, was the only sound course. But something else was also pulling at him. He could be off on his 7 A.M. jog, or at his laptop devising a strategy to take advantage of the sudden frost ravaging Brazil's coffee crop, or simply driving into La Jolla with the top down on a cool, starry night and Carla going on about the kids, when suddenly it would sneak up on him: *What if it was true?* What if Fasold was right? What if there really was an ancient treasure buried at the foot of a mountain in the middle of the Saudi Arabian desert?

It would be the find of a lifetime.

How could he walk away from that kind of opportunity? The

possibility, however far-fetched, was so exciting, it ignited so many of his lifelong ambitions, that after contemplating it for a while he came to understand he could not simply ignore Fasold's letter.

But he also refused to allow himself to be impetuous. To his orderly way of looking at things, the search for treasure, even the ancient gold buried at the foot of the most sacred mountain on the planet, was first and foremost a commercial venture. Like all business propositions, it required due diligence. Further complicating the process, the more he reread Fasold's account, the more his mind shouted out questions. Sure, he told himself, maybe there was some debate over the precise location of Mount Sinai. But Saudi Arabia? Was that possible? Did that make historical sense? And *gold?* Did the Hebrews actually take gold out of Egypt?

Williams, despite his passion, was determined to steer a steady course. It would take a lot more evidence than the readings from Fasold's frequency generator to send him off on an expedition deep into a desert halfway across the world. He would need to do some research. He could start with the Bible—wasn't there a copy somewhere in the house?—and go on reading from there. A handful of generous (and, conveniently, tax-deductible) checks sprinkled around to the nearby universities should help put him in touch with an arsenal of scholars. He would buy the best minds he could find, and even if they wound up laughing at Fasold's letter, it would be money well spent. Not only would it save him the cost of the trip to the Middle East, but it would also save him a chunk of his highly valued self-esteem. At least then he would never have to wonder if it had been the danger waiting out in the desert that had scared him off.

Because from the start, from the moment he had begun to think seriously about Fasold's account, Williams could not help but be concerned about the risks. Fasold, to his credit, had been candid. He had dangled a golden carrot, but he had also clearly raised a cautionary stick, a warning that weighed heavily on Williams. Going to Jabal al Lawz would be a dicey undertaking. Even if he made his way across the desert to the mountain, managed somehow to find the exact spot that had set off Fasold's generator, and then succeeded in excavating the treasure, getting it out of the country would still be a challenge.

Just as, for that matter, would be *his* getting out. Ron Wyatt, the letter reported, had spent 78 days in a Saudi jail. And Fasold himself had spent a disquieting week under house arrest after having been taken at gunpoint, a rifle shoved up against his chest. Then there had been the trial—a Saudi trial! a Saudi court!—and the judge's unequivocal decree: Never speak about the mountain. Never dream about the treasure. Never return—or be arrested on sight.

An image of a Saudi jail cell took to materializing without warning in Williams' head, and anxiety had turned his imagination brutal. It loomed before him as the bleakest of dim dungeons, a dark, dank, foul-smelling hole. Williams told himself he could very likely wind up as the inhabitant of just such a cell, a prisoner accused of unspecified crimes, shackled to a stone wall forever—if they didn't execute him. And then another fear rushed through him. The Saudis chop off people's heads. Still, if given the choice of life in an Arab prison or the executioner's ax, he could only wonder which fate he would wish for.

Williams was scared. However, he was also a man who had lived his life on excellent terms with his fears. He acknowledged them, respected them even, and at the same time enjoyed triumphing over them. Each small step deeper into the cave was a large, sweet victory, a measure of the quality that, in his prideful assessment, made his life special. Therefore, Williams, although jumpy, was determined not to be deterred. But he was also prudent. He was a husband and father. His life was bounded up in responsibilities. With the treasure or without it, he needed to get out of Saudi Arabia alive. As he worked toward the first tentative steps of a plan, he grew convinced that he needed a partner. It was not simply a question of success. The odds for survival itself would jump reassuringly if there were someone else along for the ride. This realization made him immediately more comfortable with the risks, and consequently Williams quickly rearranged his priorities. Before he read another verse of Exodus, before he shared Fasold's letter with any scholar, he would need to find someone to accompany him to Saudi Arabia.

But whom? What sort of man was he looking for? Williams asked himself. He thought about the men he knew and mentally scrolled down a long list of types. There were the athletes, obsessively fit, not yielding to age, preoccupied with workouts, Nautilus machines, and body fat. Heading off into a desert where the temperature could settle in at around 120, it undoubtedly would be an edge to have someone along who wouldn't wilt. Then there were the starchy, pink-faced self-made business heroes who, while puffy from rivers of martinis and expense account outings, had agile, quick-witted minds that would be invaluable if it came to thinking a way out of a jam. And there was a host of potential candidates from the easygoing circle of clubmen he knew only too intimately, men comfortable with life, who knew how to tell an amusing story and, no small gift, have a good time. What more could one ask of a traveling companion?

Yet even as his list grew, as he sorted through names and faces, he kept returning to the same bottom line. He wanted someone he could count on, someone he could trust if his life depended on it, someone who wouldn't run. And as a corollary to these criteria, his memory kept summoning up the same, defining story. Jim Irwin, the astronaut, a man who knew firsthand about the fine points of courage, had shared it with him, and his imprimatur only added to its unimpeachable power.

The occasion was a get-together—"party" was too festive a concept for a sober commander like Irwin—to mark the conclusion of the weeks of training Irwin's team had endured in anticipation of their climb of Mount Ararat. Williams, their benefactor in this search for Noah's Ark, had been invited up to the house outside Seattle to meet the men, slap a few backs, and share their optimism. It was only as the evening was winding down that Irwin led Williams into a corner and, without making too much of a show, pointed out a man across the room. The man was a hulk. He wasn't particularly tall, but his shoulders seemed wide enough to fit snugly between two goalposts, and the buttons on his lumberjack plaid shirt looked ready to burst across his solid chest. He was planted like a redwood in the middle of a group gushing with beery laughter, yet he had only a small, tight smile on his handsome face: amused, yet controlled. His name, Irwin announced, was Bob Cornuke, and with that introduction out of the way, the astronaut proceeded to tell Williams a story about the man. He told it without embellishment, the way soldiers do when they are filing a report they hope will result in one of their own winning a medal; which, in another life, was no doubt precisely what Colonel Irwin would have done.

THEY had been in Colorado a few weeks earlier, training on Pikes Peak. In the morning they had split into teams of two; the mountain was solid ice, and pairs made better progress than a long train when the going turned slick. Nevertheless, it was a slow, careful, often nerve-tingling ascent. The ice was so thick it took a lot of concerted hammering just to drive a single stake into the face of the mountain, and even the occasional narrow ledge offered little safety. It might as well have been covered with a sheet of solid glass. Only an atheist, and a diehard one at that, didn't say a prayer before taking each new step. After they had been climbing for nearly an hour, the snow came. It arrived without warning and built quickly to a fury. And, Irwin admitted without embarrassment, he cheered its arrival. The previous night all three teams had agreed that as soon as any snow started falling, they would immediately head back down the mountain. Ice was dangerous, yet part of the risk; however, climbing in snow was a fool's sport. The teams, without losing any pride, began their descent.

Cornuke knew next to nothing about climbing, so he had been teamed with Steve, the group's expert. Steve was strong, skilled, and, Cornuke's good fortune, a diligent teacher. While it was Steve's luck that he had a student who, like a wind-up machine, went off without complaint or hesitation in the direction he was pointed. That morning Steve had expertly led the way up the mountain and Cornuke, the trusting novice, had obediently followed. Despite the conditions, they made good progress. After their first full hour, when Cornuke dared to look down, he could barely make out the colored parkas of his friends; Steve and he had climbed that much higher. Then the snow came and there was no point in looking for anyone. He had a hard enough time seeing Steve or hearing his instructions.

Just as he had led the way up, Steve methodically led the way down. Yet it was a battle. The wind was singing wickedly, driving the wet snow into their faces. The rope began to feel heavy in their hands as it became coated with ice. The spikes on their boots were quickly clogged with fresh snow, and Steve made a point of repeatedly instructing Cornuke to make sure one foot was planted firmly before even thinking about moving the other. But they went on.

And then Steve fell. There was no warning, merely a quick, terrible free fall when his rope broke in two as if sliced with a knife. He went straight down, a body flying through space, legs kicking in panic, down and down, until he landed on a ledge forty feet below with a crash that nearly drowned out Cornuke's terrified scream.

Cornuke had no choice but to go down after him. He was climbing alone for the first time in his life. And there was a blizzard. By the time Cornuke made his way down to the ledge, Steve had regained consciousness. He had to struggle through waves of pain, and the words came out in slow, short bursts. Nevertheless, he managed to tell Cornuke that his leg was broken. Cornuke looked down at Steve. The man's face was ominously drained of blood. He lay flat across the ice, as inert as a doll. It seemed to take all his remaining strength to bite down on his lip so he wouldn't cry out from the pain. Cornuke, without much hope, offered a silent prayer begging that a broken leg was all Steve had to worry about; and then, somehow finding a reassuring grin, he finally spoke: "You don't look too bad. Now let me see about getting you out of here."

"I can't move," Steve insisted, nearly crying. "You go down the mountain. I'll wait for help."

Cornuke shook his head. "It's not going to be that way," he said. There was no point in explaining that by the time the blizzard stopped and a rescue crew made its way up the mountain it would be tomorrow. And by then Steve would be dead.

When Steve continued to argue, Cornuke cut him off. His voice was soft because that was the way he always spoke, and his words had the force of a promise because he meant precisely what he said. "We're going to go through this thing together. We're going to find a way to make it."

Steve began to realize he couldn't change Cornuke's mind; and anyway, when Cornuke picked him up in a fireman's carry and started tying him to his back with the rope, Steve passed out from the pain. Cornuke told himself that was probably just as well. Now Steve wouldn't feel a thing when both of them went crashing to the ground. Then, without further hesitation, Cornuke took the first step down the mountain.

IT took Cornuke nearly five hours to reach the camp at the mountain's base, Irwin told Williams. There was a blizzard. He had a man tied to his back. And it was his first solo descent. "So all things considered, he shouldn't have been too upset with his time," Irwin concluded without even a smile to signal that he was being ironic. The astronaut delivered the punch line with similar deadpan control. "Not to mention that in the process Bob had saved a man's life. The doctors said if Steve had spent another hour without being treated, it would have been his last."

His narrative over, Irwin, a man who was probably more at home on the lonely craters of the moon than in a room full of people, nodded to Williams and, without another word, headed for the door. So that left a curious—and truth be told, envious—Williams to cross the room unescorted and make his own introductions. After only the briefest of small talk, he zeroed in with the question that had been circling around his mind. "How did it feel to be going down the mountain, 185 pounds of dead weight on your back, and knowing every step could be your last?"

Cornuke considered the question for a moment before answering in his slow, soft way. "It wouldn't be accurate to say I was scared." There was another silent beat before he added, "Terrified would be more like it."

That night, with the help of several beers to speed the process along, Bob Cornuke and Larry Williams became friends. That had been nearly two years before, and they had not talked since. But now as Williams was playing with the possibility of going off into the Saudi desert to find a forbidden treasure, he began to think he could do a lot worse than having Bob Cornuke along for the trip. In fact, a dependable sort like Cornuke could, especially if the going got rough, come in very handy. He opened his address book to the Cs and hoped that Cornuke had not moved or finally stumbled off some mountain.

9

Colorado Springs, Colorado: 1987

Bob Cornuke was in his bedroom doing push-ups when the phone rang. He did them in sets of twenty-five, one-handed. He was on his third set, having just switched to his stronger right hand, and he decided he would let the machine take the call. It could be his wife calling from her new place, and he didn't want to hear about it. At least that was what he tried to convince himself. But on the fourth ring, he hurried to the alcove off the living room and grabbed the receiver. "Honey?" he asked, out of breath and full of hope.

"Not yours," Larry Williams can still remember answering back.

When both men's embarrassed laughter subsided, Williams got around to identifying himself.

"Sure," said Cornuke after only a moment. "I remember you. How you doing? What's up?"

For the next twenty minutes, Williams went through everything in Fasold's letter. He didn't exaggerate or editorialize. He laid it out as he would any potential investment—the upside and the downside.

Then it was Cornuke's turn. There was a long, thoughtful pause before he spoke. "The real Mount Sinai? Saudi Arabia? A hidden treasure? What're you smoking, Larry? It's got to be the craziest story I ever heard."

"Yeah," Williams agreed easily. Both men shared a good laugh.

"But what if it's true?" Williams asked at last.

They played with that for a while until even Cornuke had to admit the possibility was exciting. That was the opening Williams had been waiting for, and he invited Cornuke to come for a visit. It was, he was quick to make clear, just a first step. Neither of them was committing himself to anything. Still, there were a lot of questions that needed to be answered before they could even begin to think seriously about going to Saudi Arabia. Williams suggested they might as well try to work them out together. Besides, he pointed out, if there was even the possibility of their being a team, they would have to get to know each other better, to hang out.

Cornuke was unsure. He was not ready to give an answer.

"Naturally," Williams went on, "it's my treat. Same for the trip to Saudi—if there is a trip. We don't go, well, at least you'll have had a vacation in sunny California. What do you say?"

Cornuke looked around the living room. There wasn't a stick of furniture in the whole damn place. His wife, soon to be his ex-wife, had taken everything. He could go back to doing push-ups and waiting for her call. Or he could fly off to San Diego, all expenses paid. And who knows? Before it was all over he might wind up finding a treasure to boot.

"Tomorrow sound good to you?" Cornuke asked.

THIS isn't a house, this is a mansion, Cornuke decided as Williams drove him through the electric gate and into the courtyard the next afternoon. "The last time I was in a place this big," he told his host, "I needed a library card to get in." Cornuke couldn't help wondering what he had gotten into, if this trip was a big mistake. But soon enough he noticed that Williams seemed to take it all for granted so he might as well do the same. And, anyway, there was work to be done.

On their very first night together, Williams, who had been giving the matter a good deal of thought, proposed a plan of attack. He waited until dinner was over and then, with apologies to his family, led Cornuke to his crow's nest study. The evening sky beyond the glass walls was sprinkled with stars, and Williams spoke in his sound-bite voice—steely and without hesitation. But Cornuke could tell he was at the same time being very careful. It was, he felt, as if Williams was leaning back from the edge of the pool one last time before deciding either to plunge in—or to turn around and walk away.

There are questions, Williams began, that need to be answered before we can even think of traveling to Saudi Arabia. Fasold's letter is valuable as a starting point, but nothing more. The risks are too real, too steep, for us to rely on his account alone. We need to be confident we have at least a fair chance of succeeding. After all, there must be hundreds of would-be Sinais scattered throughout the Middle East. What we'll need is an independent way of verifying we're traveling to the real Mount Sinai.

Williams let that sink in, then got to his feet and began to pace across the small room, rattling off commands. Here's what we must get clear in our minds before we go any further. We need facts. We need an accurate and detailed description of Mount Sinai. We need to know specifically which geographical and physical characteristics make the mountain we're searching for unique. We need to know what we should expect to find if Jabal al Lawz *is* the real Mount Sinai. We need to know—and this was the bottom line he had been heading to all along—everything the Bible tells us about the mountain that is Mount Sinai.

But he was not done. There was a final question. He offered it with a tight, narrow smile that seemed, at least in Cornuke's mind, to suggest a challenge. "Think you could get a handle on all that, Bob?"

"I could give it a try," Cornuke answered in his soft, even way.

• • •

FROM the start, Cornuke found the problem a joy to attack. In his meticulousness, he might as well have been a detective scouring a crime scene, only now he pored over the Bible, hunting in the nuances of each passage for hidden clues. He was, as he was in everything, all discipline. After an early-morning run and then a family breakfast, he would climb the stairs to the isolation of Williams' study, open his texts, start taking notes on a yellow legal pad, and next thing he knew the sun was setting and Carla would be calling him to dinner. Williams, who all the while continued to juggle an assortment of projects and schemes, was impressed by his friend's commitment and, not least, his stamina. However, the truth was that Cornuke found the chance to wrap himself up in concentrated, focused work a blessing. It gave him something to care about; and that, in turn, helped to muzzle so many of his demons. As he filled up the pad with his tight, minute script, he began for the first time in years to feel the beginnings of some sustained peace.

10

West Hollywood, California: 1955

BOB Cornuke had first seen the pyramids when he was eight years old. He had gazed at them, along with the Eiffel Tower, Big Ben, and the Taj Mahal, through the twin sights of his grandmother's View Master. There was a hooked rug on the living room floor of her tiny, wood-frame bungalow in West Hollywood, and for hours each day he would lie on the rug flat on his belly with the View Master pressed to his eyes. What voyages he took! She had boxes and boxes of slides, all inventoried and carefully identified. He could travel around the world and, still eager, immediately ship off again.

Like any wide-eyed traveler, he had countless questions, and his grandmother was only too glad to serve as his knowledgeable guide. He would sit at the kitchen table covered with its shiny red oilcloth and, with the comforting aroma of simmering cabbage soup filling the room, listen with rapt attention as she spun tales about the world beyond California. Like her husband, she had been born in Minsk, and after more than a quarter of a century in America, her speech was still thick with the accent of her native land. For Cornuke, this foreignness reinforced her authority. And he adored her. He was mesmerized, never daring to interrupt even when he had finished off one helping of the spicy cabbage soup and his spoon was scraping against the bottom of the pottery bowl. His grandmother, meanwhile, playing to her favorite audience, would re-create in elaborate (and, he realized with a smile when he got older, fanciful) detail her visits as a young woman to Paris, London, and Moscow. And each night he would reluctantly pedal his bike back to his parents' house and go to bed, hoping to dream of the exotic places he would travel to one day. Life at home was that bad and he wanted to get away that desperately. Escape, Cornuke would later say, was nearly all he ever thought about.

When his dad was in a good mood, that is, after just a few drinks, he called himself "a mixologist." After a few more, however, he would demote himself to "a dumb bartender." By the time he got to the bottom of a bottle, he would be going on about the polio that had left him with a limp and how he was "nothing but a cripple." Cornuke would lie in bed, trying with all his might to shut out the angry sounds from the next room, hoping his father wouldn't find some reason to take off his leather belt and go after him. He wished that tomorrow could be there already and he could escape to the worlds waiting in his grandmother's house. He grew up dreaming of faraway places. It was how he managed to survive.

WHEN Cornuke was a teenager, he finally found a way to win his father's love, or at least get some sober, focused attention. To his own amazement as much as his dad's, he became a football star. The coach at Costa Mesa High, a beachfront town where the family had now settled, saw a short, broad-shouldered kid with a morose pout frozen on his face and decided on the spot that this thick-necked package could be molded into a head-banging second-string lineman. Those expectations, the coach soon discovered, were modest. In the course of a damaging preseason drill, the varsity had run out of healthy running backs. The coach looked down the bench and, quite arbitrarily, recruited Cornuke to carry the ball for the next play. His instructions were simple: Hit the hole as fast as you can.

Twenty years later, Cornuke, with a bemused shake of his head meant to suggest that he was still a bit bewildered by what happened, described how the play went down. "I hit the hole like a cannonball and kept on going. When someone tried to tackle me, I just ran over him. It seemed," he went on to explain with his customary, unselfconscious objectivity, "I had this blazing speed from right off the mark, which was really rare in a short, stocky guy." He became the starting fullback, and by the time he graduated he had set a handful of rushing records, won a full scholarship to Fresno State, and learned that high school—life itself, even—could be fun, at least for a football hero. There was, naturally, a Faustian payoff for all this previously unimagined good fortune—nerve-rattling, eye-watering physical pain.

But, unbending, he gutted it out. And by the time he was the starting fullback at Fresno State, his resolve even more than his ability to break tackles became his trademark. There would be Cornuke on the sidelines, his face fixed with a grimace, his two hands locked tightly onto the back of a bench as if all his strength and concentration were necessary to keep it from floating away. And then, with an ear-shattering bellow, he would slam his shoulder smack into the bench with so much force that the stadium itself seemed to shake. Sometimes, to the crowd's disbelief, he would finish with one shoulder only to repeat the process with the other. And the next play, his dislocated shoulders popped into place, he would be back in the game, taking a handoff, putting his head down, and ramming straight through the hole. It still hurt like hell. Worse, it would be nothing compared to the full charge that shot through his body when the frustrated opposition finally caught up with him and a bunch of bruisers piled on. But he wasn't a quitter.

In the off-seasons he routinely had operations. Nasty surgical scars were laced in jagged crisscrossing patterns around each shoulder. A lot of good the doctors did. One solid hit and it was as if he had stepped on a percussion grenade. Still, if he could stand, Cornuke was in the backfield. He later explained his stoicism with matter-of-fact logic: "When I played football, that was the only time my father admired and loved me. Therefore, pain was not an issue. He was so happy when I played. I would've endured anything for his love."

In his wounded mind, Cornuke had no choice. He was already disfigured by deeper scars. He had struggled through a more intense, more invasive pain long before he ever stepped onto a football field. *That* had been unbearable. The hurt from football was, he felt, less remarkable. In time, it would subside. He would go on playing.

BUT his body caved in before his will. By Cornuke's senior year, he was sitting on the bench in his street clothes, his shoulders demolished beyond any hope of repair. He had once talked seriously about going to the pros; now it was an ambition that, without looking back, he discarded. After graduation and a few unsatisfying detours—selling shoes, plumbing—he began to understand that he required a more consuming vocation, something he could wrap himself up in. He was searching for the power, the thrill, and, not least, the gratifying challenge he had experienced when he was running with a football. He found it in the police.

He joined the Costa Mesa force and celebrated the event by rushing into marriage with a woman he had met on a blind date. Right from the start their life together was difficult. There was never, he would come to realize, any joy in each other's presence. All he could do was throw himself into his work. Like the fullback he had been who begged to carry the ball on every play, Cornuke became the zealous cop who covered the entire city. When a report of man-with-a-gun or robbery-in-progress came over the police band, Cornuke, siren wailing, would tear off in pursuit of the action. He made a point of never wearing his jacket; that way he would always be ready to throw a punch. No matter what the weather, he drove with his windows down; that way he could hear what was happening on the street. Two years on the force and he was leading the department in arrests. His superiors, impressed by such dedication (and perhaps too grateful to worry about its roots), rewarded him with an appointment to the SWAT team.

His exploits with SWAT became the stuff of departmental legend. But just what was being celebrated was a matter of some station house debate; one cop's fearless hero was another's risk-taking crazy. Unchallenged, however, was the fact that most times Cornuke was the first man through the door. But more than any other incident, it was the time Cornuke got knifed that earned him his notoriety.

The SWAT team had rolled out on a report of shots fired only to find a wide-eyed lunatic, high on PCP was the guess, sitting at his living room window and tearing up the front lawn with shotgun blasts. The lieutenant sized up the situation, weighed the risk of an assault, and then decided the safest approach would be to give the negotiator a chance to talk the shooter out of his anger. So while shotgun blasts still ripped into the lawn, the team took cover and waited for the negotiator to arrive. When he finally showed, he grabbed a bullhorn and launched into a long monologue that repeatedly circled back to the same demand: Things will look rosier in the morning; throw down your weapon and you'll live to see it. That prospect, however, did not seem to offer the shooter any solace. He continued to howl and fire rounds. A standoff was shaping up that could drag on until either he ran out of shells or the drugs wore off.

Cornuke, crouched behind a squad car, was in no mood to wait. His bladder was about to burst. He needed to urinate desperately. Finally, without even a nod to the lieutenant, he abruptly stood up, ordered the stunned negotiator to can it, and, his sidearm still holstered, began striding up the front walk. Before he got to the door, the man came out on the porch to meet him. His bulging eyes were as big as saucers. And he had his shotgun leveled toward the center of Cornuke's armored vest.

"Where the hell you think you're going?"

"Sorry, got to take a leak," Cornuke said with some embarrassment.

That explanation seemed to confuse the man. It was the moment Cornuke needed. In one quick, fluid motion, he grabbed the shotgun and, now holding the weapon by its barrel, swung it like a baseball bat into the side of the man's head. It was a home-run blow, and he fell to his knees. Cornuke, not breaking stride, stepped over him and opened the screen door. But before he could go inside, the man, still on his knees, pulled a long-bladed knife from his boot and plunged it into Cornuke's thigh. He was preparing to do it again when Cornuke, blood seeping through his pant leg, turned and brought the butt of the shotgun down like a piston onto the crown of the man's skull. When he went down this time, he lay there motionless. And Cornuke headed into the house, looking for the bathroom.

After that, the lieutenant always made a point of going up to Cornuke as soon as the SWAT team was about to roll out. In a voice loud enough so everyone could hear, he would say, "You make sure to take a leak. Don't want you getting antsy out there." That earned a round of laughter, and, just as the lieutenant intended, helped ease the pre-battle mood. Cornuke would play along, a self-deprecating grin on his face, but the truth was, he would have preferred to forget the whole incident. It was inextricably tied up in his mind with some very rocky business.

In the hectic aftermath of his stabbing, it had been late by the time Cornuke, after a half-dozen stitches and at least the same number of beers, finally made his way home. He called out to his wife, prepared to offer a modest account of the day's adventure as an excuse for his tardiness. There was no answer. That night he lay awake in bed. And by the morning's light, still alone, he admitted to himself that his wife did not love him. An old, familiar hurt raced through him. It seemed, however, more painful this time around.

11

FIVE weeks to the day after his arrival at Williams' big house, Cornuke had completed his preliminary round of research. It wasn't everything they would need, he knew, but it would be a good start. There was enough to make a call about whether or not they stood a chance of identifying the real Mount Sinai. The time had come, he felt, to decide if they should take this any further or forget the whole thing. He picked up his legal pad and went looking for his host.

By now the two men were no longer strangers. In their differences—one a strategist, the other a foot soldier; one ambitious, the other almost humble—as well as in their similarities—a chance, both were ready to gamble, was usually worth the risk—they had forged a friendship. Cornuke found Williams in the pool, efficiently completing his daily laps. He did not interrupt. Instead, he found a sling-back chair on the tile deck and sat. He was quite proud of what he had accomplished, and he wanted Williams' complete attention when he laid it all out.

He waited until Williams, with a towel draped over his shoulders and a bottle of Evian in his hand, was seated comfortably on a chaise to begin his presentation. He was prepared to cite—quite literally—chapter and verse, but Cornuke also knew his audience. It wasn't so much that Williams was impatient as that, a perpetual whirlwind of activity, he didn't like to get bogged down. His mind was always reaching like a chess player's to the next move—and the move after that. Cornuke, therefore, didn't embellish or digress. He was once more the cop, a model of brevity. From the moment he started in, he laid out the facts with the shorthand precision of a dispatcher announcing an all-points.

"FORTUNATELY for us," Cornuke began, "the Bible gives a very good description of what we should find if we're able, in fact, to locate the real Mount Sinai.

"First off, let's consider the big picture. I'm talking basic topography. OK, we're looking for a mountain surrounded by a plain or at least some sort of campsite that's big enough to shelter and support the million or so Israelites who fled from Egypt and then wound up spending eleven months at Sinai. Another clue should be the vegetation. This mountain wasn't in the middle of your typical desert wasteland. Not only do we know for a fact that the Israelites grazed the thousands of animals they brought with them, but also that Jethro, Moses' father-in-law, kept his flock of sheep around the mountain for decades before the Exodus.

"Next, there should be an open, level expanse of land nearby. A plain big enough to have been the scene for one knock-down-drag-out battle. The Israelites fought the Amalekites for an entire day at a site not too far from Mount Sinai. And within a stone's throw from this battlefield, we should expect to find the hill where Moses, his staff raised toward Heaven, cheered on his troops.

"But these are, I realize," Cornuke went on with a candor Williams was learning to appreciate, "pretty general physical characteristics. For all we know, we could find this sort of terrain at a dozen mountains. We need to be able to identify other, more unique characteristics. Right?"

When Williams didn't bother to respond, Cornuke continued, leaning so far forward in his chair that for an edgy moment Williams can still remember thinking his friend was going to topple into the pool. "Now, admittedly this is going to take some luck, but if we're really prowling around Moses' mountain, and if things are really going our way, then there's always the chance we might be able to find some trace of what the Israelites built during their stay.

"For starters, we might come across the boundary markers. Moses, the Bible says, erected them around the base of the mountain so the Israelites would keep their distance. Now I admit, we don't know too much about these markers. Are they carved? Decorated with designs? Maybe they're simply huge stones. The Bible doesn't really say. But suppose we *can* find them. If we use these markers as our starting point on one side, walking away from the mountain, we might stumble onto what's left of the altar that was erected to support the golden calf. And on the other side, nearer to the base of the mountain, we could very well find the remains of a larger altar.

"Now this time God, according to the Bible, was a bit more specific with the construction blueprints. He instructed Moses that this altar needed to be big enough to allow oxen and sheep to be sacrificed, and it had to be built from uncut stone. OK? Now, using this altar, the big one, as our guide, we should be on the lookout for the pillars Moses had put up. Again, what specific kind of pillars is not clear. But we've got a number to guide us—twelve. One for each tribe, the Bible says.

"Are you following all this?" Cornuke asked, interrupting his own recitation. Williams' silence was, he still remembers, making him uneasy.

Williams responded with the slightest of nods, a gesture whose grudging economy seemed, when Cornuke thought about it later, to suggest a variety of interpretations. But he was on too much of a roll to worry at the time. He merely uttered a rhetorical "Great," and continued his recitation.

"But no matter how many of these artifacts we encounter, our case is still going to be circumstantial. I mean, are we going to know for sure a pile of old stones is really an altar, let alone the altar that held the golden calf? We're not archaeologists or scientists. We can't do carbon dating. The best we'll be able to determine is that this mountain *could* be Sinai. What we need to make our case is what convinces juries in any court of law—eyewitness evidence."

Again Williams merely nodded, and his silence was beginning to puzzle Cornuke. But determined, he went on. "There are certain, very specific *physical* characteristics that are mentioned in the Bible. They were there for Moses. And if we find the right mountain, they'll be there for us too. We'll see them with our own eyes."

For the first time Williams spoke up. "Such as?" he asked.

"OK," Cornuke said, fully prepared, "here's what we have to look for on the mountain. First off—a cave. In Exodus it states that when Moses was up on the mountain, he took shelter in a cave. Unfortunately, there's only a brief, passing reference to it, but I started hunting around and I hit pay dirt. In First Kings, I came across a chapter about the Prophet Elijah and how he flees for his life to escape the wrath of Jezebel. He's so scared he heads off straight into the desert, and after forty days and forty nights he winds up at Mount Sinai. Now here's the good part: While Elijah's on the mountain, he bunks down in Moses' old cave. So, no doubt about it. If we're exploring the real Mount Sinai, we should be able to find a cave big enough for at least one man to sleep in.

"Then we should also come across a brook. Or at least evidence that there once was one. The Bible says quite specifically that after Moses destroyed the golden calf, he chucked the remains into a brook that came down out of the mountain. If we find a cave *and* a brook with our own eyes on a mountain with the right topography, plus, if we get really lucky, a man-made artifact or two, well, then it's a pretty good bet we're in the right place."

"That's it?" Williams asked.

There was something else, but it was such a speculative clue that Cornuke had been reluctant to mention it. Now, however, he found himself responding to the challenge in Williams' question.

"If we're going by what the Bible says, when we get to the top of the mountain there is another proof we should find. According to Exodus, when God descended to Sinai, he was wrapped up in fire and the whole mountaintop was belching smoke and fire and quaking . . ."

"A volcano," Williams said, completing the image.

Cornuke was less certain. "Maybe," he shrugged. "It could be that Mount Sinai really was a volcano. Or it could be just metaphor, a lot of special effects thrown in to keep the story going. Or for all we know," he added without conviction, "what happened could be exactly what the Bible says happened. It's what occurs whenever God shows up on earth. If that's true, there's bound to be some trace of all that heavenly fire and brimstone on the summit."

"Sure," Williams teased. "And maybe we'll find the burning bush."

"Look," Cornuke said, his voice suddenly rigid, "I'm convinced we've got a shot. There are enough clues. If we're in the right place, we'll know it."

But Williams didn't take the bait. He rose from the chaise and began walking along the very edge of the pool. He might have been a man on a tightrope. The exercise seemed to require all his concentration.

"Hey," Cornuke called out, his anger building. "You don't buy this—fine. Thanks for your hospitality. Next plane to Denver, I'm out of here."

But Cornuke did not move, and Williams continued his silent, contemplative journey around the pool. Finally, his circuit completed, he stood beside Cornuke and said, "OK, now we know what we're looking for. But that still doesn't mean we know *where* to look."

Cornuke was stunned. "What about Fasold's letter? Jabal al Lawz?" he shot back with an intensity that surprised him. He suddenly realized that after all his research, he was very much counting on coming face-to-face with the mountain.

"It's going to take a lot more than a letter from Dave Fasold to send me running to the other side of the world," Williams said evenly. "Before I go risking my neck—and yours—I want to know if anyone else, any reputable scholars, any genuine biblical authorities, believe Mount Sinai could be in Saudi Arabia. I need to know if this is just some crackpot theory, or if it really makes any kind of historical sense."

And with that stony pronouncement, Williams started walking quickly toward the house. But he wasn't finished. He abruptly turned and looked directly at his guest. Cornuke returned his stare, adding, he hoped, some angry weight of his own to the moment. At last Williams spoke. "And let me make one other thing clear. Before I get on any plane, before I go trudging through any desert, before I go climbing any mountain, I want to make sure there really was a treasure. I want to know if anybody besides Fasold believes the gold of Exodus ever existed."

Then Williams turned once again and cut across the lawn, walking toward the house. Cornuke, full of disappointed fury, shouted after him. "Hey, I'm sorry I wasted your time. I wasn't scholarly enough for you, fine. No problemo. I'm out of here."

It was only when Williams was at the kitchen door that he answered. All traces of his previous combativeness were gone. Someone who didn't know him might have thought he was simply capricious. But the reality was that his mood depended on how much control he felt he had. He needed to work his way through all he had heard before he would allow himself to be pressured into taking the next step. Yet in the time it took him to cross the lawn, his mind had succeeded in zeroing in on a plan. He called out, "Bob, you did great. Just great. I'm impressed. Really."

"So where the hell you going?"

"Calling in the reinforcements, Bob. It's time to bring in the big guns." And with that he disappeared into the big house.

12

TWO days later, they went to see Williams' "big gun." Full of anticipation, they made their way across a sunny California campus glistening with wide lawns and crowded with bike-riding students. In a second-floor office they met with a professor noted for his research and writings in both religious thought and biblical archaeology. The session was polite, vague, and, in Cornuke's judgment, a complete waste of time. Williams, who prided himself on knowing how things were done, told his friend to be patient. "He was just feeling us out, seeing if we're serious," he explained. But Williams was not taking chances. That same day he mailed two checks, one to the university and the other payable directly to the professor.

Three more fretful days passed. Williams, although he did his best to disguise it, was beginning to find Cornuke's impatience infectious. He had made up his mind to check with his bank to learn if the professor's check had been cashed when, before breakfast, the professor called and asked to see a copy of Fasold's letter. Williams had it delivered and decided he might as well include photocopies of the legal-size pages filled with Cornuke's biblical research.

Cornuke, whose moods had taken to swinging dangerously with all the inactivity, was once again hopeful. But when a week passed and there was still no response from the professor, he began to talk about leaving. He was spending a lot of time sitting by the pool, and his wandering mind always managed to work its way back to his wife. His soon-to-be *ex*-wife, he constantly corrected himself. He wondered what she would think if she knew he was living in a mansion in southern California. He liked to believe she'd be jealous. His big fear was that she wouldn't care. Maybe, he was coming around to thinking, he should call her.

THE first time they had separated was back when he was still a member of the SWAT team in Costa Mesa. It was a rough time for Cornuke. He was mystified, not so much angry as wounded. Over the uneasy months that followed, he grew certain of only one thing: He would not let go. Divorce, he informed his wife, was out of the question. Instead, once again trying to play through the pain, he worked up an attempt at a solution. They would go to Colorado on a camping vacation, hike through meadows sprinkled with wildflowers, sleep under aspen trees in the cool, crisp mountain air. It would be, he promised, a second honeymoon, although as soon as he said the words he shuddered at the memory of their first testy one.

Nevertheless, they went and it was, miracle of miracles, a restorative week. In the calm, Cornuke began to dream of possibilities. He could, he persuaded himself, see a future—if their lives were different. California, he decided, was the problem. The solution, he excitedly told his wife, was to chuck it. They had put up with enough suffocating smog and spaced-out neighbors. Imagine what life would be like living in this sweet-smelling Rocky Mountain wonderland. Riding along on this wishful optimism, he marched into the police station of the mining town near their campsite and asked for a job. Just a week later—further proof of his wisdom, he felt—Cornuke had his badge.

After six months, the new man on the force was sending off postcards to the guys in Costa Mesa, reporting that it sure was pretty in the mountains—pretty poison. Cornuke was miserable. The half-dozen cops in the department made a point of parading about the town with their gun belts riding low on their hips, as if they were gunfighters itching for the chance to draw, and their uniform sleeves rolled up to expose their pumped-up biceps. But after watching them keep the peace, Cornuke decided these mountain men weren't tough guys. They were bullies.

When he played back in his mind all he had witnessed, he realized he might as well have been ticking off the counts in an indictment. Count 1: Some hapless drunk flipped two officers the bird, so they handcuffed him, threw him to his knees, and proceeded, quite methodically, to slam his head against the sidewalk until the street was running red with blood. Count 2: A long-haired kid wised off, so they threw him into the back of a squad car, yanked the earring from his ear, squirted mace in his face, and when his arms started flailing, they beat the crap out of him for resisting arrest. And the list of horrors went on and on.

At first Cornuke, aware that he was the new man, had tried a light touch, letting loose with a stern "Whoa now, you really think that's necessary?" when things looked as if they were turning mean. But it was only a matter of time. By his eighth month on the job, when he saw a patrolman raising his nightstick high as he prepared to bring it down on the skull of a panhandler, Cornuke intervened. "Don't," he warned and grabbed the cop's arm in midflight. The cop fought it, but Cornuke held tight until the nightstick fell to the pavement. That evening the chief wanted to see him.

"You're an outsider, so I can imagine it takes some time learning how we do things in my town," Cornuke can remember the chief saying. He realized the man was trying to be conciliatory.

Cornuke, however, wanted to get right to the heart of the matter. "Can't imagine I'll ever learn your way," he cut in.

Now the chief was ready for a fight. "That could be a problem."

"No problem," Cornuke said without emotion. He took off his badge, slid it across the desk, and walked out.

It wasn't long after that when his wife again decided it was her time, too, to walk. Their marriage had been dragging on for years like a terminal illness, yet Cornuke was unprepared and even surprised each time it threatened finally to die. He went into a deep and inconsolable mourning.

He began moving without conviction through a series of jobs. In Denver, he hooked up with an ex-fireman who wanted to be a professional boxer. Cornuke trained with him, managed him, and then said an abrupt good-bye when he became convinced his fighter had agreed to take a dive. An opening in a real estate office took him to Colorado Springs, and for five months he was riding high, making the best money of his life. Then, after seven months, he was out of a job. Real estate, they told him, was like that.

It was a friend of a real estate friend who had hooked him up with Jim Irwin. The trip to Mount Ararat was a bright spot, but three weeks later he was back in Colorado Springs, wondering if he would ever again find the calm that would allow him to sleep through an entire night. In time, he found work as a part-time investigator for a lawyer. He was good at tracking things down, and was even thinking about trying to get a private detective's license. When he wasn't thinking about the woman who was soon to be his ex-wife.

Then, out of the blue, Larry Williams had reached out for him. And for the first time in a long while, things seemed to be working themselves out.

Only now Cornuke was once again staring at the phone, thinking about calling his wife. Or maybe, he suddenly began to consider, he should surprise her, get on a plane and knock on her door. He was close to making a reservation on the next flight to Colorado, when Williams appeared.

"The professor just called," he announced. "We're on for tomorrow, eleven sharp."

13

"Do you believe in the supernatural?"

This time the meeting was at the professor's house, and when they were seated in the study, those were the professor's first words. He asked the question amicably, like a doctor routinely inquiring about previous illnesses. But Cornuke and Williams were no longer able to contain themselves. Without even the pretense of disguise, they exchanged long, wondering looks. It had been going like this, one small unsettling turn after another, ever since the professor had greeted them at the door.

A short, plump man on the far side of middle age, the professor had bounded across the entry of his cheerless gray ranch house dressed as if he was heading off to play a set of tennis. A pair of white shorts exposed legs like sausages, and a pristine polo shirt, complete with a trademark alligator, stretched over a well-rounded belly. It was a getup that, considering what was at stake, considering the risks they were contemplating taking, struck the two friends as frivolous. Williams, however, was quick to rein in his misgivings. The man's scholarly credentials were impressive, and this was, after all, southern California.

But in the next moment things skidded further downhill. With his guests still standing in the narrow entry, the professor officiously announced that there were "ground rules." If both men did not agree to them, he added flatly, they would have to leave.

It was the acid tone as much as anything that Cornuke can still vividly recall. He felt as if he had been ambushed. He had spent two unsteady weeks waiting for this morning, and now the great professor shows up dressed in tennis shorts and coming on like some nightmare defense attorney. *Ground rules?* Cornuke, who tended to personalize things, was ready to walk; but a sharp look from Williams brought him back in line. It was a struggle, but Cornuke did not say a word. And Williams, who over the years had done too many deals to get caught up in personalities, tried to offer up a pleasant smile and said, "I'm all ears."

The professor's demand was succinct and nonnegotiable. He insisted on complete anonymity. The two men, still standing like uninvited guests in the airless hallway, listened without comment as the professor explained his reasoning. There were strict laws, he said, prohibiting the removal of antiquities from Saudi Arabia. "Without casting aspersions," he said, he would feel more comfortable if he was not connected in any way, even as a consultant, with their expedition. In addition to any possible legal ramifications, he also had to consider, as the two friends said he puffily put it, "my position in the community of scholars." His career would be irreparably damaged by even a hint of a scandal involving the theft of artifacts. Therefore, in return for his assistance, the professor required that his name remain, and now he affected a theatrical tone, "a deep, dark secret."

Cornuke was stunned by the implications of the professor's pronouncement. It had never occurred to him that they would be breaking any laws by taking the treasure out of Saudi Arabia. The way he saw it, if the gold belonged to anyone, it belonged to the Jews. And to Williams' practical mind, the professor's concerns were squeamish. His morality was that of a treasure hunter: finders keepers.

What was a problem, Williams was ready to concede, was precisely *how* he would get the treasure out of Saudi Arabia. He had given the matter a good deal of thought, and the best plan he could come up with was simply to cross that particular bridge when, and if, he was fortunate enough to come to it. If he got that far, he was confident that he would be able to persuade someone—Bedouin smugglers, a customs official?—to help him get a few nondescript crates out of the kingdom. Anyway, he reminded himself, this was his concern—not the professor's.

Therefore, if all the professor wanted was his name kept out of things, Williams was ready to comply. But he was also a businessman. He could not make a concession without receiving something in return. If you'll renounce all claims to any portion of what we might recover, he said, it's a deal.

After a round of solemn handshakes, the professor finally led them out of the hallway and into his study. The shades were up and at high noon spirals of dust swirled about in the strong sunlight. Books were everywhere, spilling out of floor-to-ceiling bookcases and stacked in short piles that spread haphazardly across the wooden floor like stepping-stones. The professor took a seat at his desk, turned on a desk lamp that, to Cornuke's eyes, threw off an unnecessary glow, and pointed to the two high-backed chairs directly across from him. It was immediately after the two men were seated that, without further preamble, the professor had asked his unexpected question.

WHEN there was no response, the professor repeated, "Please, gentlemen, do you believe in the supernatural?"

Williams figured they had gone this far; and, no small matter, his check had been cashed. There was, he decided, no place to go but forward. "No, I don't buy into that mumbo jumbo at all," he answered. And Cornuke stopped sulking long enough to agree. "Same here. I've got no truck with any of it."

"Good," they would remember the professor saying with approval. "Any other response and I would have said, 'Thank you very much, gentlemen, but there's really nothing further for us to discuss.'"

"Really?" Williams said, ready to play the straight man. "I can't wait to hear why."

The professor merely nodded, and then, as if a curtain was being raised, he began his discourse. He spoke without notes and, they thought, with obvious pleasure, a man accustomed to parading his knowledge before an audience.

"The supernatural," he said, "is all that's at the root of the present location of the *alleged*"—and he soaked the word so deeply in innuendo that Cornuke and Williams' spirits instantly soared—"Mount Sinai. There's not an iota of biblical or historical evidence to support the determination that, as so many ignorant people seem willing to believe, Mount Sinai rises above St. Catherine's Monastery in the Sinai Peninsula. That site is nothing but a tourist scam. In fact," he insisted to Cornuke and Williams' amazement, "it was probably the longest running con in history. Sounds harsh? Well, let me explain how that site, one mountain out of all the peaks in the Middle East, came to be chosen as the holiest spot on earth.

"Once upon a time back in the fourth century," the professor continued as if he were telling a fairy tale, "the Roman Emperor Constantine the Great was heading into battle when, to his colossal surprise, he suddenly had a vision. It was just before the battle of Milvian Bridge outside Rome, and he saw a large, shining cross in the sky. Emboldened by this sign, he fought valiantly and led his troops to a great victory. After that, the lucky emperor began having supernatural visions on a fairly regular basis. He grew convinced that he was 'the new Moses' and that his wisdom was unimpeachable, the direct result of these 'divine impulses.' But after one of the supernatural messages persuaded him to order the executions of his wife, Fausta, and his son, Crispus, he could not help getting a little down in the dumps. Fortunately, another well-timed vision gave him a prescription for atonement. The emperor awoke one morning and remembered that during the night a particularly vivid dream had revealed to him—the new Moses, after all—the exact location of Mount Sinai. He immediately sent his mother, Helena, to the Middle East to commemorate the mountain he had 'foreseen.' Helena, guided by her son's rather vague instructions, established a church at the foot of a rugged mountain in the south-central Sinai Peninsula. That was how the mountain that's now known throughout the world as Mount Sinai was 'discovered.' Two centuries later, in 527 A.D., the Emperor Justinian established the monastery of St. Catherine on the site of Helena's small church, and the rest is history. Or, more precisely, legend."

"That's it?" Cornuke heard himself saying, amazed, but also on guard. "All this time people have been flocking to that mountain, thinking it's holy, all because the mother of some fourth-century nut job decided it was the real thing?"

The professor offered a small, yet emphatic tilt of his head.

"But what about the Jews?" Cornuke asked. "Don't they buy into the same legend?"

The professor's reply was terse and forceful. "Not at all," he said. "There is absolutely no Jewish tradition as to the geographic location of Mount Sinai. For centuries rabbis and talmudic scholars have stated without equivocation that the precise location of the mountain where Moses received the Ten Commandments was unknown. A mystery."

"But couldn't, just possibly, the traditional site be the real mountain?" Williams asked. He didn't want this to be true, but he felt he needed to get all the facts.

"Let me see if I understand your question," the professor replied patronizingly. "You're asking if there are any biblical facts to justify the selection. You're wondering, to put it bluntly, if Constantine, or his vision, or even his mother for that matter, had somehow managed to anoint a suitable candidate."

"Just what I was driving at," Williams said, realizing he had no choice but to play along.

"Well," the professor said, "Helena did get something right—

she did manage to pick a mountain. Other than that felicitous similarity, the site she chose has no resemblance at all to the Mount Sinai in the Bible."

He reached for some papers on his desk. Cornuke thought for a moment the professor had broken off to swat at a fly, the way he began waving the pages in the air. But then he saw these were his own handwritten notes, and his stomach started to sink as he anticipated what the professor would have to say about his attempt at biblical research.

"Mr. Cornuke's work is a fine blueprint," the professor declared, and Cornuke felt as if he had just scored a touchdown. "He has accurately detailed what anyone should expect to find at the mountain. And what's also quite interesting is that not a single one of these pieces of physical evidence—the cave, the grazing ground, the brook, the large campsite, for example—can be found at the St. Catherine's site. In fact, none of these identifying criteria can be found at *any* mountain in the Sinai."

The professor paused to hunt through the piles of books stacked on his desk, finally settled on a thick volume, and opened it to the place where a green pencil had been wedged between the pages. "'If the record of Exodus is strictly historical,'" he read in a surprisingly loud voice, "'we must seek a locality where six hundred thousand fighting men, or some two million souls in all, could encamp or remain for some time, finding a pasture and drink for their cattle, and where there was a mountain (with a wilderness at its foot) rising so sharply that its base could be fenced in, while yet it was easily ascended and someone could be seen by a great multitude below. In the valley there must have been a flowing stream.'"

The professor looked up from his book, directly at the two men. "Given your unique interest in the matter, gentlemen, this is the most important part. Let me read the next line in its entirety. 'The peninsula Sinai *does not* furnish any locality where so great a host could meet under the conditions specified.'"

For a moment no one spoke. Williams remembered that it was as if "a wind filled with great possibilities blew into the room." And he thought maybe, just maybe, Dave Fasold was onto something. Cornuke was even more optimistic.

The professor then revealed that he had been reading from, of all things, the Encyclopaedia Britannica. It was, he took pains to make clear, neither an obscure nor even a scholarly source. Yet even the encyclopedia's editors, writing for a general audience, had little respect for the notion that Mount Sinai was located at the traditional St. Catherine's site. Or, for that matter, anywhere in the entire Sinai region.

"Perhaps you're familiar with Sherlock Holmes?" the professor asked, once again confusing the two men by his seemingly incongruous question. "The story about the dog that didn't bark? In that tale, of course, silence was the clue which enabled Holmes to crack the case. Well, in the late 1960s and 1970s, when Israel controlled the Sinai Peninsula, the area was intensively and systematically explored by archaeologists. And do you know what they found? Nothing. The region was an archaeological blank. No remains of any kind were discovered in the entire area for the thirteenth to twelfth centuries B.C.E., the era of Moses' and Israel's entry into Canaan. Oh, they found evidence of Egyptian mining sites. But nothing at all indicating that a large group of men and women had made camp, fought ferocious battles, and traipsed about the desert for forty years. And so there we have it. The sound of the dog not barking. The fact that archaeologists didn't find anything is proof enough to me that the Exodus did not take place on the Sinai Peninsula. More to the point—Mount Sinai is not there either."

14

WITH that unqualified and conclusive pronouncement left hanging in the air, the professor signaled that he was finished. He stared with obvious impatience at his watch. The implication, at least to Williams, was clear: duty—or tennis?—called.

But while Williams was encouraged by what he had heard, he was still unsatisfied. Besides, he decided that by now he knew the professor's game. The man was deliberately cagey. He would tell all, but only if pressed. So Williams chose to ignore the professor's deep fascination with his watch and asked one more question. "So, are you telling us that Mount Sinai is in Saudi Arabia?"

"Well, those are your words. Not mine," the professor said.

"OK. What would you say?" Williams countered. He was determined to be a model of patience.

"I would say precisely what the Bible says. Mount Sinai is in Midian."

Williams considered that for a moment and then asked, "All right. Where is Midian?"

"Very good," said the professor, and he clapped his hands together in a parody of applause. Both men no longer had any doubts that he was mocking them. "At last you have asked an interesting question."

Now that the professor had been suitably coaxed, all his previous reluctance was gone. He spoke fluently, a man enjoying himself. His starting point was the Bible.

"The story told in the Book of Exodus," he said, "is really the story of two distinct escapes from Egypt. The first is Moses'. You will remember that he was an Israelite born in Egypt. The pharaoh had ordered that all Hebrew males should be put to death at their birth. But Moses' mother hid him for three months until, no longer able to, she placed the infant in a basket by the banks of the Nile. As Fate would have it, it was at that moment that the pharaoh's daughter came down to the river to bathe, and she spotted the basket floating among the bulrushes. She looked at the crying baby and was filled with compassion. She rescued the infant, and when he was older she brought him to the palace to be raised as her son. And so Moses, although born a Jew, grew to manhood living in the luxury and privilege of the Egyptian court. The course of his life appeared comfortably set. But one day he happened to be walking in the brick fields and saw an Egyptian overseer flogging a Hebrew slave. He became enraged and killed the Egyptian. He hid the body in the sand, but the pharaoh soon learned of the murder. He ordered Moses' death, and Moses wisely decided to run for his life. That was the first escape."

The professor interrupted his narrative with a question. "All right, gentlemen," he said, "you have just killed someone and the pharaoh himself is looking for you. Where would you go? You wouldn't remain in Egypt, would you? You wouldn't hide in areas where the pharaoh's armies were encamped. Of course you wouldn't. You would get out of the country. You would get as far away from Egypt and Egyptian authority as you could."

"Makes sense," Cornuke agreed.

"Of course it does," the professor continued. "Nevertheless, it is a simple logic that many historians have ignored. And here's why it's so important. The southern part of the Sinai Peninsula was under the total and complete control of the Egyptian army during the time of Moses. The desert was swarming with soldiers. The army was there in such force because it was protecting the pharaoh's most valuable possession—the royal mines loaded with copper and turquoise. Now, this is not simply historical conjecture. It is fact confirmed by evidence uncovered from numerous archaeological excavations. Also bear in mind that these mines in the southern part of the peninsula were significant operations. According to records discovered by archaeologists, there were twenty-five classes of quarry workers and eleven separate ranks of supporting bureaucracy at each site. And within forty miles of St. Catherine's Monastery, the traditional Mount Sinai site, there were a number of mines, all protected by large Egyptian forces.

"Therefore," the professor concluded, "I think we can logically assume that Moses did not go off to hide in the southern Sinai Peninsula. Or, for that matter, in any other region patrolled by Egyptian soldiers. If he had, could he have lived, as the Bible says, in peace and anonymity for the forty years following his escape? Of course not. So, let us consider—where did Moses go? And the answer, gentlemen, is right there in the Bible."

Williams and Cornuke waited as the professor took an oversized volume down from an eye-level shelf, hunted for the appropriate chapter and verse, and then read in his strident stage voice: "'But Moses fled from the face of Pharaoh, and dwelt *in the land of Midian.*'" He waited a moment, then repeated, "The land of Midian," on the off chance that the two men might have missed the carefully enunciated phrase.

The professor closed his Bible, and they listened attentively as he went on. "It was in Midian, while a fugitive from Egypt and the pharaoh, that Moses married the daughter of a Midianite priest and shepherd, had children, and lived in quiet contentment until something extraordinary happened. God spoke to Moses from within the burning bush. And where was this bush, a bush that glowed with fire but was not consumed by the flames?"

Once again the professor looked down at his Bible and read: "'Now Moses kept the flock of Jethro his father-in-law, the priest of Midian; and he led the flock to the back or west side of the wilderness, and came to Horeb or Sinai, the mountain of God.'

"There we have it, gentlemen, the first mention in the Bible of Mount Sinai. The mountain of God. The site where God appeared to Moses in the burning bush. And where is it? The Bible is quite clear about this. It's in Midian, gentlemen. Where Moses had fled. Where he tended his father-in-law's sheep. And where he had lived in safety for forty years, a fugitive from Egyptian law and authority."

The professor, caught up in his own argument, went on confidently. "Now, we've already deduced, I believe, that it defies logic that Midian could have been in the southern part of the Sinai Peninsula. Too many Egyptian soldiers. Nowhere for Moses, on the lam, if you will, to hide. Still, in case we missed the fact that Midian was a separate country, a land removed from both Egyptian territorial boundaries and authority, the Bible drives that point home, too. For example, when"—the professor scanned the pages of his Bible while he continued talking—"Jethro, then Moses' prospective father-in-law, asked his daughter why she was home so early one afternoon, she dutifully responded: 'An *Egyptian* delivered us from the shepherds.' That is, not one of the local Midianite boys but someone from another country, an Egyptian—Moses. And when Moses was on Mount Sinai for the first time, getting his marching orders from God, this is what the Bible says: 'The Lord said to Moses *in Midian,* Go *back to Egypt;* for all the men who were seeking your life are dead.'

"Could the Bible have been any clearer?" the professor demanded. "Midian, land of Jethro and the mountain of God, was one country. Egypt, where Moses was being sent, was another. Further evidence: Moses, while living in Midian, was always cognizant of his immigrant status, his perpetual sense of dislocation. He even named his son Gershom. In Hebrew that translates as *ger,* 'a stranger,' and *sham,* 'there.' Life for Moses in Midian was no melting pot. He, and his son, were strangers in a strange land. He missed the faraway land of his birth—Egypt.

"So much, then, for the first escape," the professor said, but he was too caught up in his argument to consider even a moment's pause. "The second escape in Exodus was even more momentous. This time the fugitives were the twelve tribes of Israel, a flock that after four hundred years in Egypt had grown, if the census in the Book of Numbers was accurate, to well over a million men, women, and children. And where did Moses lead his fellow fugitives? He took them *away* from Pharaoh's armies. He took them *out* of Egypt, following the same route he traveled forty years earlier. He returned, and the Bible is quite specific about this, to the land of his father-in-law. And to Mount Sinai, the very mountain where he first spoke with God in the burning bush. Moses and the twelve tribes returned to Midian."

"So now," the professor concluded, "we have gone full circle. We are back to Mr. Williams' question: Where is Midian? Come, I want you to see this with your own eyes."

He abruptly rose from his desk and walked to a closet on the far side of the room. The two friends joined him as he pulled open the door. Taped inside as if it were a pinup was a map colored in washed-out, pastel shades.

"I want you to look at this carefully," the professor instructed. The two men leaned closer and saw that it was a map of the Middle East. It was fairly recent. The configurations of each country, one soft-colored shape bordering on another, were at once familiar.

As they looked, the professor resumed his lecture. "Let's return to the question, where is Midian, home to both the Exodus and Mount Sinai? Well, the Midianites were like all true Arabs a nomadic people. Nevertheless, the consensus among scholars is that Midian occupied the land bordering the Gulf of Eilat's eastern shore."

"The Gulf of Eilat?" Cornuke asked.

"Excuse me," said the professor. "The Gulf of Eilat is now

known as the Gulf of Aqaba." He pointed to a thin, baby blue crescent on the map.

Williams and Cornuke peered closer. They were suddenly excited, but Williams realized it was important to hear it from the professor. He needed to be certain. "The land east of the Gulf of Aqaba," he said, "that's Midian. Is that what you're saying?"

The professor bent his head slowly forward in agreement.

"And that's—Saudi Arabia," said Williams, trying to control his excitement.

"Exactly," the professor said.

ANOTHER, less demanding investigator might have stopped then and there. And that, in fact, was Cornuke's inclination. He was ready to celebrate. In his mind, the professor had confirmed if not the specifics then at least the possibilities in Fasold's letter. The old man had been quite clear: Moses and the Israelites had fled to Midian. Midian was east of the Gulf of Aqaba. Therefore, Mount Sinai was in present-day Saudi Arabia. All that remained, Cornuke felt, was to go off and bring home the prize.

But Williams would not be rushed. Success, he was fond of saying, was 110 percent preparation. There were still a few things on his mind. Besides, it would be bad business not to get his money's worth of wisdom from the professor. The man had, after all, cashed a sizable check. Cornuke was chanting, "I knew we were onto something. I just knew it." Yet Williams focused on the professor and in a voice that was firm, even a bit intimidating, he raised what he realized was a very impolite question.

"It's reassuring that you believe Mount Sinai is in Saudi Arabia. But that's just one man's opinion. Do any other scholars support your view? Other authorities? No offense meant, of course."

"None taken," said the professor tersely. Cornuke, however, appeared to be boiling over ominously. "You really think this is necessary, Larry?" he said. "I mean, we've gone over everything. No need to get insulting."

The professor intervened, quickly cutting Cornuke off. There was, he announced with a sly smile, something he wanted to read to the two men. It was an interview in the *Bible Review.* "In case you're not familiar with the *Review*," he explained, "it is a well-respected, authoritative, scholarly publication. In the pages I'm about to read, the *Review*'s editor Hershel Shanks, a noted scholar in his own right, is having a conversation with Professor Frank Moore Cross. Now Dr. Cross," the professor declared with genuine respect, "is a *giant* in the field of biblical scholarship. He is the Hancock Professor of Hebrew and Other Languages at Harvard University and has written several classic books and articles on the ancient world. He is a man celebrated for his stores of knowledge, an eminent authority, to quote the *Review,* in"—and now the professor began to read from the photocopy that he dug out from a pile of papers on his desk—"'biblical history, the decipherment and dating of ancient texts, the history of religion, the development of the biblical canon, ancient languages and culture, the development of the alphabet, the Dead Sea scrolls, archaeology on both land and sea, historical geography—the list could go on.'

"Satisfied?" the professor asked; and this time Williams had no doubts about the irony in his thin smile.

"Just the sort of authority I was hoping to hear from," he acknowledged. "What does he have to say?"

"Well, in this particular interview Dr. Shanks is exploring Professor Cross's beliefs about Israelite origins. Allow me to read a few of the relevant questions and answers."

> *Shanks:* Where is Midian?
>
> *Cross:* . . . It is in the northwestern border area of what is now Saudi Arabia. . . . The notion that the "mountain of God" called Sinai and Horeb was located in what we now call the Sinai Peninsula has no older tradition supporting it than Byzantine times. . . .
>
> *Shanks:* So you would place Sinai in what is today Saudi Arabia?

Cross: . . . Yes, in the northwestern corner of Saudi Arabia, ancient Midian.

"All right," Cornuke cheered; and even Williams clenched a fist in triumph and uttered a soft *"Yes!"* But the professor ordered quiet. There was more, he said, and he continued to read.

Shanks: Isn't the movement of the Israelites into Saudi Arabia just in the opposite direction from where they wish to go?

Cross: . . . We cannot think of Israel leaving Egypt and making a beeline for the Promised Land. If the tradition of their long period in the wilderness has a historical basis, then the historian must ask how this tradition survived. . . . If the Israelite contingent from Egypt survived long in the southern wilderness, it was because they headed for an area in which there was civilization, irrigated crops, the means of sustenance. Southern Edom and Midian supply this need, and so I believe they headed there . . . [to] northern Midian . . . and where, in my view, the mountain of God was located.

The professor looked up from his reading. "And now, gentlemen, here comes the $64,000 question." He read:

Shanks: Do you have any guess as to what mountain might be Mount Sinai?

Cross: I really don't know.

The air seemed to go out of the room; but before the two friends could get caught up in this sudden change of pressure, the professor spoke. "Ah, but there's more." He picked up where he had left off:

Cross: I really don't know. There are several enormous mountains in what is now northwestern Saudi Arabia. Jabal al Lawz is the highest of the mountains in Midian—8,465 feet—higher

> than any mountain in the Sinai Peninsula. But biblical Mount Sinai need not be the highest of mountains.

"There you have it," the professor announced. "From the mouth of one of the world's foremost scholars."

"He's not saying Jabal al Lawz is Sinai," Williams pointed out.

"No," Cornuke shot back immediately. "It's just the one place on earth he happened to mention."

"Dr. Cross has never been there," the professor said. "He's never seen Jabal al Lawz with his own eyes, close up, as did your friend, Mr. Fasold. And yet Dr. Frank Moore Cross, the Hancock Professor at Harvard University, is saying your mountain, Jabal al Lawz, is a realistic candidate to be Mount Sinai."

"So now what do you have to say?" Cornuke goaded his friend.

Williams remained silent. He was busy playing back all he had heard. He was encouraged. He was almost there. But he still had one other large concern. "What about the treasure?" he asked. "Before I decide to go off to Saudi Arabia, there's one more thing I need to know. The gold of Exodus—did it ever really exist?"

15

THE professor excused himself and went off to cancel his four o'clock tennis game. When he returned, he suggested they go out into the yard. He needed, he said, "to get rid of the cobwebs." Once they were outside, the professor set a leisurely pace, and Cornuke and Williams fell in shoulder-to-shoulder. They followed, more or less, a straight line, tracing the route of a white picket fence. When the fence ended in a right angle, they turned and continued in their unhurried fashion in this new direction. The sky was a cloudless blue, and the air carried a sweet scent from the cluster of orange trees the professor's wife had planted as seedlings decades ago.

As they walked, the professor talked. He began with what sounded to Williams like an apology. The great difficulty in biblical scholarship, he said, was that so little could ever be decisively and positively known. What in the Bible was fact? What was tradition? What was tradition reshaped into legend by the literary talents of ancient poets? So much of my work, he said with what sounded like a weary sigh, is in the end speculation. And with that uncharacteristically candid introduction out of the way, an indemnification of sorts, Williams worried, he began to explain about the treasure that was taken out of Egypt. He talked about what the Bible said, about what it cryptically implied, and about what, to the objective student, remained ambiguous. He spoke of the Hebraic tradition, about what the great rabbis with the imprimatur of their spiritual authority have added to the folklore over the centuries, and about what their occasionally conflicting commentaries have subtracted. But finally, he suggested, since the Bible was a story, since it was a mix of historical fact, legend, and literary license, it seemed only proper that he draw on these sources and techniques to weave together a story about the gold of Exodus. It was, he said with total sincerity, the only way to get close to truths buried as deeply as the ancient treasure itself. He was a fluent storyteller, and Williams and Cornuke would vividly remember the tale the professor told them in his garden that afternoon.

> In the last hours of daylight on an afternoon in 1250 B.C.E., Bezalel, a 13-year-old boy from the tribe of Judah, watched helplessly as a mob beat his father to death. It was all at once awful, devastating; and yet, even as he watched in absolute terror, he also could not help thinking that it was, above all other things, so unfair. Hur, his father, had escaped so many determined and powerful enemies. For what? To die in the wilderness, in the shadow of Mount Sinai, and, most incredible of all, at the hands of his own people.
>
> Why? Bezalel continued to demand even after he had placed his father's body into a shallow grave not far from the mountain. It made no sense. If, Bezalel told himself, his father had died a slave in Egypt, in the brick fields at the hands of a cruel overseer; or if the sea had not miraculously parted and the Egyptian soldiers in their chariots had taken their revenge; or if while in the wilderness manna had not dropped from the sky and water had not poured from the rock; or if the Amalekites had triumphed—these were deaths, however painful, the boy could have accepted. But to have come out of Egypt, to have escaped across

the desert to freedom, to have felt the earth shake and to have seen the holy mountain smoking and quaking as God descended upon it, and then to be killed—that left the boy inconsolable. But that was what had happened.

Before Moses had gone off to Mount Sinai for the second time, he met with the elders from the twelve tribes. "God has summoned me to receive His law," he announced. "Until I return, my brother Aaron and Hur of Judah will be in charge." The next morning Moses, accompanied by only Joshua, disappeared into the thick cloud that surrounded the mountain. Weeks passed. There was no message from Moses, no sign that he was still alive. And all the while the people, strangers in a strange wilderness, grew fearful.

In their anxiety, they turned to Aaron and pleaded that he make them a god whom they could worship, a god who would protect them. Aaron, confused, wary, decided to ask the people to give him their golden rings and earrings. He would use the ornaments to make them a god. It was the only plan he could conceive. His hope was that the people would be reluctant to part with any of the gold they had taken out of Egypt. But he was wrong. They pulled golden hoops off their ears and rings from their fingers.

And so Aaron, hoping to keep the peace, melted down all the metal; and out of this shining, molten mass of pure gold, he sculpted a golden calf. When he was done, he placed the idol on an altar and declared that tomorrow would be a feast day. Except now Hur, of the tribe of Judah, spoke up. "Moses will return," he promised the people. "The Lord our God has taken us out of Egypt. He has protected us and brought us safely to Mount Sinai to receive His word. Do not turn from Him." Suddenly a rock was thrown. It struck Hur, and blood began dripping down his face. He continued to plead with the people, but more rocks were thrown. The crowd surged forward with fists and stones and sticks. When it was over, Hur was dead. Bezalel retrieved his father's body and buried him the next day, as the people danced around the golden calf.

The boy was still trapped in his grief, still tormented by the ironies in his father's death, when Moses returned from the mountain. All at once, it was as if Moses' hot anger was Bezalel's own avenging sword. He watched excitedly as Moses toppled the golden calf into a raging fire. But that was not enough! The metal was ground into a fine golden powder and Moses, still seething, scattered it like precious rain into the brook that ran out of the mountain of God. In time a speckled, golden stream snaked through the camp. "Drink!" Moses ordered. And the boy watched as the idol worshipers drank handfuls of water laced with bits of pure gold.

But Moses' anger still raged. "Whoever is on the Lord's side, come to me," he shouted. When the men from the tribe of Levi rushed forward, Moses sent them off throughout the camp to kill the idolaters. Thousands died by the sword that afternoon. Moses ordered the Levites not to spare even the relatives of those who had worshiped the calf. They must pay too. And still Moses demanded more. As the Levites raced through the camp with their swords held high, as fresh blood seeped into the ground and ran into the golden brook, as anguished, piercing cries from the dying and the fearful filled the plain, Moses announced that a final gesture of atonement was required. There were a million or more people stretched out before him, and he ordered the entire camp to strip themselves of the jewelry they were wearing. The children of Israel were told to leave these jewels and ornaments scattered on the ground, a sacrifice for their sin. At this moment, as the avengers roamed through the camp, their swords wet with blood, who would even think of hesitating?

On Moses' command, rings of heavy gold, necklaces dotted with emeralds, rubies, and sapphires, thick silver bracelets, these prizes that once were Egypt's—all were removed. Jewels fell in a sparkling shower to the ground. Some were thrown toward the mountain; a volley of golden rings and pieces of shining jewelry. And wherever they landed, they were to remain, discarded forever, ignored and abandoned—testimony that the children of Israel were in mourning for their sin. Yet when they were done, even after they had stripped themselves of all their ornaments, as they stood before Moses without a single jewel or piece of precious metal adorning their bodies, their fear remained strong.

They tried to imagine what would happen next. But Moses only ordered that his tent be moved away from the camp, closer to the mountain, and his anger subsided.

It was not long after this that Moses had Bezalel brought to his tent. Although Moses had found some calm, the boy was still full of rage. "Why did my father have to die, after all he had gone through?" he blurted out to Moses.

Moses let the boy cry. When Bezalel's tears had stopped, he explained that Hur's death had not gone unnoticed by God. Just as an earthly king rewards a loyal officer who has given his life to defend him against traitors, Moses told the boy, so does a heavenly king. Hear this, he announced: The Lord has reserved for all of Hur's children, from this moment on and for every generation to come, a great place in the world.

The boy was overwhelmed. A great place in the world? What could that mean? Would he be a king? A general?

Moses said, "I have been told you do skillful work with your hands. That you can carve wood. Mold precious metals. Set gems."

The boy agreed. "It is a skill I learned in Egypt." But he did not see what his talent as an artisan had to do with the great place in the world that had been promised to him. More out of politeness than any real interest he asked, "Who speaks to you of my work?"

"God," said Moses.

As the boy listened in astonishment, Moses explained that God had chosen him to build the children of Israel's most sacred possession. Bezalel, son of Hur, was to construct to God's precise specifications, out of the finest gold, silver, and gems, an ark of the convenant to hold the laws of God, vessels for use in the service, and a tabernacle where the priests would worship.

Bezalel was about to say he was unworthy. He was only a boy. He did not possess the skill, the artistry that such holy work required. But before Bezalel could protest, to his own amazement, he said, "Moses, our teacher, as a rule a man first builds a house and then brings the vessels into it. Can it be that the Holy One said, 'Make a tabernacle, an ark, and vessels?' "

Moses smiled. The wisdom of the Lord had filled the heart and the mind of the 13-year-old. He was certain Bezalel's hands would also be guided by God.

And soon the work began. Moses assigned Oholiab, of the tribe of Dan, to assist Bezalel. Oholiab was older, a man nearly his father's age, and a friendship grew between them. The boy confided to Oholiab that, despite the enormity of the challenge, despite his own unworthiness, he was determined to create a tabernacle of great beauty and majesty. A temple to worship God, and a work of art in memory of his father. But as Bezalel drew his plans, he began to worry. It did not seem possible that there would be enough gold, silver, and gems to embellish his work in the glittering manner demanded by the Lord. Frantic, the boy rushed to share this new concern with Oholiab.

"God has provided," Oholiab assured him. "Just as He promised." Oholiab told the boy that when the Lord had first appeared to Moses in the burning bush, He had promised that the Israelites would not leave Egypt empty-handed. "And, Bezalel, son of Hur, it has come to pass. The wealth of the pharaohs had been handed over to their slaves. The riches of Egypt now belong to the children of Israel."

"But how did this happen?" wondered Bezalel.

"You wouldn't know, would you? You were just a child in your father's home at the time of the Exodus," Oholiab said. So he shared with the boy what he had witnessed with his own eyes. On the night the children of Israel left Egypt, the people had gone from house to house, and the Egyptians gave them all they had.

"Gave?" challenged Bezalel.

Oholiab told the boy that it was all freely given. But he also shared a secret. When God had cast darkness down upon Egypt to demonstrate His power, the elders entered the Egyptian homes. Hunting about as quietly as house cats, they searched out where the valuables were hidden. They did not take anything. But when the moment came to leave Egypt, they knew what to ask for. Not that it mattered. By then the Egyptians were so eager for the slaves to leave that if an Israelite asked for one golden necklace, they forced two into his hands. It was as if God had opened the Egyptians' hearts. They wanted to give their wealth to the Jews. On the night of the Exodus, as millions of Jews marched out of Egypt, every family brought with them many Libyan asses loaded down with the spoils of Egypt.

"And yet soon there was more," said Oholiab. "More gold. More silver. More gems." The boy listened as Oholiab recounted that when the water closed over Pharaoh's chariots, the sea churned up glistening with the spoils of war—chariots decorated with gold, jewel-encrusted harnesses, silver amulets. The wealth of the pharaohs floated forlornly in the suddenly calm sea, the scattered remains of all that no longer was. By the thousands, said Oholiab, people dived greedily back into the sea. They gathered up armfuls of the spoils, only to dive back in for more.

Bezalel explained that he had been with his father. They were just glad to have escaped the pharaoh's soldiers. They had not looked back.

"Many lingered," Oholiab assured him. They would have remained there for days, hunting for every piece of treasure. But Moses said, Enough. At last he ordered them to move ahead. And they obeyed.

"Do not worry, Bezalel, son of Hur," the older man said. "There is enough treasure in this camp for our work. We will be able to honor the Lord."

The next day Moses spoke to the entire encampment. He asked the children of Israel to come forward and give whatever they, in their hearts, felt was a fitting contribution to the further glory of Bezalel's work. And so each morning a long line snaked from Bezalel's tent and stretched across the plain. There were over a million people in the camp, and for months one Israelite after another offered his tokens of respect. Many, eager to show their love and commitment to the Lord, lined up day after day. A glistening hill, a mound that climbed taller than a man's head, soon stood outside Bezalel's tent. It was a dense pile, one object stacked on top of another. And it was solid with treasure, the bounty of Egypt: gold and silver, sapphires and emeralds, onyx and turquoise. And across from it was another tall mound: more rings and brooches, necklaces and armlets. And next to this was still another rich pile. What high tribute! A civilization's glory liberated to honor the one true Lord. The riches of the pharaohs brought out of Egypt and now gathered together at the foot of the mountain of God.

The Israelites' generosity was so great that in time Bezalel found he had a totally unanticipated problem. "The people," he told Moses, "bring much more than enough for us to do the work which the Lord has commanded us to do." So Moses issued a proclamation that was circulated throughout the camp. The people were not to give any more tokens of tribute.

And they obeyed. But Bezalel was still concerned. "What am I do with the surplus?" he asked Moses. "What am I to do with the piles of gold and silver, with the hills of emeralds and sapphires that remain?"

Moses took some time to consider this problem. Nothing can be returned, he said at last. He explained that it would be a cruelty to return a gift given freely and from the heart. Those who had acted only out of kindness would be forced to suffer an embarrassment.

"But I cannot use the surplus," Bezalel interrupted. With great tact and respect, he pointed out to Moses that God's instructions were precise, down to the last talent of gold. "I will build only exactly as the Lord commanded," the boy said.

"As you must," agreed Moses.

But that did not solve the problem.

At last Moses made a decision. He ruled that whatever was not used by Bezalel would remain at Sinai. It was God's tribute, freely given in His honor by His chosen people. It must stay forever at His mountain.

"And so it shall be," said Bezalel.

"And so it has been," said the professor as he concluded his story. "For more than two thousand years, the gold of Exodus has been buried somewhere near Mount Sinai. At least, that's what the legend says."

The sun was beginning to set and a breeze rushed across the yard. The professor, still in his tennis shorts, felt the cool wind and suggested they go back inside. But Williams could not wait. He asked, "But is it all just a legend? Is there any historical fact to the story?"

"Well," said the professor, "much of the story is told in the Bible. The Book of Exodus tells of the Israelites' plundering Egypt, the sea closing over Pharaoh's army, the golden calf, the Jews being stripped of their ornaments, Hur's death, and Bezalel's complaining that the offerings were too much. The rest," he said with a philosophical shrug, "is commentary and tradition." After a moment, he added, "And conjecture."

Williams let out a small, sarcastic "Great."

"It's worth considering," the professor chided, "what Theodor Reik, the great psychoanalyst, said about biblical scholarship. He called it 'conjectural history.' After all, nothing in the Bible is known for certain. Did Moses live? Did the Red Sea divide? Did a million Jews escape from Egypt? Did God give the Ten Commandments on Mount Sinai? We *believe,* that is one thing. But to *know,* that is another."

The professor let the two men struggle with the implications of all that for a moment. Then, his voice flat with resignation, he went on. "Biblical historians must live with uncertainty. The best we can do in attempting to re-create the biblical past is, as Reik called it, conjectural history. We don't put forth definitive answers, but rather plausible, fruitful conjectures."

"If I come back from Jabal al Lawz with a backpack full of gold, I'd say that goes a hell of a lot farther than just a fruitful conjecture," Cornuke insisted.

"Point," conceded the professor. They were now walking back into the house. "You will have gone quite far, indeed, in proving that the Bible is a historical document and that the Exodus is a true story—*if you find the gold.*"

"Not if," Cornuke said defiantly.

CORNUKE and the professor disappeared into the house, but Williams, without offering a word of explanation, lingered for some time in the yard. The stars were just beginning to shine, and he could hear the Pacific rolling in on some unseen beach. Alone, he thought about Frank Moore Cross and the Bible and the gold. When he joined the others, his mind was set. But that was his secret. After all his years in business, he had learned that there was no upside in signaling your intentions too soon.

He reclaimed his seat in the study. "OK, I agree," he began. "Plausible—that's the key word. I know the Bible tells us the Jews plundered Egypt. But is there any historical record? I mean, it has to have been one of the greatest rip-offs in history."

"That's precisely what the Egyptians tried to argue a few hundred years later," the professor answered. "They filed a lawsuit with Alexander the Great, demanding that the Jews return the gold and silver their ancestors had taken out of Egypt. Except an Israelite by the name of Gebiha turned out to be a pretty shrewd lawyer. He argued that the Jews were slaves in Egypt for, the Bible said, 430 years. Pay us, he demanded, the wages that were due for the toil of 600,000 men for more than four centuries, and then we'll see who owes whom anything. Alexander, to his credit, ruled in the Jews' favor."

"You got that, Larry?" Cornuke said. "It was the Egyptians who went to Alexander. If something wasn't taken, why would they go to all the trouble to try to get it back?"

"OK, let's say the Bible is accurate," Williams conceded. "The Jews took Egyptian spoils with them into the desert and to Mount Sinai. Fine. But a treasure? What kind of loot are we really talking about?"

"Mr. Williams," the professor said, "if you can retrieve even a water urn and can show that it was used by the Jews during their exodus, that piece of pottery alone would be priceless to historians and theologians. But if you're referring to intrinsic value . . ."

"Dollars and cents," Williams cut in. "A ballpark estimate."

"That's impossible," the professor snapped. But after a thoughtful moment, he spoke again. "Perhaps this might interest you. Do you know what is considered to be the most magnificent, and at the same time the most valuable, treasure ever discovered? King Tut's gold," he said, once again answering his own question. "Howard Carter found in the Egyptian King Tutankhamen's tomb a fabulous fortune in gold and gems. There was exquisitely designed jewelry, artifacts fashioned with a most delicate and intricate workmanship, and gold. Lots of gold. All told, Carter found about four hundred pounds of gold."

"I don't see what that has to do with what we're looking for," Williams said.

"Perhaps nothing. But then again," the professor said, "perhaps a good deal. King Tutankhamen died in 1350 B.C.E. That's within a hundred years of Moses' lifetime. Now the riches in the good king's tomb demonstrate beyond a doubt the vast wealth of Egypt. Four hundred pounds of gold is proof—not conjecture. And here's why all this 'loot,' as you put it is, is relevant. It gives us a pretty reasonable idea of the treasure that could have been liberated from the Egyptians just a hundred years earlier.

"So let me attempt to answer your question in another way. According to the specifications cited in the Bible, about 1,980 pounds of gold were used by Bezalel in his work. Is this true? Is it possible? Could the Israelites really have had that much gold? That's about five times the amount of gold that was found in King Tut's tomb. But now I ask you, is it good conjectural history to assume that over a million Israelites were able to carry off more than five times the treasure in one pharaoh's tomb? I'd say that's plausible. And," he concluded, clearly taken by the prospect, "very conservative."

Cornuke jumped in. "Which makes it real plausible that, as the Bible also tells us, there was one heck of a fortune of gold and gems left over when Bezalel's work was done. A fortune that must still be at Mount Sinai. The *real* Mount Sinai." Cornuke looked over to his friend, hoping for encouragement. "Makes sense, doesn't it, Larry?"

But Williams didn't react. His face showed nothing. "You couldn't tell what he was thinking," Cornuke, still evidently troubled by the moment, would say later. Williams simply rose from the chair and told the professor, "You certainly have given us a lot to think about. Thank you." And after a polite handshake, he headed to the door. Cornuke, grim and confused, followed.

It was only when the two men were in the car, just starting out the driveway, that Cornuke said cautiously, "Well, what do you think?"

"Think?" Williams repeated as if he didn't understand the question.

"Look, Larry, are you in or not?"

"In or not?" Williams echoed dumbly.

The top of the car was down and the cool night was rushing all around them. Yet Cornuke would not let himself be distracted. He was all control, all concentration. He waited, hoping his heavy silence would force his friend to speak. At last Williams turned toward him.

"Bob, my boy," he announced with an exhilarating confidence, "you and I are going to make history."

16

McLean, Virginia: 1985

Two years earlier, there had been another eventful stroll through a backyard garden. It had taken place in suburban McLean, Virginia, just a short drive from the White House. Two married couples had finished an elaborate Sunday lunch in the wood-paneled dining room of a redbrick Georgian mansion. The food had been served by liveried waiters on heavy silver trays, and the wines had been chosen with much thought. They were about to move to the library for coffee and brandy when the host asked if anyone, perhaps, would like to join him for a tour of the gardens. It was a casual enough invitation, but the wives realized they were not being invited to come along. They were not insulted; both women understood the nature of their husbands' work.

The afternoon was wintry, the sky pale and threatening, so the guest put on his topcoat and hat before he went outside. The host, young enough to have been his son, made do with his sports jacket. The younger man led the way, and once they were outside, neither of them had any interest in the garden. It had been only pretense, and a thin one; at this time of year, the flower beds were moribund. They continued to walk beyond the boxwood hedges and down a sloping, faded lawn. They wanted to get as far from the big house as possible, away from their wives, and the servants, and the teams of security men on the flagstone terrace with Uzis under their coats. They wanted to make sure no one would hear what they had to say.

When they had gone far enough, the older man took a small card out of his pocket. On the card were the handwritten numbers of a bank account in Geneva. If you're on board, he told his host, then $3 million should be deposited in this account. The white-haired man giving the instructions was William J. Casey, director of the CIA.

Prince Bandar bin Sultan, the Saudi ambassador to the United States, took the card, gave it a quick look, and then put it in his pocket. You can count on us, he said. The money will be deposited in Geneva.

The Saudi government had agreed to pay $3 million to have a man killed. The money would finance the assassination of Sheik Fadlallah, the leader of the Party of God. Fadlallah was a terrorist who had been involved in the planning of three bombings of American facilities in Beirut. Casey wanted the sheik dead. But he didn't want to ask permission from the president or inform Congress. And he didn't want anyone in the agency who someday might have to answer questions under oath to know about the hit. He wanted the CIA to be, for the official record at least, totally uninvolved in the assassination of Sheik Fadlallah.

He had shared this problem for the first time with Prince Bandar a few days earlier. It was a meeting between two friends, and at its conclusion Casey had asked for a small, discreet favor. The prince had listened attentively, and then said he would need to discuss the matter with his government. Come to my house for lunch on Sunday. Bring your wife, the prince had suggested. I'll have an answer by then. And now, in the course of a meandering, digestive stroll on a gray Sunday afternoon, it had been settled. The Saudi Intelligence Service would recruit and finance a hit team to kill a man at the request of the director of the CIA.

The two men began the walk back up the lawn toward the lights of the house. "I'll burn the card," volunteered Bandar. He wanted Casey to appreciate that he, too, knew something about tradecraft. He wanted to show the director of the CIA that he knew how to keep a secret. Most important, he wanted to emphasize what had gone unspoken: The Saudi Intelligence Service would do all that was required. It was a very good friend.

"Don't worry," said Casey. "We'll close the account at once." It was his polite way of informing the younger man that the CIA, thank you, could handle that end of the operation. But as they approached the terrace flanking the house, Casey came to a sudden halt. "I just want you to know," he told the prince, "that I appreciate what you're doing. This country does not forget its friends."

It was the nearest Casey ever came that day to stating the terms of the deal. Yet his words were a tacit acknowledgment of a large, outstanding debt, and a solemn promise that it would be paid upon demand. Their bargain struck, the two men rejoined their wives.

ON March 8, 1985, a car loaded with explosives blew up near the apartment house in the Beirut suburb where Fadlallah was living. Eighty people were killed and more than two hundred others were injured. But Fadlallah was unharmed. Nevertheless, Bandar had tried to fulfill his bargain with Casey. It was not long before the Saudis asked for something in return.

Bandar was no longer involved. Perhaps it was because this time he would have been the supplicant and the role embarrassed a man who, after all, was also a prince. Or perhaps he had caught on that in the world of intrigue a cushion of deniability—a "cutout," as they say in the trade—made good operational sense. Or maybe things were simply as they seemed: On instructions from the Higher Officers' Committee, Bandar was being kept out of the loop. But whatever the thinking, the initial discussion was between a high-ranking member of the Saudi Intelligence Service and a CIA operations officer. Over a seemingly casual lunch at the Saudi embassy—Big Macs on sterling silver trays and Havanas with the brandy was the usual fare—the Saudi operative revealed what his government wanted as payback.

The kingdom, he began, was growing increasingly concerned about the activities of Islamic fundamentalists living in the United States. He appreciated, or so he claimed very convincingly, that in this country students and other "rabble" had the right, protected by the Constitution, to free speech. He would not presume to interfere with that. Nor, for that matter, was he asking the CIA to take any action. In fact, *in*action, a turning of the back, a walking away, was all he was hoping for.

The CIA man might have looked puzzled; or, equally likely, the Saudi simply realized he was not making himself clear. The moment had arrived to talk more directly. He said that it would be in the best interests of the Kingdom of Saudi Arabia, and, therefore, also in the best interests of the United States, if the Saudi Intelligence Service could keep a close watch on this scum. Again, he emphasized that he wasn't asking the CIA or, for that matter, the FBI to do any of the dirty work. That, he realized, would be illegal. And it was with similar tact, as though he were only pondering some very remote possibility, that he brought the conversation to its conclusion. He posed what he insisted was a strictly hypothetical question: If the Saudi Intelligence Service, solely for informational purposes, began keeping tabs on the dissidents and terrorists living in the United States who were fomenting trouble inside the kingdom, would that pose any problems? Could, again hypothetically, the service conduct its monitoring activities without fear of stepping on any official toes?

Let me get back to you on that, said the spook without much hope.

Yet when he ran it by the director, he was surprised to hear how easily Casey acquiesced. "You tell the Saudis," Casey barked, according to the certain memory of a man familiar with what had been said in the room, "it's their people's ass if they get caught bugging a phone or steaming open a letter. Other than that, I've got no problem."

But in time, Larry Williams and Bob Cornuke would.

17

Colorado Springs, Colorado: 1988

ONCE more, Cornuke was back in training. And on his own. Two days after the meeting at the professor's house, he had returned to Colorado, while Williams remained in California to get, he said, his varied affairs in some kind of order before they headed off. "Give me a couple of weeks, a month tops, and I'll have things under control. We'll be on a plane to Saudi before you know it," Williams had solemnly promised when he deposited Cornuke at the San Diego airport. But Cornuke, who after his stay at his friend's house had insight into enough of these deals to appreciate their constantly spinning circles of complexity, was not so sanguine. If Larry says a month, it'll stretch to two, he told himself sadly. But before the plane landed, a new, more resourceful Cornuke had worked out a plan. He would take advantage of the delay to prepare. Time, he vowed to himself, would be on his side. He would make sure that he was ready for whatever was out there.

He set out to get himself not merely into shape, but into *great* shape. I'm the man, he cheered himself on, when he awoke at six to begin his first day of training. He looked forward to the old, familiar pain of pushing his body to its limits. As he headed off with a stopwatch around his neck to do wind sprints—100 yards, 10 seconds rest—he was convinced it would be just like preseason. That was before he found himself standing at the side of the track, vomiting up his breakfast.

Cornuke was disappointed, and humbled. This was, he began to realize, like nothing he had ever done before. It was harder, much harder. He was, he found himself forced to admit, within shouting distance of his fortieth birthday—middle-aged!—and yet his plan was to drive himself as if he were a 20-year-old. Nevertheless, he stubbornly refused to make concessions. The ex-jock took comfort in repeating a bit of motivational wisdom his college coach had purloined from, he had said, some old Chinaman: A journey of a thousand miles starts with a single step.

Well, Cornuke reasoned, since he would he heading off on a journey of some 6,000 or so miles, with stops along the way for mountain climbing and digging up a buried treasure, more than just one first step might be necessary. He began with two-mile runs. Twice a day. By the time two months had passed, he was doing ten miles. Twice a day. In the third month, he strapped on a knapsack loaded with rocks before heading out each morning. In the fourth month, still waiting, he climbed a 14,000-foot mountain in the dead of winter. He was also lifting weights and shoveling driveways packed with snow. By the time six months had passed, it was spring and he was, he judged with considerable pride, in the best shape of his life—body and mind. The exercise had helped to fill up the empty spaces in his life. He was ready. But he was still waiting for Williams' call.

WILLIAMS, meanwhile, was having his own very difficult time. It was the first occasion in his life when he felt completely and utterly stymied. He was an optimist, as might be expected in a man whose life had been blessed by luck. Yet after the past six frustrating months, even he was close to giving up hope.

Cornuke, it seemed, had been wrong. The delay—and this, of course, was the reason for the sea change in Williams' outlook—had nothing to do with the hectic demands of his many ventures. Those were worries, Williams liked to say, that would never go away—thank God. There was, however, one large and apparently insurmountable problem—the Saudis. They refused to grant Cornuke and Williams visas. They did not want them to enter the kingdom.

For the past six months, Williams had been locked in a losing battle with Saudi officials. It had begun modestly, on the day Cornuke flew back to Colorado, with an initial phone call to the consulate in Los Angeles. He naively requested that he be sent the forms for a tourist visa. The man at the other end of the line was terse to the point of rudeness. We do not allow tourists to come to Saudi Arabia, he announced with a ferocity that in itself would have discouraged most vacationers. But Williams pressed ahead, asking just who was welcome. The official recited a discouragingly short list. One, anyone invited by a citizen of the kingdom. Two, anyone hired for a legitimate job within the kingdom. Three, anyone on a pilgrimage to the Holy Mosques. And with a curt "thank you" (for what, Williams wasn't sure) he hung up the phone.

But Williams was not deterred, at least not yet. The next day he drove the 405 up to Los Angeles and went to the consulate. He had spent the night writing a brief, and somewhat cryptic, letter addressed To Whom It May Concern, Consul's Office, Kingdom of Saudi Arabia. The letter explained that he was an archaeologist—that was sort of true, he convinced himself—and he wanted to "inspect"—it had taken him a while to settle on that neutral-sounding euphemism—biblical sites in the kingdom. He filled out some forms and attached his letter to the top page with a paper clip and handed the whole package to an unsmiling woman behind a desk.

To his surprise, five weeks later he received a note asking him to set up an appointment at the consul's office to discuss his visa. He drove up the freeway to Los Angeles the next day. But it was not a very encouraging interview. This time the lady was smiling, very friendly, but her message held not even the smallest possibility for a concession. I am sorry, Mr. Williams, but the kingdom is not allowing archaeologists in at this time. Yet Williams, the master salesman, would not surrender. He put on his most charming, his most sincere, candidate's smile and told her about all the fascinating biblical research he had done, and what he had found. Dutifully, she took notes. He went on and on, all the time doing his breezy best to win her over. When this didn't seem to be working, in desperation he tried the politician's last resort—the truth.

Not that he told her the *whole* truth. He didn't mention the treasure. Or that Fasold's frequency modulator had registered readings that promised gold, and lots of it, in the plain surrounding the mountain. Or that Wyatt had seen a piece of shiny jewelry dug up from the sand. But he did tell her that he and his buddy, another scholarly sort, were intending to visit Jabal al Lawz, a remote mountain down the road from Tabuk. They believed—and he said this in a whisper, almost conspiratorially—that it was the real Mount Sinai.

All the while, the rather pretty young woman filled up pages with running notes on the conversation. But when Williams had finished, the best she could offer was a big smile and a noncommittal "I see." As she walked him to the door, she explained in the kindest way possible that the decision, of course, wasn't hers. All she could do was to write up a memo detailing his proposed "research trip" to Jabal al Lawz, and pass it on to the proper authorities. "You should hear soon enough," she promised with another fetching smile.

Two months later was not nearly soon enough by Williams' clock, but the news he received was even more depressing: Visa denied. Yet even now he did not give up. He began speaking with friends, calling in favors. He sent the message out that anyone who had a way for Larry Williams and a buddy to get into Saudi Arabia would climb to the top of his list. And this was, it went without saying, a summit filled with glittering possibilities.

After three more long weeks, a British commodities broker Williams traded with came up with an inchoate plan. "Come to

London," he suggested. "There's a Saudi embassy here. We know a few people in the oil business. It'll work out, you'll see," he assured Williams with impressive confidence. It was all Williams had to hang on to, so he had no choice but to consider it as a serious strategy. In the end, he realized it was all pretty pie-in-the-sky. However, it got him thinking: Why not call the London embassy? So he did. And since he had already shared the whole story—or at least an expurgated version—with the Saudi official in Los Angeles, he once again went through his theory about the sacred importance of Jabal al Lawz. It had the same effect in London as it did in Los Angeles. There were only three reasons that would convince the Saudi government to allow foreigners to enter the kingdom, the Saudi embassy official emphatically confirmed over the transatlantic connection. And traipsing off to some mountain in the desert was definitely not one of them.

The call to London left Williams more distressed than any of his dealings with the Los Angeles officials. It seemed as if even he, the one man at the table who always had an ace up his sleeve, had finally run out of cards to play. Saudi Arabia seemed impossibly far away. He was as down as he could remember himself being, his equilibrium rubbed raw by the frustrations, and in this irritable state he called up Cornuke to talk over their mournful prospects.

As soon as Cornuke came on the phone, Williams, ready to jump on anything, started complaining about the connection. "What's that clicking? You hear that, don't you?"

"Of course," said Cornuke wearily. "Past couple of weeks or so they've been working on the lines or something." It was, he felt like saying, the least of their problems.

But Williams would not be pacified. "They've been working on the damn phone lines out here too. The whole country's falling apart. Every time I pick up the phone, there's this goddamn click-click."

"Probably the SEC bugging your line," Cornuke joked. That got a laugh, and the conversation quickly turned to their visa problems. Their mutual complaints about the phones, in fact, might have been forgotten, relegated to the dustbin where all the small annoyances of daily life are quickly discarded, if two seemingly unconnected events had not occurred in rapid succession.

The first was the arrival of a letter. David Fasold, the man whose original letter to Williams had ignited his dreams about Jabal al Lawz, had something to report. Out of the blue, Fasold said, he had gotten a call from, of all places, the Saudi embassy in London. How they got his number, he didn't know and had been too nonplussed to ask. But, he wrote, this Saudi guy, very cordial, asked if I was thinking about returning to Jabal al Lawz. He said he had heard that some Americans were planning a trip, and, more to the point, he wanted to know if I was one of them. "Farthest thing from my mind," Fasold said he had told him. The official immediately responded that this was wise. Then he brought up the fact that Fasold had promised not to return to the kingdom. And just to make sure he got the message, the official warned that if Fasold was contemplating entering the country illegally, that would definitely be considered as a very "provocative"—and Fasold had the feeling the word had been chosen with care—act. With that, just as mysteriously as it had begun, the conversation was over and the Saudi hung up. "Larry," Fasold demanded when the two men spoke on the phone after Williams had digested the letter, "what the hell are you getting yourself into?"

Williams thought a lot about that for a few days. The waiting was gnawing at him. And so was the challenge. More than ever he was convinced that across the world was the find of a lifetime—the mountain of God, and a treasure, the gold of Exodus, thrown in for good measure. It seemed the Saudis were getting anxious too. Williams liked that. It was a good sign. Better than that, it was just what he needed. Like the cavalry, his old optimism, his faith in his ability to break the back of any challenge, reared up and rushed to the rescue. Suddenly, the impossible was scaled down to size. And as a consequence he called Cornuke and announced his impetuous decision. "Pack your bag. We're flying to London in two days. I haven't figured out a plan, but I have a hunch we'll get lucky. We'll find a way to get into Saudi Arabia."

. . .

ALTHOUGH it was not as well known as either the Mossad or the Shin Bet, Aman was the largest and, many in the trade believed, the most valuable of all the Israeli intelligence agencies. Its job was to eavesdrop on the world. In its ability to monitor electronic, radio, and telephone communications, the agency functioned much like America's National Security Agency.

And also like the NSA, it was divided into two main departments. The Collection Department was responsible for signals intelligence. Signit, as it was known in the commonly used shorthand, included the interception of radio transmissions and telephone conversations. Prime targets for the Israeli signit specialists were Arab consulates and embassies throughout the world. Aman's goal was to know everything these diplomats, Israel's enemies, were sending off to the attention of their political superiors, and what instructions they were receiving in return.

It was the job of the Production Department to sift through the information that had been collected from all over the world. It was the largest department in the agency, employing nearly 3,000 people, almost half of the entire Aman staff. Yet its job was still daunting. Out of the millions of scraps of information that came into its headquarters, out of the countless intercepted phone conversations and diplomatic communiqués, it had to decide which were significant. The Production Department had to determine if a small, seemingly innocuous telephone call or routine dispatch disguised a large threat to the state of Israel.

It is a matter of much debate in intelligence circles about where Aman first picked up the crucial signit about the two Americans' proposed trip to Jabal al Lawz. Some insist that the Israelis, with so many targets to aim at, were spread too thin to pay much attention to the low-level goings-on in a consulate in west Los Angeles. They believe that an analyst in Aman's Production Department must have stumbled on a conversation held with an official in the Saudi embassy in London. In fact, according to this argument, when the Saudis reached out from London to ring up David Fasold in

Florida, they might as well have put an announcement about the proposed trip to Jabal al Lawz on the front page of *Ma'ariv.* But even if Aman's antennae had missed something coming out of Los Angeles or London, they would certainly not have ignored a signal sent from Riyadh. As soon as the Saudi Intelligence Service in Washington received orders to pay attention to Cornuke and Williams, it was only a matter of time before the Israelis joined the crowd. And if the two men were of such interest to Israel's enemies, then the Jews were bound to be curious about them too.

There is, however, no debate about how intensely Israel pursued any information it could get about Project Falcon. After the Production Department had passed on to the upper echelons of military intelligence a signal mentioning the two Americans' proposed trip, a decision had been made. From that moment on, regardless of Williams' wishful confidence, he and Cornuke would no longer have to count on mere luck to get them to the mountain.

Part Three

INTO THE MIDST OF THE SEA

18

10 Downing Street, London, England: 1988

PRIME Minister Margaret Thatcher was furious. The director-general of MI-5 had the floor, and as she listened to his report, the meeting was rapidly turning into a war party. MI-5, the British Security Service, was responsible for counterintelligence within the borders of the United Kingdom. And the subject under discussion was the covert activities of the Mossad in England.

The MI-5 brief focused on three incidents, all of which had occurred within the past eighteen months. They were presented in chronological order, starting with what had become known in the British press as "the Vanunu Affair."

In the fall of 1986, Mordecai Vanunu, a former technician at the top secret Israeli nuclear installation at Dimona in the Negev Desert, arrived in London. Vanunu had become disillusioned with Israel, Zionism, and even Judaism itself. As a result, he had a story he wanted to tell—to the highest bidder.

While it was not much of a secret that Israel had a facility that could produce a low-grade atom bomb, Vanunu wanted the world to know that a huge arsenal of advanced thermonuclear weapons had already been manufactured at Dimona. Further, he had spectacular proof. He had surreptitiously shot two rolls of color photographs inside the closely guarded facility. When *The Sunday Times* offered him more than $50,000 for his story and the snapshots, a deal was made.

As Vanunu worked with reporters and editors of the paper to prepare an article for publication, word of his activities reached Israel. Israeli Prime Minister Shimon Peres responded by issuing an executive order. The Mossad was instructed to arrest Vanunu and to do whatever was necessary to bring the traitor back to Israel to stand trial.

Two teams of Mossad operatives, perhaps a dozen men and women, immediately flew to London and, under a variety of covers, began staking out the city. After a few unsuccessful days, the pair of agents posing as a television crew covering the picket lines outside the *Times*' Wapping plant spotted Vanunu. He was crouched down in the backseat of a taxi that was leaving the newspaper building. The bearded cameraman quietly repeated the license plate number into a walkie-talkie. And by the time the cab pulled up to the hotel where Vanunu was registered under an assumed name, it was being followed by a staggered procession of cars, taxis, and motorcycles.

For the next three days, the Israeli watchers tracked Vanunu, waiting for the right moment. When a team of pavement artists reported that he was making his way through Leicester Square on foot and without his usual escort from the *Times,* the decision was quickly made to launch phase two of the operation—the introduction of "Cindy."

It is not known precisely how Cindy managed to strike up a conversation with the lonely foreigner in a strange city. What is known, however, is that Cindy was a bleached blonde partial to high heels and low-cut dresses that stretched tightly across her fleshy figure. She claimed to be an American makeup artist enjoying a European vacation. And it is also a matter of record that within minutes of her meeting Vanunu, it was agreed that they would have dinner that evening.

At dinner, Cindy showed a lot of cleavage and followed a careful script. She was flirtatious, given to deep, dreamy looks. Vanunu only had to place his hand casually on the table and she would reach over to caress it with her finger. But she refused Vanunu's invitation to come back to his hotel. Two more dates followed a similarly coy, teasing pattern. Finally, when her handlers decided she had seeded enough frustrations to overwhelm the most cautious of instincts, she was instructed to proceed to the next phase of the operation.

It began with an invitation: Why don't we go on a quick holiday together, she urged, maybe a short trip to Rome? It would give us a chance to be alone, to get to know one another. She knew the perfect hotel, very romantic. She would make all the arrangements. Who could blame Vanunu, so expertly manipulated, for disregarding the advice of the editors at the *Times* not to leave the country? When Cindy said she would be waiting outside his hotel with a car that would drive them to Heathrow Airport, how, despite all his fears of Israeli reprisals, could he refuse?

The moment Vanunu climbed into that car, he was trapped. He was not seen or heard from for forty days. Then the Israeli cabinet secretary, Elyakim Rubenstein, issued a brief statement to the press: "Mordecai Vanunu is legally under arrest in Israel, in accordance with a court order following a hearing in which a lawyer of his choice was present."

The Sunday Times still ran its exposé about Dimona. But, arguably, it was the paper's follow-up story that caused more of a stir. It described how the Mossad had kidnapped Vanunu on British soil, drugged him, packed him into a crate, and, under the pretense of diplomatic baggage, flown him to Israel.

The second incident cited in the MI-5 brief occurred not in England but in West Germany. It was certainly less sensational than the Vanunu affair. And it was largely played out behind the scenes, without the excited scrutiny of the British press. Nevertheless, in its small way it, too, was very effective in hardening Her Majesty's government.

It all began in Bonn, when a conscientious citizen happened to find a leather shoulder bag lying in a phone booth and dutifully brought it to the police. The police opened it and found documents belonging to the Israeli embassy in Bonn, an Israeli passport, and eight British passports. They immediately contacted the embassy. But by the time an official arrived at the police station to retrieve the bag, it had been determined that the eight British passports were forgeries. The British government demanded an explanation, not that one was necessary. MI-5 was convinced this was proof that the Mossad was arrogantly—and illegally—using British identities as covers for its spies. Even an official apology from the Israeli government did little to assuage the building tensions. The Mossad, the British were becoming convinced, was out of control.

The final incident in the MI-5 brief sealed the case. On July 27, 1987, a Palestinian critic of Yasser Arafat was shot to death on a sunny London afternoon just steps from the busy boutiques of King's Road. It was assumed that this bold assassination was the result of a PLO hit team, but Scotland Yard could not find the killers. Ten months later, a 28-year-old Palestinian, Ismail Sowan, was arrested in an unrelated case—and an unexpected subplot emerged. The murder, according to Sowan, had been committed by a team led by one of Arafat's bodyguards. The killer had used Sowan's apartment in Hull as his base of operations, storing weapons and 68 pounds of explosives in suitcases in his bathroom. As the daily Scotland Yard interrogations continued, Sowan revealed something else. He was working for the Mossad and had infiltrated the PLO terrorist group on instructions from his handlers in the Israeli embassy. The Israelis even paid the rent on the apartment. They knew about the hidden weapons and the pounds of explosives. And, Sowan implied, they were aware of the hit team as it stalked its target in the streets of London.

"Intolerable," said Prime Minister Thatcher when the director-general's briefing was concluded. Within the week she took action. On June 17, 1988, an Israeli embassy attaché, Aryeh Regev, was expelled. Another diplomat, Yaakov Barad, out of the country on vacation, was prohibited from returning. The usually circumspect British Foreign Office identified the two as "Mossad men." It was an unprecedented and well-publicized reprisal against an ally's intelligence service. The game was not usually played that way.

Equally unprecedented, however, was the Israelis' reaction to their public humiliation. The Mossad had always been oblivious to criticism. The agency defined its role pragmatically: It would do whatever was necessary to ensure the survival of the Jewish state. World opinion, the fine points of international law, even at times the moral high ground itself—all were philosophical restraints that were irrelevant to the realities of Israel's daily life-and-death struggle. But after the angry British reaction to its operations, the Mossad seemed surprisingly chagrined. The agency informed MI-5 that it was voluntarily removing three more operatives from the London embassy. The Mossad station in London, the agency promised, was being dismantled.

At the time, the British Secret Service congratulated itself. An arrogant and reckless bunch of Jewish spies had been brought into line. It had been easy enough. All that was necessary was for the Iron Lady to shake her fist. Well played, they heartily applauded.

It was not until years later, after a provocative briefing by the CIA, that some officials of MI-5 began to wonder if it had been too easy. Perhaps, these intelligence backbeaters began to theorize, Israel's voluntary dismantling of its Mossad station in London had been a shrewd bit of distraction. Perhaps it had been a gesture designed to lull the British Secret Service into a deep, self-satisfied complacency. For in the same week that the Mossad somberly announced it was sending its agents home, it was busy conducting a covert mission of the highest priority in the streets of London. There was no shortage of manpower. It was standard Mossad tradecraft all the way—teams of static watchers, roving pavement artists, forgers, break-in boys, and even a couple of Cindys. In its design and execution, it was similar to the bold adventures in the past on British soil that had so infuriated Her Majesty's government. And its targets were Larry Williams and Bob Cornuke.

19

Heathrow Airport, England: June 1988

WHERE was he? Where the hell was he? Williams' commodity broker pal had promised, no, *insisted,* that he would have his driver, Francis, waiting for them the moment their plane touched down. "No bother at all, old chap," Warren had purred across the transatlantic connection in an accent that, for all his clubby Brit-speak, remained steeped in his previous life in Indianapolis. True, it had been the shortest of calls, but Williams prided himself on his ability to intuit the motives of all the Warrens of the financial world. The broker, he was certain, would seize the chance to show another player how his own fortunes were prospering. These bountiful days Warren commanded the services of a driver. Only now, after an exhausting day (and sleepless night) in the air followed by a snaking forced march through customs, it was nearly eight in the morning London time and Francis, the trophy driver, was nowhere to be found.

Williams, with increasing ill temper, searched the length of the terminal. Cornuke scouted the cars lined at the curb outside. Then, exchanging routes, they went off again. And still no Francis, which was an annoyance. But it was also something more. Warren, bursting with mover-and-shaker confidence, had also pledged to Williams that he most assuredly would, one way or another, get them their visas to enter Saudi Arabia. Yet after not even an hour in England, their faith in Warren—and his ability to deliver on the possible, much less the impossible—had fallen precariously.

The flight to London had been uneventful, and that would always be, Cornuke was convinced, the very best thing that could be said about any trip in an airplane. He had spent most of the journey obsessively replaying the encounter he had had with his wife—not ex; nothing was final until the court ruled, he constantly reminded himself—on the day before he had left Colorado. He had persuaded himself that since he would be out of the country for who knew how long, since he was heading off into some real danger, and since, not least, the whole adventure was such heady stuff, it would only be right to tell her about it. There was also something else—he missed her. So he called and boldly suggested dinner, and when she said she was too busy, he settled gratefully for a beer.

He arrived at the bar a half hour early, and she was twenty minutes late. They found a booth and in his soft, understated way, careful not to come off as some starry-eyed adventurer, he laid out what he and Williams were setting off to accomplish. He didn't play up the risks, but at the same time he felt it would have been dishonest to omit the serious trouble both Wyatt and Fasold had gotten into. When he was done, she said simply, "I never worry about you, Bob. If your plane fell out of the sky, you'd be the one person to walk away." Then she drained her beer, told him to have fun, and, without a farewell wave or even a smile, was gone.

Still, considering the way things might have gone, he had left the bar feeling pretty good. After all, she had expressed confidence in his ability to triumph over any kind of adversity. But on the plane ride across the ocean, when falling out of the sky seemed less remote a possibility, he started thinking about her words in an entirely different way. From this perspective, it was just another chorus of her old, hurtful song. He was so stony in his emotions, so rock hard in his detachment, so unfeeling, that even a 30,000-foot drop wouldn't put a dent in his impervious shell. When he looked at things this way, it didn't help his mood at all.

Williams, meanwhile, was lost in his own thoughts; and these, too, followed a familiar pattern. One moment he was nearly giddy with excitement as he contemplated what might lie ahead. A history-making discovery! And, as if further reward were even necessary, the gold of Exodus! But soon his mind would head down another fork in the same road and he would see things with a bleak objectivity. There would be no visas, no trip to the mountain, no treasure. He was, on a whim, flying off on the wild-goose chase of a lifetime.

Landing in early-morning England, however, seemed literally to ground both men's spirits. There was a sudden sense of things moving forward, of things happening, of an impending rush into action. But then, just as suddenly, there was no Francis, and it was as if for lack of a single, insignificant brick a tower of great expectations had come crashing down. For a jet-lagged Williams especially, there was no longer any getting around the oversized reality of what they were hoping to accomplish. Or, no less disturbing, the inordinate faith he had put in others—Fasold, the professor, Cornuke even, and now Warren. What a fiasco, he chided himself.

But all at once a thin man, his shirt undone in a V deep enough to expose a gold chain and a field of dark, wiry hair, came running toward them at a pace that seemed in itself an apology for being late. With the fluid movements of an athlete, he picked up their bags and announced, "Come, I've got a car." Relieved, they followed him out of the terminal.

It was only after they were in his brilliantly polished car, heading away from the airport and toward the city, that the driver, a sky-blue peaked cap now on his curly head, turned to them and said, "I'm Peter."

He spoke the words with so much gaiety that for an instant Williams thought he might have been singing a song. "What happened to Francis?" he asked testily.

"Francis?"

"The driver. Warren's driver."

There was no reply.

"You work for Warren," Williams said. "I mean, Warren sent you to meet us. Right?"

"I'm going to get you into London in a jiffy. You'll be at your hotel before you know it. You must be exhausted." Peter offered up this rush of words with a dazzling smile, but no one was fooled. He had ignored the question.

Cornuke, who after all had been a cop, jumped in. It took some doing, but in time Peter genially confessed that he did not know Warren, had never heard of Francis, and had, in fact, simply rushed over to offer his services when he saw two American gentlemen looking for a taxi.

"How did you know we were Americans?" Cornuke pressed.

"Two big, handsome men. What else could you be?" Peter explained and let loose with a peal of high-pitched laughter. When no one joined in, he quickly added, "The shoes. Always can tell what country someone's from by their shoes."

Both Cornuke and Williams automatically looked down. Williams saw a pair of black leather loafers. Cornuke wore size 11 hiking boots. Not a bad trick, Cornuke decided.

They drove on in silence until they were approaching the city. "I'll take you by Buckingham Palace," Peter volunteered.

"Great," Cornuke said.

"You don't even know where we're going," Williams said suspiciously.

"The Hilton," Peter said.

"How did you know that?" Williams demanded.

"Where else would two handsome American gentlemen stay?" Peter replied. And this time they joined him in his laughter.

After they had turned a green corner of Hyde Park and pulled into the hotel's drive, Peter announced his fee. "Five pounds. A real bargain."

It certainly was, Williams, who knew London well, was pleased to note. Still, when Peter offered his services as their driver for as long as they were in town, day and night, Williams was reluctant to accept. "I'll give you a real good price," Peter insisted. But more out of instinct than for any practical reason, Williams refused.

Soon the doorman was getting their bags out of the trunk and the two men were standing by the car. Williams, a generous tipper, handed Peter a small pile of pound notes. That was when Cornuke, who had seemed lost in his own thoughts, spoke up. "It's not foolproof," he said to Peter.

"Excuse me?" said Peter warily.

"Your system. The shoes," Cornuke said. And he pointed to the Nikes on Peter's feet.

"Oh," Peter said with a quick laugh. "That's easy. I'm Lebanese."

20

AT this moment, sleep seemed treasure enough. The two friends had flown across an entire continent, continued on over the Atlantic Ocean, and in the process had passed through eight time zones. They went immediately to their separate rooms, did not even consider unpacking, and it was evening when, still surprisingly groggy, they emerged. More out of habit than appetite, they agreed to have dinner. They stuck to the hotel, settling on a table in a far corner of a nearly deserted restaurant. The room was so dark that it appeared bathed in its own thick, cozy nighttime. Even the waiter seemed to whisper in a voice sweet enough for a lullaby. They ate rubbery steaks without interest, didn't complain that the beer was warm, and then hurried back to their rooms for more sleep.

In the morning they were finally refreshed. "I'm ready to climb mountains," Cornuke announced cheerfully when he joined Williams in the lobby. But instead he polished off an English breakfast drenched in enough grease, his friend calculated with a shudder, to galvanize any man's arteries. Williams stuck to yogurt, and between spoonfuls he told Cornuke that he was getting ahead of himself. "Without a visa, you can forget about climbing any mountain, at least in Saudi Arabia. We can't get the Saudis to let us in, we might as well head home."

"Got any ideas?" Cornuke asked. He wasn't worried. He was certain his inventive friend would think of something.

Williams had, in fact, a dozen or so possible schemes percolating. But none was any better than the wishful one that had brought him to London in the first place. "Let me call Warren," he said at last.

It was a lengthy conversation, and Warren, drawing on his salesman's repertoire of personalities, did most of the talking. It started out with a bewildered Warren apologizing that his car had inexplicably broken down on the way to the airport; and then moved on to a stalwart Warren assuring, guaranteeing, and even swearing on the lives of his children that he would deliver their travel visas; and it ended with a sincere Warren, bubbling over with friendship, insisting that they come to his office right this minute.

Williams agreed. Maybe this is going to work out after all, he told himself as he hung up the phone. Then he realized that he was becoming as mercurial as any of the politicians he had attacked when he was living out another fantasy. In this complicated mood, hopeful yet full of doubts, he and Cornuke left the hotel. But no sooner had they taken a step beyond the revolving glass doors of the Hilton than they heard someone shout their names. "Mr. Williams. Mr. Cornuke." And there was Peter running toward them as if he were greeting two long-lost friends.

"This is great. Just super," he said. "What luck. I'll take you anywhere you want to go. Right this way."

He didn't wait for an answer. He simply turned and headed off in a trot toward his car. The two friends, after an exchange of amused shrugs, followed. For a moment, Williams wondered how Peter knew their names, but then decided he must have overheard them yesterday when the doorman had taken their bags.

It was a bit of a walk. Peter's midnight-blue car was not in the

Larry Williams, investor, politician, and treasure hunter, in Egypt before heading off on his great adventure.

Former SWAT team member Bob Cornuke. When Williams needed "someone he could count on, someone he could trust if his life depended on it," he recruited Cornuke.

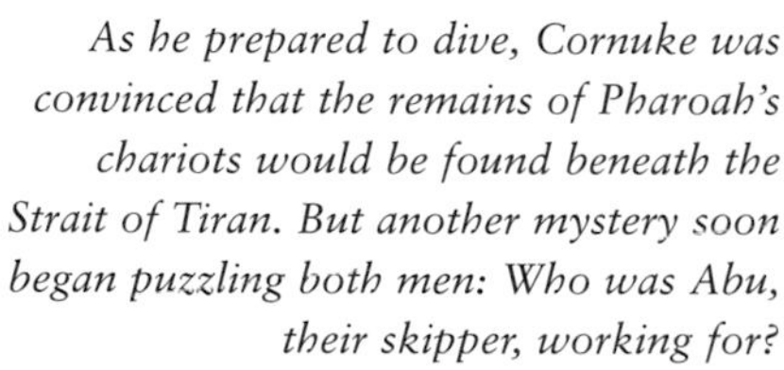

As he prepared to dive, Cornuke was convinced that the remains of Pharoah's chariots would be found beneath the Strait of Tiran. But another mystery soon began puzzling both men: Who was Abu, their skipper, working for?

Cornuke and Williams standing on the underwater land bridge that extended across the Strait of Tiran toward Saudi Arabia—the site of the Red Sea crossing. The ship in the background was trapped high and dry on the continuation of this pathway.

"Then they came to Elim where there were twelve springs and seventy palm trees and they camped near the water." (Exo. 15:27)

Cornuke and Williams camped there, too, near the town of Al Bad in Saudi Arabia, on their way to Jabal al Lawz.

The caves in Midian where Moses lived with his wife and children—and where Williams and Cornuke discovered a Saudi military facility, part of the top-secret Project Falcon.

Between the Saudi coast near the Strait of Tiran (the site of the Red Sea crossing) and the town of Al Bad (the biblical Elim), Cornuke and Williams discovered an alkaline well—the Springs of Marah.

"Then Moses led Israel from the Red Sea and they went into the Desert of Shur. For three days they traveled into the desert without finding water. When they came to Marah . . ." (Exo. 15:22–23)

The mountain of God, as it was first seen by Williams and Cornuke.

"The Lord came down upon Mount Sinai, on the top of the mountain; and the Lord called Moses to the top of the mountain; and Moses went up. . . ." (Exo. 19:20)

Williams and Cornuke discovered that Mount Sinai had been turned into a heavily guarded secret Saudi military encampment. If they were caught climbing the mountain it would mean jail, or worse.

"Take heed that you do not go up into the mountain or touch the border of it; whoever touches the mountain shall be surely put to death." (Exo. 19:12)

"Then came Amalek"—as the Amalekites, a fierce tribe of desert nomads, were known—"and fought with Israel at Rephidim. And Moses said to Joshua, Choose us out men, and go out, fight with Amalek. Tomorrow I will stand on the top of the hill with the rod of God in my hand." (Exo. 17:8–9)

They found the great plain near the mountain of God on which the battle had been fought. But they did not expect to find a new force of Amalekites.

Weary to the point of exhaustion, yet exhilarated, Williams stood in the plain near Jabal al Lawz, where the Israelites had camped. In his mind, the Bible was no longer simply a story. It had all happened just as it had been written in Exodus.

"And Aaron said unto them: 'Break off the golden rings. . . . And he received it at their hand, and fashioned it with a graving tool, and made it a molten calf . . . (and) he built an altar before it." (Exo. 32:2–5)

The mound of rocks that could have been the altar of the golden calf near Jabal al Lawz, now fenced off by the Saudi government.

On the altar rocks were distinct drawings of cows: not sheep, not animals that were native to the desert, but cattle, in a land where there were no cattle—unless they had been driven there by the fleeing Israelites.

Cornuke found a spot where the fence stretched across a soft, silt-like bed of sand. Using his knife, and then his hands, he dug a crawl space. They wriggled under and were inside the compound.

"And you shall set bounds for the people round about, saying, Take heed that you do not go up into the mountain. . . ." (Exo. 19:12)

Williams tripped—literally—over a boundary marker, but he did not heed its warning. He and Cornuke were determined. They had come too far to turn back now.

Halfway up the mountain, the wind started to moan, attacking them, slapping hard at their faces. As they climbed higher, their path led them straight to a long, craggy wall of solid rock.

From the top of the mountain, they could see beyond the plain and across the desert, nearly all the way to the Red Sea. It was as if the entire Book of Exodus was spread out before them.

The cave of Moses was their only hiding place from a Saudi patrol, but Williams would not enter. He felt a presence. Only later did he begin to suspect that they had unknowingly stepped into a larger drama, and that their lives had been manipulated by an ancient feud between Jews and Arabs.

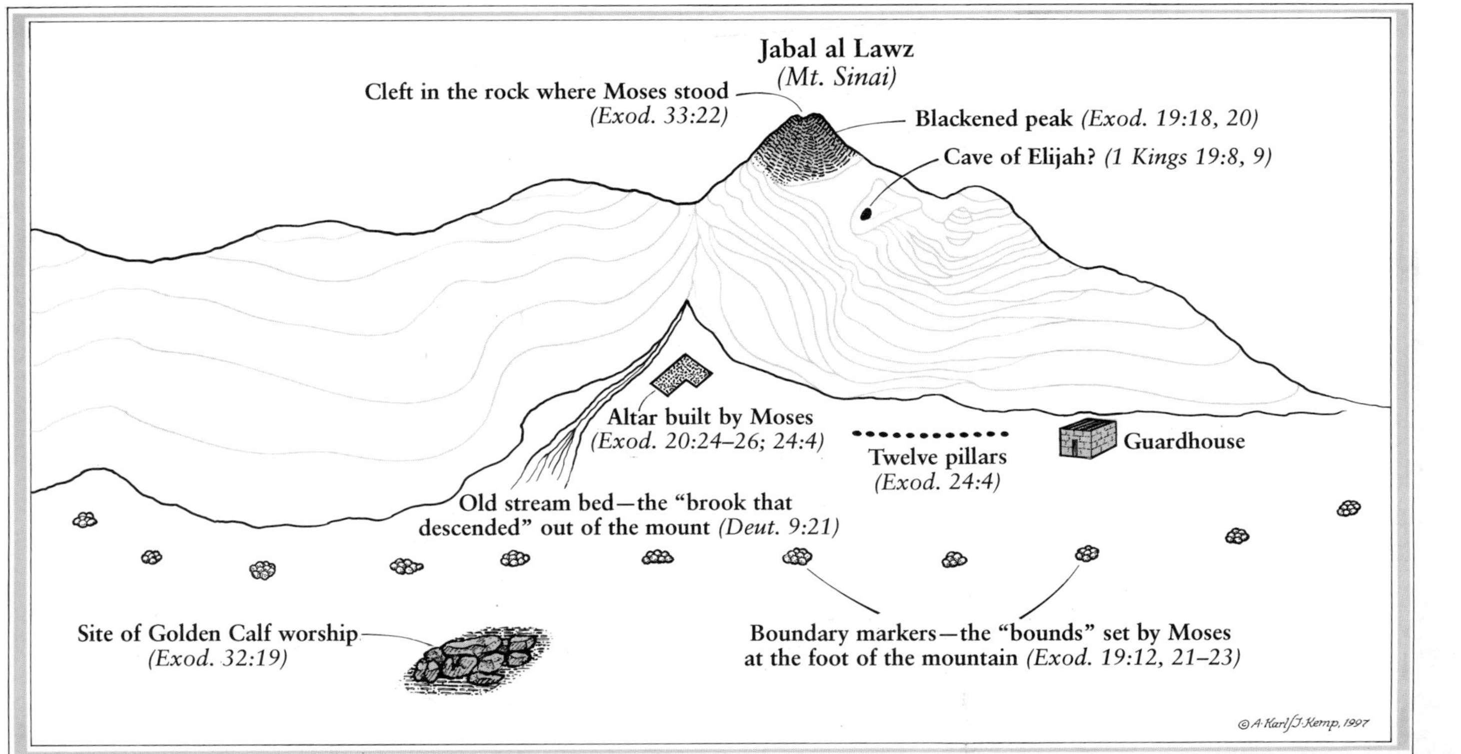

Using the Bible as their guide, Williams and Cornuke found the visual proof they had been searching for—Jabal al Lawz was Mount Sinai.

line of cabs in front of the hotel. It was parked around a corner and then down a long block.

When they finally reached the car, Peter, standing erect as any soldier on parade, was holding open the back door. Except for a soft black leather coat that nearly reached his knees, he was dressed the same as yesterday—carefully pressed blue jeans, white shirt with the top three buttons rakishly undone, and Nikes.

"How do you expect to get business if you don't line up outside the hotel with the others?" Williams asked before climbing into the backseat. It was the sort of practical question that genuinely intrigued him. There was also something else bothering him. Had Peter been waiting for them?

Peter laughed as if Williams had told an uproarious joke.

"No, really. I wasn't kidding," Williams said. "I mean, what's the point of hanging around the hotel if you don't get in line? How are you going to make any money?"

"I can tell you're a businessman," Peter said once he was sitting behind the wheel. "So I'll let you in on my secret." He turned his head and looked at them as if he was about to utter words of great consequence. "If you queue up, you must take whoever comes out of the door. I only want to take certain people. I only drive rich people. The big tippers." But then he admitted with a laugh, "I was waiting for you to come through the door."

"Who says money can't buy love?" Cornuke said, nudging Williams.

Williams, however, was not amused. He could not help thinking something was up. "What if we hadn't left the hotel?" he asked. "Or suppose we didn't need a cab? What if we wanted to walk, or maybe we had cleared out bright and early before you showed up? Then what would you've done?"

"Ah, but Mr. Williams, none of those things happened."

"But how could you be sure?"

"Well," said a suddenly somber Peter, "I was certain I would see you. You know why?"

The question filled the car until Peter spoke again.

"'Because, Mr. Williams, I'm a very lucky man."

Peter had better be, Williams thought, if he was going to risk his livelihood on hunches. Still, he reminded himself, who was he, a man preparing to head off into the desert to find a long-lost mountain and its treasure, to dismiss the efficacy of luck? Looking at things that way, Williams decided it was as good an answer as any. His suspicions were somewhat assuaged. And in a moment Peter had his blue peaked cap on his head and they were driving along the park toward the address in Belgravia that Williams had given him.

WARREN had thin, oily, unconvincingly dyed jet-black hair that rose in a single, swept-back ridge from the center of an otherwise bald head. He was tall and lean, and his chalk-striped double-breasted suit was tapered vainly at the waist. He wore, as always, a Hermès tie, and today the puff of silk in his breast pocket was a complementary fire-engine red. His shirt was striped, but the collar was a solid white. He showed a lot of starched cuff, and they were fastened with hefty gold links shaped like anchors. Williams took one look at Warren—at the entire, careful package—and in an instant recognized perhaps for the first time why going to Jabal al Lawz was so important to him.

This could be me, he realized; and, in fact, in a not-so-distant life it had been. With a clarity so precise it made the moment solemn, Williams understood that he had been given his opportunity to escape the Warrens of the world forever. Even more, he was aware that he needed—and it *was* a need, a passion as deep as his love for his family—to declare himself a different sort of man. Williams looked at Warren and at the busy room stretched out in front of them with its rows of bright young men in shirtsleeves and suspenders glued to their computers as they watched fortunes rise and fall with each incandescent tick of the market, and he knew he had no choice but to go off and climb Jabal al Lawz. It would be his legacy, his gift to himself—the defining act of his life. And so, without warning, months of vacillation were finally resolved. Doubts became irrelevant. In an instant, his mind was irrevocably set. He would go to Saudi Arabia no matter what.

But all this, like so many important realizations in the course of one's life, went unspoken. Instead, there was a round of handshakes; a tour of the trading floor, where Williams oohed and aahed about how impressive the whole enterprise was, which was true; a bit of small talk about the wives, kids, and, not least, the markets; and then, as gracious as any king in his palace, Warren led them into his office.

They sat in cordovan leather wing chairs that gave the two friends a good view of the hunting prints fixed in precise vertical rows along the wood-paneled walls. The conversation, under Warren's subtle guidance, drifted into what Williams realized was a very careful interrogation of his opinions on where the market was heading. Cornuke, restless to the point of boredom, began an intense study of a large print depicting the field at some obscure meet. He had risen to his feet for a closer inspection when Warren, abruptly switching gears, announced it was "time to get down to business." He had, he said proudly, "a foolproof plan" to get them their visas. Then he pushed a button on his desk, gave a muffled order into the intercom, and the next thing the two men knew, Warren's plan walked through the door. His name was Nikoli.

NIKOLI, while Warren's partner, was no Warren. It was as if all the available taste and discipline had been used up in the process of molding a presentable Warren. Nikoli, left to his own instincts, ran to sloppy excess. He had a wayward mop of curly black hair and a body that spread out thickly from his hips so that he rocked like a bowling pin when he walked. His tie was undone, helping to give the impression that he had been interrupted in the midst of some very strenuous physical activity. His gargantuan white shirt billowed like a mainsail out of trousers slung low beneath a jutting prow of belly. He was never at rest, either mopping his brow with a handkerchief or raking his thicket of curls with stubby fingers. But when he finally focused on the matter that was foremost in Williams' and Cornuke's mind, he was cut from the same confident cloth as Warren.

"I know gaggles of Saudi princes," Nikoli began. "We're all in the oil business together. It made me rich and them richer. That's the best kind of friends you can have. Everybody's a winner. They just love Nikoli. I'm their favorite Turk. When they come into town, my phone doesn't stop ringing. It's one big party. I eat, gamble, hell, I'm out all night carrying on with them. I'll get you your visas. Just tell me when you want to leave. You've got my word. And Nikoli's word is something you can count on, right, Warren?"

"Good as gold," purred Warren.

And with that out of the way, a previously immovable roadblock cleared with one effortless swat of Nikoli's beefy hand, Warren suggested that they adjourn for lunch. He mentioned his club, but after another look at the casually dressed Americans, a little Greek place where they knew Nikoli seemed a more suitable choice. But just as they were heading off, one of Warren's soldiers from the trading floor, a blondish young man in pin-striped pants, polished shoes, shirtsleeves, and suspenders, came rushing in for a short, whispered conference with the boss. Warren listened, nodded authoritatively, issued some concise instructions, and then, as the young man was hurrying back to the trading floor, ordered him to wait. "Larry," he called to Williams across the room, "a little opportunity has come up in copper that just might be up your alley."

While Cornuke busied himself once more in his study of the rows of colored prints on the wall, Williams, huddled between the twin pillars of Warren and Nikoli, listened to the scheme. "I'm in for thirty contracts," he agreed without hesitation when Warren concluded; and, the truth was, his mood at last was so confident and resolved that he would have agreed to just about anything.

THEY were seated in the Greek restaurant, platters of food before them and well into their second bottle of ouzo, when the blond young man, this time wearing his suit jacket, made his way to their table. After a brief consultation, Warren, with a poker face, told Williams he had some good news and some bad news. The bad news was that he had filled on only twenty of the thirty contracts. The good news, he went on after a lugubrious pause that was pure theater, was that copper was up limit and Williams had walked away with a $25,000 profit. Not bad for a two-hour investment, he crowed.

Cornuke was floored. Williams, while pleased, could not help believing that more significant than any money was the precedent: Warren would deliver. He would get them their visas for Saudi Arabia. And as if reading Williams' mind, Nikoli looked up from his plate to announce, "See, you can trust us. We'll go out gambling tonight. Maybe give back some of that money you made. Maybe make some more. Who knows, by then I might even have your visas."

AFTER making plans to meet up later that evening at the hotel bar, the two friends left the restaurant and went their separate ways. Cornuke, vividly remembering the View Master slides of the Tower of London and Parliament he had studied as a child, was eager to see the real things. Armed with directions from Warren, he waved good-bye to Williams and, dodging traffic, ran across the street to find a bus stop. But as he stood in line, a familiar blue car pulled up, and there was Peter sticking his curly-haired head out through the open car window and insisting that he would take him wherever he wanted to go. At first Cornuke was surprised, but as things worked out, he couldn't have been happier. He couldn't have wished for a better tour guide. Peter seemed to know everything about getting around London.

Williams, meanwhile, was doing his best to spend at least some of the money he had made over lunch. If Nikoli was right, they could be flying to Saudi Arabia as soon as tomorrow. He might as well get his shopping in while he could. His first purchase was a pair of night-vision binoculars at a store not far from the restaurant. He thought they might come in handy in the desert. With that out of the way, he moved on to Bond Street. He went from store to store, amassing piles of cashmere sweaters, kilts, blouses, and, finally, even scarves for his wife and daughters. As the saleswoman totaled up the latest bill, Williams began chiding himself. Scarves! They would really come in handy in southern California. But his thoughts were interrupted when he noticed a reflection in a mirror above the display case. It was a man with a neatly trimmed beard, a fit-looking dark-haired guy, and he seemed to be staring very intently at him.

There was also something else about the bearded man. It took a moment before Williams could bring it to mind. Then he had it. He had seen the man before in another of the stores down the block. Nothing odd about that, necessarily, but catching the bearded man focused so directly on him made Williams uncomfortable. He turned to face the man. And as soon as he did, the bearded man dropped his head and walked briskly out of the store.

Williams did not give the incident another thought until later that afternoon. He had emerged from the Underground near Marble Arch and was walking leisurely back to the hotel. On his way, he stopped at a store window to look at a magnificently colored Oriental carpet. But at the same time, he could not help noticing something else. Reflected in the window, he saw a row of vehicles that had stopped for a red light. Right over his shoulder was the bearded man, sitting on a motorcycle. And this time Williams had not the slightest doubt that the man was staring directly at him.

21

IN the hotel bar, a gray-haired pianist was working his way through a saccharine medley of Beatles songs. "All you need is love . . . love," he crooned pleasantly. Williams stood by the door, waiting a moment as his eyes grew accustomed to the darkness, and then scanned the room for his friend. He found him at a far table wedged against a wall decorated with wine barrels. Cornuke had a pint in one hand, a roguish grin on his face, and two sultry women positioned as close as bookends on either side. "Love is all you need."

As Williams weaved his way through the crowded room, he was able to get a better look at the women. One was short, a not particularly pretty brunette with a long, straight nose. But she had merry eyes, seemed broad in the hips, and had her legs crossed recklessly so that her skirt rode high to expose an ample thigh. No doubt about it, she was very tempting.

The other, though, was glamorous. Tall, with an athlete's honed thinness, she sat erect, her back as straight as a model's. Her hair was blond, or at least had been dyed to a soft shade of yellow, and her features were precise and confident. She kept her hands on the table, long fingers locked together as if she were holding cards for a rubber of bridge. A different sort altogether than her friend. And, Williams decided without any real interest, much more to his liking.

But in the next moment, that appraisal, however casually made, led him somewhere unexpected. It was a setup. The women had been carefully chosen, types knowingly matched to types. The short, fleshy brunette for Cornuke, the taller, more refined blonde for him. Had Warren? No, Nikoli, self-proclaimed host to the libidinous Saudi princes, had fixed them up with dates. After all their talk about wives and kids? Williams, more amused than shocked, figured there was only one worldly way out of this awkward situation. He would just have to announce straight off that he was a happily married man and send the blonde at least on her undoubtedly expensive way.

"You must be Larry," the brunette said eagerly when Williams joined them.

"Did Nikoli tell you that?" he snapped, and immediately regretted his tone.

"Nikoli?" she repeated, and Williams decided her accent might have sounded English back in San Diego, but not in London. She looked at Cornuke. "I thought you said your name is Bob?" She seemed annoyed, or at least confused.

"Larry, this is Claire," Cornuke said, gesturing toward the brunette. "She and Susan here"—he gave a small nod in the other woman's direction, and she responded with a breathtaking smile—"are from South Africa. They're here on vacation. They don't know Nikoli."

Williams was still on guard. "How about Warren? You ladies happen to be friends of ol' Warren, everybody's favorite hustler?"

"I'm afraid I don't know Warren either," said Susan politely.

Williams sat in the chair next to the blonde. "Well, I guess I got things sort of mixed up," he said, although he was far from certain. "This weird thing happened to me today. Left me a bit out of sorts,

I guess." He was about to explain, but for some reason—the way Claire seemed to be inching closer to Cornuke? the way Susan aimed the full wattage of her smile directly at him?—he found himself holding back.

"Bob was telling us the most amazing story about Mount Sinai," Claire said brightly.

"Are you really going to Jabal al Lawz?" Susan asked. South African or not, the name of the mountain, Williams couldn't help noting, seemed to slide off her tongue like a native. "It sounds so exciting."

"I'd love to hear all about it," Claire said, moving in even closer to Cornuke. Her leg pressed against his, but she made no attempt to move it.

Williams told himself not to be hostile. Either they were whores who prowled the hotel bars or, despite their disclaimers, they had been sent by mischievous Nikoli. Either way, it was no big deal—if he put an end to it right now.

"Ladies," Williams announced with a formality that even he found surprising, "I'm afraid Bob and I have a prior engagement. We have to be going."

"Really? I was so interested in hearing more about your trip," said Claire, nearly begging.

"Like I said, there are people waiting for us," Williams said, and rose from the table. "Come on, Bob."

When Cornuke stood, Susan extended her hand to Williams. "Well, perhaps we'll meet again," she said and made a point of looking him directly in the eye.

"Perhaps," he agreed without conviction.

"How did you hook up with those two?" Williams asked his friend after the bill had been paid and they were leaving the bar.

"I don't know. I was sitting there waiting for you and they came over and asked if I was from the States. They had some kind of bet or something about whether New York was the capital of the country. Wanted me to settle it. The next thing I know, they're sitting with me."

"Smooth," said Williams sarcastically. Cornuke looked embarrassed, but Williams continued. It bothered him that Cornuke had been telling strangers about their plans. "Then you started going on about Jabal al Lawz?"

"You know, it's really funny. They asked me why I was in London, so I explained how we were just stopping here on our way to Saudi Arabia. You know, just being polite, really. But they wanted to hear all about it. Asking me all kinds of questions. They were really interested."

"Right," said Williams. "a couple of hookers fascinated by the search for Mount Sinai."

That seemed to unsettle Cornuke.

They were making their way through the lobby. "My money's on Nikoli," Williams said. "Ten to one, he sent them. Anyway, it doesn't matter who they were. You shouldn't be talking about Jabal al Lawz." He let that sink in for a moment. "And you would think Nikoli would know better. I'm a married man."

"Me, too," Cornuke added weakly.

They were on the street, about to hail a taxi to take them to the gambling club, when Peter appeared.

"My lucky night," he exclaimed. "Right this way."

"Persistent little guy," muttered Williams. But in his mind he was beginning to put all the pieces together.

IT seemed as if the only sounds in the room were the click of the ball in the spinning wheel and the shuffle of chips as they were moved about the baize-covered roulette table. These people took their gambling very seriously, Cornuke decided. Williams had bought him a hundred dollars worth of chips, but he could not bring himself to place a bet. He watched as Nikoli and Warren, dressed in tuxedos no less, ordered bottles of champagne and began placing piles of chips stacked inches high about the table. Without a word Cornuke drifted from their circle and set off on his own.

Williams, too, was not a gambler. When he took risks, in business or, for that matter, in life, he always made his moves after a succession of thoughtful calculations. But as he watched colossal sums being risked solely on a hunch, without even the pretense of a theory, he was totally fascinated. The complete randomness of success or failure was so alien to the way he believed things worked that he was mesmerized by each spin of the wheel. He did not place a single bet at the roulette table, but he stood at Nikoli's side for more than an hour. Finally, after Williams calculated that about $70,000 had been squandered, the Turk, with a brave shrug, moaned, "That's enough punishment for one night." Williams, suffering as if the losses were his own, followed him to the bar.

The club's bar was as homey as a country house, with nicely frayed Orientals, pine paneling, and a picture of a horse that could have been a Stubbs above the mantel. Nikoli ordered another bottle of champagne, insisted on opening it himself, and after this was done with great ceremony, he drained his flute in a single swallow. Two more quick glasses and he seemed more at ease.

"Quite a show," said Williams when the moment seemed right.

The champagne had made Nikoli happy. "Win some. Lose some. Life goes on," he said with a big smile.

So Williams thought now would be a good time to ask him about the women. "You wouldn't have happened to send a couple of girls over to our hotel, would you?"

"Girls. I know plenty of girls. No problem. That can be arranged. What kind you like?"

"Come on, Nikoli. Level with me. You sent a couple of hookers over to meet us, didn't you?"

"You want girls, you got them. Just tell me what kind you like. Or maybe you want me to surprise you. Don't worry, you won't be disappointed. Nikoli's got very good taste."

Williams couldn't determine if Nikoli was drunk or purposefully obtuse, or maybe both. He decided to let the matter slide. After all, he still needed the man's help.

"Forget the girls," he said quickly. And he moved on to what was really on his mind. "How are we doing with those visas? Any of your Saudi friends able to help us out?"

"Those Arabs are busy running around spending their billions, screwing their brains out. Can't expect them to drop everything. They're going to get back to me, I guarantee it. Nothing to worry about."

"You're sure about that?" Williams asked. And as soon as he spoke, he was embarrassed by the urgency in his voice.

But Nikoli did not seem to notice. "Larry," he said, "relax. Nikoli's going to get you your visas. Like I promised, you're going to be sweating your ass off in Saudi before you know it. Just got to let me handle things. OK?"

"OK," Williams agreed, appeased. After all, he reminded himself, not even twenty-four hours had passed since the meeting in Warren's office.

"Good," said Nikoli heartily. "Now how about we go back in and you can watch me get even?"

Williams' mood, however, had shifted. "I'm going to call it a night," he said. Nikoli nodded and quickly stood. Suddenly he was in a hurry to get back to the table, and with only a small wave, he trundled out of the bar.

BOB must have gone back to the hotel, Williams decided. But when he stepped outside, he saw the dark blue car parked at the curb. Cornuke was in the backseat, and, one more surprise, Claire and Susan were huddled on either side of him.

Williams squeezed in and found himself pressed closely against Susan. Even in this tight space, he observed, she managed to keep her perfect posture. "So what's going on here?" he asked, trying to keep things light.

Cornuke explained that he had been watching Telly Savalas play blackjack—"He's not so tough as he looks on TV," he couldn't help adding—when all of sudden someone tapped him on the shoulder and he turned to find Claire and Susan standing there. They went off to have a drink, but the bar was so expensive that they wound up sitting out in the car, talking and waiting for Williams. "We've been here maybe an hour or so," he concluded, perfectly happy with his good fortune.

"I can't believe it," Claire said. "You guys are really going off to Saudi Arabia to find the real Mount Sinai."

Williams refused to follow her lead. "How did you ladies happen to come here?" he asked.

"The concierge at the Hilton," Susan said. "Very 'in,' he promised. Trendy."

"We saw Telly Savalas," said Claire quickly.

"I heard," Williams said without bothering to disguise his exasperation.

"We could go for a drink," Claire suggested. "And talk some more."

Peter started the car and pulled into traffic.

"I think I'll just go back to the hotel," Williams said. "Peter," he instructed, "please take the ladies anywhere they want to go."

"We could go back to the hotel," Susan said. She spoke the words softly, and she was so close that Williams could feel her breath on his ear.

Her suggestion went unanswered.

Then Claire spoke. "I heard they have glass showers in the rooms. The kind you can see through. I've always wanted to try one."

This time Williams' voice was steel. "I'm going back to the hotel. By myself. Got that?"

"Me too," Cornuke agreed abruptly. "It's been a long day."

"Are you sure?" Susan said, still leaning into Williams.

But suddenly Peter's voice was booming from the front seat. "I am dropping the gentlemen off at the hotel. I will take you ladies home. It has been decided."

He spoke with authority, and it very effectively put an end to the evening.

THERE was a large manila envelope, perhaps 20 by 15 inches, lying on the bed in Williams' hotel room. That was the first thing he noticed when he came in. He looked at the return address: Horizon Research, Searchlight, Nevada. He had been expecting this. Excited, he picked it up. That was when he saw it had already been opened. The flap had been cut neatly, as if with a knife. There had been no attempt to reseal it.

Immediately he began to inspect his room. The manila folder on his desk had been moved. It was no longer directly underneath the brass lamp. He quickly shuffled through the papers—notes on his meeting with the professor, a copy of Fasold's letter, a concordance of relevant biblical passages, a map of Saudi Arabia. Everything appeared to be there. Yet a search through his luggage convinced him that it, too, had been examined. Then he had another anxious thought, but he found the metal detector he had brought with him and the night-vision binoculars he had purchased that afternoon. Both were in the closet, approximately where he had left them.

When he finished with his inventory, the only thing that was missing was his watch. It was gold, a Patek Philippe. A present from his wife, and worth a small fortune. He cursed himself for having thought it would be safer in his room. Still, the more he thought about it, he could not help feeling that the watch had been taken only as an afterthought. His room had been searched. His papers had been examined. And he stayed up a long time that night wondering why.

22

Searchlight, Nevada: 1988

WILLIAMS slept fitfully, unable to work out precisely what was going on. He shared the night with visions of a lurking Peter in his blue cap, the intense, bearded man on the motorcycle, and Susan bending her swan's neck to whisper in his ear. In the morning, closer to an answer but still troubled, he was glad to put aside new mysteries for ancient ones. He ordered breakfast in his room and then dumped the contents of the envelope mailed from Nevada onto his desk.

Inside were four photographs about the size of hospital X rays, each at first glance a jumble of contrasting colors, and a typed letter. He studied the photographs one at a time. They were aerial shots, taken from space, he knew, by a French satellite equipped with a high-resolution infrared camera. He arranged them in a line as if he was dealing a hand of solitaire, and together they formed a map of the Middle East. He stood above it, looking down for a while. From this perspective it was as if he, too, were off in space, lost in thought.

Then he went to work. He placed his index finger in the upper-right-hand corner of the first satellite shot. This was his starting point: Egypt. Moving his finger slowly, as if each inch he traveled required a great exertion, he began to trace an invisible line across the Middle East. He followed the long, western edge of the V-shaped Sinai Peninsula, hugging close to the coast of the Gulf of Suez; proceeded to the sharp point of the V where the Sinai was wedged against the Red Sea; then started to move up the eastern side of the peninsula; but stopped suddenly and moved across a narrow channel of water in the Gulf of Aqaba; and, back on dry land, headed for a short distance up the coast of Saudi Arabia, only to hook quickly east until he finally came to a stop at the highest point in the area—the mountain known as Jabal al Lawz.

This, Williams was certain, was the route the Israelites had taken when they fled from Egypt on their way to Mount Sinai. It was not the traditional Exodus. Most people—laymen *and* biblical scholars—assumed the miracle of the Red Sea crossing had happened just outside Cairo at the Bitter Lakes, or perhaps farther south in the western branch of the Red Sea, the Gulf of Suez. From there, the commonly held theory went, Moses had lead the twelve tribes down the Sinai Peninsula to the mountain near the present site of St. Catherine's Monastery. But everything that Williams had read, studied, annotated, lived with for all these months—in the Bible, in the volumes of history and archaeology that the professor had shared, and, not least, in Fasold's letter—convinced him they were wrong. He knew: Mount Sinai was in Midian, and the Red Sea crossing had occurred just west of Saudi Arabia at the Gulf of Aqaba. And soon he would prove it. He stared at the four satellite photos, at the route he had just traced, and could not help feeling a sudden excitement. If he was right, if this was the way to Mount Sinai, then in front of him was—*a treasure map*.

He now turned at last to the letter. He had been deliberately avoiding it, but finally he told himself, whatever it said, it was his own doing. He had asked George Stephens, his old friend from the days when he had hunted for less consequential veins of gold and silver, to cast his professional eye over these satellite shots. Stephens, who had learned his trade in the military, would be able to study the infrareds and come up with a pretty good idea of whether there was any trace of the trail made by the tribes of Israelites who had trekked through the desert to Midian. At the time, it had seemed like a pretty inventive way of checking out Fasold's letter. Only now, months later and determined to go ahead with this expedition, he did not want to deal with conflicting evidence. So before he went any further, he made a silent vow: Regardless of what Stephens had found, he would climb Jabal al Lawz. Still, he could not help offering up a small wish. Let it be good news.

A coldness came over him, his defense whenever he had to put his money down or pull it abruptly out of some deal, and he began to read.

"First, there is a clear trail that comes into the photograph from the left side. It is south of the traditional Mount Sinai, and it goes right to the water's edge at the Strait of Tiran, at the Gulf of Aqaba."

Which was exactly the area where he believed the Red Sea crossing had occurred, Williams told himself, suddenly eager to read on.

"It is impossible to tell the exact age [of the trail] from the photographs, but it is certainly thousands of years old. That is for sure!

"It was used heavily, and has some real width to it at parts."

As well it should, since perhaps a million people had fled Egypt, Williams thought.

"There are some very large campsites along the way, on the other side of the strait, where it seems to come out of the Red Sea . . . the trail goes right down the strait and resumes on the other side."

Into Saudi Arabia!

"It goes about 11 miles south of the crossing site, then turns up north. There are three major campsites, or areas where there were towns or gatherings of many people. I can't tell you what went on there, only that there were large congregations of people."

And Moses led Israel onward from the Red Sea, and they went into the wilderness of Shur.

"Finally, the trail turns east, about halfway up the gulf, and heads inland, going right to the area you marked on your map as representing Jabal al Lawz. There is a huge, well-used campsite there."

Just as you would expect to find at Mount Sinai, Williams told himself, his sense of triumph complete.

But there was a final paragraph, added as if a footnote to the more momentous information that had preceded it. Back in his cautious, uncertain days, a time and mood that now seemed to Williams as long ago as the Exodus itself, he had asked Stephens to pull the satellite infrareds of the area around St. Catherine's. If there was something to the traditionalists' theory, he figured he had better find out. But now with a calm that came from total confidence he read on:

"There are several pathways around that mountain [at St. Catherine's], but no major camping sites. And based on my study of and interpretation of the density of the colors in the photographs, I'd say the trails there are no more than three hundred to four hundred years old, at most. The trails there don't even come close to the size and apparent age of the one that goes into and out of the Red Sea."

With that, Williams put down the letter and, exhilarated, returned to the satellite photos placed edge to edge in front of him. No doubt about it. He was staring at a treasure map.

IT took all of Williams' self-control to put off phoning Nikoli the moment he finished Stevens' letter. Instead, he dropped to the floor and started doing push-ups. The exercise, he hoped, would bring him some calm. When he was done, he hid the photographs under his mattress—a precaution that after last night's break-in seemed necessary—and rounded up Cornuke. They went for a rambling walk around Hyde Park.

Williams began by announcing that he was certain his room had been searched when they were out the night before.

"Searched?" Cornuke repeated. "What would anyone have been looking for?"

"They took my watch," Williams said. "It was worth some real money."

"Then there's my answer."

"I don't know. I just feel they were hunting for something else."

"You think those girls fit into this somehow?" Cornuke wondered.

"Wouldn't surprise me," Williams said. "I just don't know why anyone would go to all the trouble." They would just have to be more careful, he warned, then moved on to his other news.

Stephens' interpretation of the satellite infrareds had confirmed their theory, Williams said. "He nailed the Red Sea crossing just where we expected it to be. And if the Israelites crossed over at the Strait of Tiran . . ."

"Then they're in Saudi Arabia," Cornuke said, completing his friend's sentence.

"And heading right to Jabal al Lawz," Williams said.

The fact that they were right, and that they were preparing to go to the holiest spot on the planet, seemed, for an instant at least, to overwhelm them. When the moment had passed, Cornuke spoke. "How about we check in with Nikoli. See if he's had any luck?"

Williams thought about that. "No," he decided, "let's give him some more time. Don't want to spook him."

So they walked on for a bit and wound up having tea in a somber, wood-paneled reception room in a hotel on the other side of the park. It was quite a production, the waiter clearly enjoyed his work, and Cornuke was impressed. But Williams seemed preoccupied and finally said, "I'm going to call Nikoli."

As soon as he got on the phone, Nikoli started to equivocate. "You got to understand," he said, a convincing twinge of embarrassment in his voice, "your Arab is a very lackadaisical sort of guy. Maybe it's the desert, all that heat beating down on him day in, day out. Who knows? But whatever it is, you've got to believe me on this. He can't be rushed."

Williams, however, was in no mood to listen to excuses, even if they were reasonable. His annoyance and frustration spilled out. "But you promised, Nikoli. You told us very specifically you'd have our visas by today. No problem, you said."

"And there isn't a problem," Nikoli insisted. "You're going to get your visas. Like I promised. It's just going to take a little longer than I anticipated."

"How long, Nikoli?

He hesitated. "A week maybe. But that's at most."

"You're sure?"

"Just give me a week. Maybe less. I'll get you your visas."

"So what are we supposed to do? Hang around London twiddling our thumbs?"

"Hey, you want some company? It can be arranged. I've got a lot of friends in this town. Maybe you take one of them on a trip. Go to Paris, or maybe Marbella. A trip would do you good."

"I'll call you in a couple of days, Nikoli," Williams said without enthusiasm and then hung up.

But by the time he had walked from the phone kiosk and was making his way toward the tufted settee where Cornuke was sitting, an idea had started to take shape in Williams' head. Perhaps, he had begun to think, they should take a trip after all.

23

Cairo, Egypt: 1988

THE noise from the plane's engines was drowning out Cornuke's voice, so Williams had to undo his seat belt and move closer. Cornuke did not notice. He continued in a flat monotone, too wrapped up in what he was reading to be aware of anything else.

"'And Moses stretched out his hand over the sea; and the Lord caused the sea to go back by a strong east wind all the night, and made the sea dry land, and the waters were divided. . . .'"

He looked up from his Bible. "This is my favorite part," he told Williams, quite seriously. Then he continued in a stronger voice: "'And the children of Israel went into the midst of the sea upon dry land; and the waters were a wall unto them on their right hand, and on their left.'"

It was just two days later, but in their tumultuous world it might have been years. After his disappointing conversation with Nikoli, Williams had bounced back with a sudden inspiration. He had suggested to Cornuke that they head off on a short trip, while Nikoli finished "pulling strings," or, as Williams, still annoyed, added at the time, "whatever it is shifty Turks do to persuade horny Arabs." Cornuke, who was growing restless with his tourist's itinerary of gambling clubs and royal palaces, immediately seconded the plan. And now the two friends were on a plane to Cairo. They were on their way to discover the precise spot where the miracle Cornuke was reading about had occurred over 4,000 years ago.

When he had finished chapter 14 of the Book of Exodus, Cornuke closed his Bible. "It's all here," he said, "all the clues we need to find the crossing site. They're right in the Bible."

"And on the satellite photos," Williams said. "We just follow the trail on the photos right to the bottom of the Sinai Peninsula."

He lowered his tray table, found a blank piece of paper, and drew an inverted triangle. "This is the Sinai," he explained. "And down here, just about at the tip, is Sharm al Sheikh." He made a small dot. "That's where we're heading. And right by it, just up a bit, is the Strait of Tiran." He drew a series of fluttering waves. "Egypt's on one side." He drew a jagged coastline. "Saudi Arabia's on the other." Then he made a big X in the middle of the strait, at the spot where even on this crude map the distance between the two countries was quite narrow. "That's our target area. That's where the satellite photos say the crossing took place."

"If we find a chariot wheel or piece of armor from one of Pharaoh's soldiers, we've got our proof. God parted the waters at the Strait of Tiran, and the Israelites marched right across into Saudi Arabia. Case closed," Cornuke said. He was really that confident.

"They've been diving up north in the Bitter Lakes for years, hoping to come up with something," Williams said. "Never found a damn thing, of course. They were diving in the wrong place. I can't wait to see what's lying forty or fifty feet beneath the strait."

All at once Cornuke seemed uncomfortable. "Dive?" he said. "I can swim, sure. Snorkel, I guess. But scuba, that's what you're talking about, right? Tanks and all that stuff?"

Williams nodded his head.

"Well," Cornuke said, "I've never done that."

Williams hadn't counted on this. It had just never occurred to him. "Well, I'm not an expert," he said finally. "But I've dived a bit, years ago when I was hanging out in Hawaii. I'm not certified or anything. But you're an athlete. I should be able to teach you."

Cornuke thought about that. "Great," he said, relieved.

In a moment he was back reading through his Bible, and Williams was asking the stewardess if she could find him a glass of red wine that wasn't too sweet.

THEY stayed only one night in Cairo, but both agreed that was too long. The city was hot, dirty, and tense, full of clogged streets and honking traffic. When they left their hotel, the air smelled like gasoline, and sly voices in doorways called out to them, "Sahibs?" There were stray dogs in the market, angry and aggressive animals; it seemed wise to give them room. At dinner the only thing Cornuke could identify on his plate was the cockroach that scurried across.

In the morning, they boarded a bus that would take them down the Sinai Peninsula, toward the Red Sea. The bus had been painted red, but an older undercoat of blue dominated in spots, so that it was actually colored in an odd camouflage design. "Psychedelic," Williams joked as they took seats all the way in the back. "Let's just hope it runs," Cornuke worried. After a day in Cairo where everything had seemed broken, he was quick to have doubts. The thought had crossed Williams' mind, too, even before he noticed the windows were all open. He had been assured the bus was air-conditioned.

They waited in the hot bus for nearly two hours. There was no way of knowing when it might suddenly leave; and even if someone had told them a departure time, they wouldn't have believed him. The other passengers waited, too. They were mostly women dressed in black with small children. They sat very quietly, not talking to each other or their children. When the driver finally arrived, there was no explanation for the delay. He simply shut the doors and started the engine. No one went to the trouble of closing a window, Williams saw.

Soon they were traveling down a highway, heading into the Sinai Peninsula. As they entered the desert, they quickly felt the force of a new heat. Outside the bus miles of flat sand stretched to the horizon, the land ancient in its emptiness and isolation. And for the first time since their arrival in Cairo, their uneasiness lifted. They began to feel a sense of anticipation about what they were setting out to do. In the distance was history. Moses and the twelve tribes had walked here. Looking out over the lonely, dusty land, the bright desert sun cruelly highlighting the starkness, they began to imagine the terror, the excitement, and the wonder the Israelites must have felt. The tribes had left behind a land in Goshen that was green and rich, and each new day Moses was leading them deeper and deeper into the unknown, deeper and deeper into a scorched and empty world.

"Think about it," Cornuke said solemnly as he stared out the window. "The spectacle of a million people—men, women, and children, their herds of livestock, their pack animals carrying the gold of Egypt—marching across this very land. And remember, the Israelites weren't just wandering. They were running for their lives. Pharaoh and his army were right on their heels. Chariots were in hot pursuit. And where was Moses leading them? To a dead end—the Red Sea."

"Well," Williams said slowly, "now you've touched on something I've been thinking over a bit. Something kind of significant considering we're out to prove the crossing point was down by the tip of the peninsula, not up north."

"Go on," said Cornuke, immediately curious.

"You're wrong," Williams said. "Pharaoh's army wasn't right on their heels."

THE bus sped down the asphalt road, its driver seeming to take a malicious pleasure in overtaking other vehicles at the last possible moment. The children up front were out of control, and their mothers made no attempt to bring them into line. Worse, the heat was inescapable, a dense, thick presence. Nevertheless, Cornuke's concentration was complete, fixed on Williams' every word.

"Read the Bible and do your math," Williams said with the authority of someone who made his living with numbers. "You'll see that Moses and the Israelites had a pretty good head start on the Egyptian soldiers. Hear me out and you'll see why this is so important."

There were three points to Williams' "head-start argument," as he called it. First, he pointed out that the Book of Exodus made it clear that Moses, shrewdly, had never told Pharaoh that the Israelites were leaving Egypt. All he had done was request a "three days journey into the wilderness that we may sacrifice to the Lord our God." So, Williams reasoned, it wouldn't have been until the fourth day at the earliest that Pharaoh's spies reported that the slaves were continuing farther out into the desert. And it undoubtedly would have taken those spies a day or so to get back to court. Therefore, Williams reasoned, let's be conservative and assume that at least five days had passed before Pharaoh realized the Israelites were fleeing from his realm.

His next point was, he said, one of "simple military logistics." When Pharaoh decided to go after the tribes, he couldn't have left that very day. It would have taken him time to mobilize his troops. The Bible—Williams borrowed his friend's copy and searched until he found the specific chapter and verse—said: "And he made ready his chariots, and took his army. And took six hundred chosen chariots, and all the other chariots of Egypt with officers over all of them." "So," he asked Cornuke, "how long do you think it took the Egyptians to ready a force of six hundred chariots? Plus an army, according to many estimates, of as many as eighteen thousand cavalry and eighty thousand foot soldiers?" Williams quickly answered his own question. "Let's say four days," he ventured. And that too, he insisted, was a conservative estimate.

His final point, Williams admitted, involved a bit of guesswork. "If I've been correct so far," he said, "the Israelites had at least a nine-day head start on the Egyptians. How long do you think it took for Pharaoh's army to catch up with them?" And once again, he answered his own question.

He started by reading a verse from the Book of Exodus: "'The Lord went before them by day in a pillar of cloud to lead them along the way, and by night in a pillar of fire to give them light, that they might travel by day and night.' Therefore, according to the Bible," Williams said, "the Israelites, about a million or so of them, were traveling during the day *and* night through the desert. Pharaoh's army no doubt moved a lot quicker, but presumably they only marched during the day. Yet the Israelites already had a nine-day lead. And even while the army was making up this lost time, the Jews were not standing still. They were still fleeing, going deeper into the desert. So, it probably would have taken at least another ten days for the Egyptian chariots to close in on the tribes. That meant the Israelites had been traveling for approximately nineteen days before Pharaoh's army could have caught up with them." He asked if Cornuke appreciated the significance of that calculation.

This time he waited for his friend's answer. A pleasant breeze coming off the Gulf of Suez filled the bus. The highway had emerged from the desert and now ran parallel to the coast. They were getting closer to the tip of the peninsula.

"I see what you mean," Cornuke said after a moment or two. "If the Israelites had gone nineteen days before they came to the Red Sea, then that's more proof the crossing took place a good distance out of Goshen. It supports our theory completely."

"Exactly," Williams said. "The other traditional crossing sites, up by the Bitter Lakes, or even south in the gulf, were two, maybe three days out of Egypt. Way too close if you pay attention to what the Bible says. I'm telling you, Bob, everything's falling into place. I'm certain we're on the right track."

24

Strait of Tiran, Egypt: 1988

THE water in the Red Sea was not red, but blue, tranquil, and warm. And while the nearby desert was desolate, empty of all apparent life, the sea was teeming with activity. It was home to a rainbow of vividly colored fish, prowling hammerhead sharks, and huge sulking manta rays. Intricate gardens of coral, luminous and filigreed shapes, rose from its soft, sandy bottom. The Bible's ancient waterway, adventurous vacationers were beginning to find out, was an ideal spot for a contemporary sport—skin diving.

In the early 1980s, the Navco Corporation announced that it was planning to build a series of vacation villages for divers along the undeveloped Red Sea coast. The potential was enormous. In their presentation to local officials, the principals raised the possibility of a whole series of resorts, a string of Club Med–type villages along the warm blue waters of the historic Red Sea.

The group, headed by two energetic Americans who made frequent allusions to their substantial Wall Street connections, began by leasing a beachfront site in Sudan. It was an immediate success. Even before the construction was finished, vacationing divers started to arrive. It seemed as if Navco had made a very shrewd investment.

Profit, however, was not Navco's motivation. In fact, there were no Wall Street investors. The majority of the funding came from the Mossad. And the divers who began to appear at the Red Sea resort were not vacationers. They were members of Israel's naval commando force.

The Red Sea resort was owned and operated by the Israeli Secret Service, which ran it as a safe house for a network that was smuggling Jews out of Ethiopia. Mossad agents secretly transported these refugees across North Africa to this holiday village. At night, when the sea was dark and calm, the Ethiopians were crowded into small boats and guided by the frogmen to Israeli ships anchored off shore. It was a short voyage across the gulf to Sharm al Sheikh. The town at the southern tip of the Sinai Peninsula was Israeli territory, captured in the 1967 war. From there the refugees were flown in cargo planes to Air Force bases in central Israel. More than 2,000 Ethiopian Jews had escaped to the Promised Land through this clandestine Red Sea route.

It was such a successful operation that the Israeli government ordered the Mossad to enlarge its scope. Under this new plan, transport planes landed secretly in the Sudan to pick up refugees. The beachfront safe houses were no longer used. But there was also another reason for abandoning the late-night voyages across the Red Sea: The 1982 Camp David Accords had returned the Sinai Peninsula, including Sharm al Sheikh, to Egypt.

The Navco Corporation, however, did not disband. Its principals, the same group of visionary Americans still boasting of their deep-pocketed connections, soon announced their intention to build a holiday village for divers across the gulf in Sharm al Sheikh. Navco architects, engineers, and diving instructors began to flock to this Egyptian town on the Red Sea to explore the investment possibilities. From the start, they were very enthusiastic. The beach was wide and blanketed with soft, fine sand. The diving, they said, was possibly the best in the world.

The Mossad, too, was impressed with the natural resources of this coastal town. Sharm al Sheikh was the perfect outpost to monitor naval traffic going through the Strait of Tiran. Or, for that matter, anything else on the Sinai Peninsula that might be of interest to the state of Israel.

AT first Cornuke and Williams had not realized they were entering the town. There was an abandoned tank, a plastic bag stuffed into its cannon, on the side of the road. A little farther on they started seeing people. They passed pairs of long-robed Bedouins, but soon these gave way to groups of hippies, deeply tanned, wiry, shaggy figures. Their dress was vaguely military, faded fatigue pants and flak jackets worn over bare chests. They stared at the passengers in the passing bus with bold, muggers' eyes. And there was an occasional glint of weaponry, the sun reflecting off a revolver riding low on a hip or a rifle slung over a shoulder. To Cornuke the scene and mood seemed to belong to a grim, postapocalyptic future world, something out of a Mad Max movie. But then he saw the sea and he knew they had arrived. This was Sharm al Sheikh.

Back in London, Williams had been told at the Egyptian consulate that renting gear and a diving boat would be simple enough; in fact, the smirk that had accompanied this guarantee seemed to imply that for American dollars you could get anything you might want in Sharm al Sheikh. In Cairo, just to be sure, he had reconfirmed the feasibility of this plan. But now that he found himself in the middle of this dusty, coolly hostile town, his confidence began to ebb. Perhaps that was why Williams was grateful when, out of the mulling clusters of hippies, a man with frizzy Medusa-like strands of sun-tinted brown hair sauntered over and, in a flat, unaccented voice that seemed to owe a lot to cowboy movies, muttered, "Howdy."

Later Williams would throw out the possibility that he instinctively felt comfortable with this stranger because he was reminded of himself a few aimless lifetimes ago, back when he was hanging out in Hawaii: the same dedicated nut-brown tan; the same shaggy, barefoot, keep-on-truckin' attitude; even the same tight strand of love beads worn like a talisman around the neck. But whatever the reason for this immediate affinity, Williams, and Cornuke too, quickly found more substantive reasons to appreciate the stranger. He introduced himself as Abu, and not only did he most certainly know a shop where they could rent scuba gear, but, talk about lucky days, he also just happened to own a charter boat. And further proof that, as Abu put it, "Allah was smiling on all of us," his boat was available. The couple who had chartered it for this week had canceled at the last moment. In fact, his whole purpose in coming to town was to scout up a customer.

"Look," Abu said moving very deftly to the bottom line, "this could work out for all of us. I'll give you a bargain price. You can have me and the boat for as long as you want. It's a very fine boat. You won't do any better. What do you say?" he demanded, trying to close the deal. The two friends exchanged looks. If they were being hustled, it was, they felt, a harmless, even charming con. After all, they needed a boat. Where was the downside? "You got a deal," Williams told Abu. "Just lead the way."

IT was night, the end of a perfect evening. Cornuke had decided to sleep on deck, in the bow. There was a thin breeze, the air fresh, almost cool, and with a taste of salt. Abu's boat was anchored in the strait, but not far from shore. It rocked lazily in the water, a comforting rhythm. Above Cornuke's head was a canopy of stars, all shining, he wanted to believe, in celebration of the adventure that was soon to begin.

When the two friends had boarded Abu's boat earlier in the day, their attitude had not been so serene. One hard look and they were instantly uneasy. It was a stubby, ancient little tug. The sun and wind had had their way with it for so long that now it was either beyond repair, or, equally disconcerting, Abu was not seaman enough to care. But when they went to stow their gear, Williams, who had a weekend sailor's appreciation for these sorts of things, noticed that there were two glistening engines that in a pinch could probably power a destroyer, a parabolic radar antenna stuck so unobtrusively atop the cabin roof that it might as well have been deliberately hidden, and a huge radio down in the hold that, he would almost bet, could pick up the Dodger games on a clear night. And, one more surprise, when it was dinnertime Abu proved to be a resourceful chef. Despite the closet-sized galley, he whipped up a tasty version of moussaka. They ate on deck, in the open air, with licorice-tasting ouzo served in water glasses to wash it down, and a delighted Cornuke declared it their first meal in days that didn't stink of lamb.

After the sun had set and the last traces of color were fading from the sky, Williams and Cornuke had stayed on deck, looking toward the shore. The sky was turning dark, but a kerosene lantern gave off a circle of light that illuminated the two men. Williams leaned against the cabin, while Cornuke, still full of energy, crouched like a catcher, holding his Bible in one hand so that it rested on the wooden deck. Soon he brought it up close to his face and began to read aloud. The words carried across the inky water, and, it seemed, across even time itself.

"'Speak unto the children of Israel, that they turn and encamp before Pihahiroth, between Migdol and the sea, over against Baalzephon: before it shall ye encamp by the sea. For Pharaoh will say of the children of Israel, They are entangled in the land; the wilderness has shut them in.'"

When he had finished the verse, Cornuke said, "That's the place. 'Between Migdol and the sea.'" He pointed to the sprinkling of lights glowing on the shoreline in the distance. "There were a million Israelites camped on that beach. 'Entangled.' Hemmed in by mountains on one side and the Red Sea on the other. No place to run. And they could hear the rumble of Pharaoh's chariots getting closer. Moving in on them."

All at once the two men saw it spread out before them: the approaching Egyptian army, mighty, eager for vengeance; and the Israelites, trapped, their backs to the sea, helpless and waiting. The moment was so real to them that they could sense the Israelites' terror, and they, too, were afraid.

It was a while before Cornuke could continue. But now when he read, it was no longer simply an ancient story.

"'When Pharaoh drew near, the Israelites looked up, and behold, the Egyptians were marching after them; and the Israelites were exceedingly frightened and cried out to the Lord.

"'And they said to Moses, Is it because there are no graves in Egypt that you have taken us away to die in the wilderness?'"

After he closed his Bible, Cornuke rose from his crouch and walked to the side of the boat. He stared at the dark sea, trying to imagine what had happened next: the very sea beneath him being parted and forming high walls of water, and a million Israelites marching across in flight from the Egyptians. It seemed impossible, yet he believed it had happened. And in the morning he would prove it.

They called it a night not long after Cornuke had finished the chapter from Exodus. Williams went below, but Cornuke preferred the open air. This was God's sea, the same water with which he had crafted His miracle, and Cornuke wanted to spend the night breathing its smell.

He lay there enjoying the night, full of eager anticipation for tomorrow's dive, his first ever, when a stray thought slipped into his mood. Wouldn't my wife love this? And that idle question provoked others, and he was trapped. He stayed awake for hours, entangled in his own wilderness.

DOWN they went, descending with a splash into a warm, deep, hidden world. Even on this first dive, Cornuke had no fear. His strokes and kicks were strong. His movements were careful but never self-conscious. He kept his breathing steady; there were none of the beginner's rushed, greedy pulls from the regulator feeding oxygen into his mouth. Williams swam close—hovered, actually—throughout this remarkable initiation. He was pleased but at the same time knew better than to take credit for his pupil's rapid progress. Whatever skills he possessed as a teacher were not responsible for this sort of performance. Endowed with an athlete's grace and instincts, Cornuke was, he decided, a natural diver.

The reality was more complex. Even before he had hit the water, Cornuke had locked his mind into such a determined place that the possibility of his being tentative, of, in fact, his being anything less than expert, was an impossibility. He was totally dedicated to his quest. If he had to climb a mountain or descend to the ocean floor, he would do whatever needed to be done. And so on each successive dive, Williams, teacher and team leader, took him deeper, gave him more freedom, and Cornuke never faltered.

Soon both men were gliding purposefully through the soft, warm waters of the Red Sea. Their attention was constant, their eyes alert for some tarnished object poking through the sand. They were convinced that something was down there, a relic waiting to be salvaged from the depths of its 4,000-year-old hiding place.

But after three days beneath the sea, the search was proving exhausting and, much more disheartening, totally futile. The only discovery Cornuke and Williams had made was that an iron will and a sense of mission can take even the most dedicated explorers only so far. However, their certainty in their hypothesis remained unshaken. They still firmly believed that the Israelites had crossed over to Saudi Arabia when the waters in the Strait of Tiran had parted. But experience was teaching them that proving this theory would be a formidable, if not impossible, task. After long days of swimming through the curtains of half-light that shrouded the lower depths, after sifting through acres of fine sand that amounted to, quite literally, mere drops in the bucket, after seeing how the centuries since the Exodus had contoured the seafloor with new hills and valleys, they were coming around to the realization of what they were up against. It would take another miracle.

By the night of their third day, the time had come to make a decision. They sat down on the deck, an open bottle of ouzo between them. Their glasses were filled but remained untouched.

"We could go on looking forever and still not find anything," Williams began.

Cornuke's answer was an almost imperceptible nod.

"Jabal al Lawz—that's our main target. We don't want to lose sight of that," Williams went on.

Cornuke still refused to be provoked.

"The sooner we get back to London, the sooner we can get into Saudi. Nikoli must've gotten our visas by now."

Again, Cornuke responded with one of his tight nods.

"OK," said Williams. He was growing exasperated by his friend's stony silence. "Are you ready to head back to London tomorrow?"

"No," Cornuke said resolutely. "One more day. What've we got to lose?"

"Nothing," Williams answered quickly. "One more day it is." He suddenly seemed quite pleased. He raised his glass. "To luck," he said.

"To luck," Cornuke echoed. But just to be sure, both of them offered up their own silent prayers before draining their glasses.

25

CORNUKE kicked his fins powerfully and angled down toward a protruding mound of sand. Something had caught his eye. As he descended, out of a corner of his face mask he had a glimpse of Williams. About forty yards of clear blue water separated him from his friend. Williams was swimming lazily, head down, surveying his own stretch of seabed. Cornuke waved to him, but Williams was too involved in his investigation to notice. It was their final day, and they had tacitly agreed to loosen up a bit on their buddy system routine.

It took Cornuke just a few more strong kicks to reach this high underwater hill. It had appeared to be shaped like an inverted triangle. But as he got closer, he saw that the summit was actually a series of jagged peaks separated by small valleys. And wedged between two of these peaks, in the crevice, was something. It was standing straight up like a flagpole.

Excited, he swam over and began to clear away some of the sand with his hands. A rod—that was his immediate guess—was caked with a thick, rusty slime. He had a diving knife strapped to his calf, and he used it to scrape out a thin, clear strip. He tapped the blade against this fresh spot, and a sharp, solid *ping!* echoed through the water. It was the sound metal would make. Or, he told himself, gold.

But when he tried to pull the object from the sand, it would not budge. He tugged with all his might, until he thought his lungs would burst from the exertion, but without result. It was wedged too deeply in the sand. He realized he needed more leverage and experimented with several positions until he found one that seemed promising. He spread his feet, planting one on each of the narrow peaks on either side of the crevice, and, bending at his knees, he gripped the object as if it were a baseball bat. And he pulled. Finally, it moved. He tried again, and it yielded a bit more. Encouraged, he focused his energy and, concentrating, gave it one, long sustained pull. With this colossal effort, it broke loose.

As it was freed from the sand and muck that had imprisoned it, a cascade of rough silt was churned up around Cornuke. It was thick, opaque, and swirled around him like a tornado. Suddenly, it was impossible to see. There was a dark solid wall outside his mask. Alone, perhaps fifteen feet beneath the sea, he had a moment of panic. But the turbulence subsided, the silt settled, and he could begin to see again. And then in the same moment, or at least it happened so quickly that it felt that way, his eyes focused on two things. First, the object he had pulled so hopefully from the sand was nothing but a rusty anchor, and not even all that old. And second, in the distance, perhaps twenty or so yards away, a hammerhead shark was swimming toward an unsuspecting Williams. The shark had its nose down, going in for the kill.

Cornuke tried yelling, but his cry was reduced to a sputter of soundless bubbles. Williams floated along obliviously, the slow kicks from his flippers creating a small wake. And all the while the shark continued to home in on this movement, a mean, purposeful machine.

Cornuke started to swim furiously toward his friend, but he was too far away. There was not enough time, and too much water was separating them. Yet he threw himself into it and his body responded. He was back in college, the halfback blasting off the mark with instant speed. It was as if he willed himself to cover the distance. And still Williams was just beyond his reach. A sudden lunge and the shark could rip its teeth into the fleshy part of Williams' leg. Without thinking, certainly without a plan, Cornuke made his own lunge. Fortunately, he came in from the side and tackled high, grabbing a totally surprised Williams around the shoulders. They came together with the force of a collision, and for a moment the wind seemed to be knocked out of both of them. They fell in a free fall, drifting down in the water. While above them the shark went on its way, a hunter deprived of his prey.

The two friends continued in their soft, half-floating fall. Tumbling slowly, as if gravity had failed, they drifted down until all at once they hit bottom. For a moment Cornuke thought it was the ocean floor. But he quickly decided that was impossible; they had in actuality not descended very far at all. Williams, who had come to realize the narrowness of his escape, pulled himself to his feet. Even in his flippers, the surface beneath him felt hard and firm. He took a small step, then another, and another. In a moment, Cornuke was next to him. They were walking side by side across the shallow water in the Strait of Tiran, toward Saudi Arabia.

THEY had found an underwater land bridge. It was not sandy or even muddy. Except for some coral growth, it was smooth and solid. It appeared to stretch ahead and behind them, west to east from Egypt to the coast of Saudi Arabia. And it was wide enough for trucks. Or chariots. Or, for that matter, a million Jews fleeing for their lives.

But the Israelites walked on dry ground in the midst of the sea, the waters being a wall to them on their right hand and on their left.

Cornuke knew his Bible. He knew that the Book of Exodus had carefully described the crossing site as a stretch of dry, solid ground in the middle of the Red Sea, a roadway that took the children of Israel out of the desert and into the land of Midian.

And they had found it.

It was not the proof they had expected, but they were not disappointed. They were certain that with the right equipment—and it would take nothing less than deep-sea mining machines—relics from Pharaoh's soldiers, an army swallowed up by the Red Sea, could be found hidden in the sands of the ocean floor beneath the Strait of Tiran.

They had found the land bridge that the Israelites had crossed 4,000 years ago when the waters parted and rose up in high walls around them. It was there just as the Bible had said it would be. Mount Sinai was out there, too. It was simply a matter of looking in the right place. More than ever before, they believed that with all their hearts.

WILLIAMS, in his wet suit, was walking on water. That was the way it looked to Cornuke through the viewfinder of his camera. It had been Williams' idea to take the photographs of him standing on the land bridge. It would be something to commemorate their discovery and, he added, evidence to wave in front of all the doubters. So Cornuke, doing his best to keep his balance, stood with his camera raised in his hands in the stern of Abu's Zodiac boat; it was the craft they used whenever they left the tug to go to their dive sites. Williams, his back to Saudi Arabia, grinned triumphantly, while Cornuke started shooting away.

He must have snapped a dozen shots, all pretty much the same pose, when Williams began waving his hands. Cornuke, who was caught up in the significance of their discovery, had no time for shenanigans; and yet there was his friend acting like one of those jerks in the stands at a baseball game who would shift into overdrive whenever a TV camera panned the crowd. But then he realized Williams was yelling something. It took Cornuke a minute to make out the words. "Behind you. The tug," Williams was shouting.

When Cornuke turned he saw Abu's tug, about four hundred yards off. And next to it was a steel-gray Egyptian gunboat.

It was only when they were both back in the Zodiac and heading toward the tug that they were able to make out more details. There were two Egyptian sailors on board the tug, standing by the cabin and talking to Abu. One was gesticulating like a man in the middle of an argument. The other stood erect and silent—with a machine gun cradled in his arms. As they got closer, Williams picked up on something else. There was an Israeli flag flying from the mast of Abu's tug. He was sure it had not been there before.

When Cornuke and Williams climbed on board the tug, Abu told them to get below. "Let me handle this," he said. He barked the words like an order, and his tone took the two men by surprise. The Egyptians, however, did not want them to leave the deck. They insisted that the two men stay where the sailor with the machine gun could see them.

At the same time, Abu made an effort to conduct his discussion with the Egyptians as far away as possible from Cornuke and Williams. The two friends, anxious and unnerved, stood motionless near the cabin. It seemed wise not to do anything to spook the man holding the machine gun.

Abu, however, continued to pace slowly up the deck, talking nonstop. Neither of the men could hear what he was saying. They still did not know what the problem was, and could only watch Abu's performance with fascination. In the course of his monologue, he seemed to assume a variety of moods. He was calm, then in the next moment apparently overwhelmed by fear; insistent, then hesitant; indignant, then supplicant. Cornuke, who was no stranger to hostage situations, came to realize that there was a pattern to Abu's nervous pacing about the deck. He was shielding his two customers, making sure his body was always in front of them and straight in the line of fire.

After another ten minutes of discussion, the voices became softer, less strained, and it was clear to a relieved Cornuke and Williams that some sort of agreement was being worked out. Abu, finding a meek, defeated tone to fit the moment, reached into his pocket. Williams decided that a fine or, even more likely, a bribe had been settled on and Abu was about to pay up. Then the man with the gun spoke up. It was the first time he had spoken, and the sound of his voice, hard and forceful, seemed to startle everyone.

Abu listened and his face darkened. He attempted to argue, but the sailor pointed his weapon toward Cornuke and Williams. It did not seem like a threat, or at least that was what the two men wanted to believe, but the gesture convinced Abu. "Get below," he told them. Williams started to protest. He didn't want to leave Abu alone on deck with the two sailors. But Abu repeated stiffly, "Just go." It was only after he saw that his customers were cooperating, walking toward the cabin steps, that Abu explained, "They want to finish our transaction in private."

In the cabin, they found two more things to think about. The radio was on. And lying on the table across from it were an M-16 and two grenades. Cornuke studied these clues and offered an opinion: When Abu saw the gunboat bearing down, he must have sent word to someone—friends? authorities?—that he had some uninvited guests.

"And the gun? The grenades?" Williams asked.

"If the Egyptians don't take a bribe, I guess our hippie friend has a backup plan," said Cornuke.

They thought about that until they heard the engines of the gunboat as it pulled away. Abu was waiting for them as they came back on deck. "What was that all about?" Williams asked.

"Need a permit for diving," Abu explained. "We didn't have one, so I paid a fine." His manner was breezy, even nonchalant. He's a real chameleon, Williams thought.

But there was something else on Williams' mind that he had almost forgotten. "What about the flag? This an Israeli boat? I didn't know that."

Abu laughed. "Well," he began, "registry—that's a tricky business. Very confusing stuff. But an Israeli flag, you know, can come in handy. Makes the Egyptian Navy think twice. You start shooting, you might wind up with an international incident or something. Sort of slows everybody down."

Anyway, Abu said, it was time to get dinner together. He wanted to make something special for their last night. Then he headed below.

"I figured things out," said Cornuke when they were alone on deck. "Our friend Abu, you know what he is?"

Williams waited.

"He's a smuggler," Cornuke announced, certain he was right.

As things turned out, there was still one last thing to do before they left Egypt and returned to London. It was Cornuke's spur-of-the-moment idea, and Williams agreed that he was curious, too. And so on their way up the Sinai Peninsula to Cairo, they made a side trip. They wanted to see the mountain that claimed to be Mount Sinai.

In the plain where some believe the Israelites had camped while Moses met with God, a hotel complex had been built. It was called St. Catherine's Tourist Village, and it advertised "150 air-conditioned suites, El Safsafa Restaurant, El Monagah Cafeteria, Garcious [*sic*] Gardens with Various Desert Flora, Videio [*sic*] Hall, Indoor Games Hall, and a Shopping Center." To their eyes, the mountain, especially when compared to the looming neighboring peaks, seemed low and undistinguished.

They discovered that there were steps carved into its face. Cornuke could not help saying that the climb seemed as eventful as a walk up to the bleacher seats in a stadium. Along the way there were refreshment stands that sold herbal teas, juices, bottled water, and biscuits. When they reached the summit, there was another tea shop, run by a Bedouin. The two men walked across a mountaintop where many people were willing to believe God had given Moses the Ten Commandments. There was trash scattered everywhere—bottles, cans, food wrappers, cigarette butts, and human waste. The stench was powerful.

The experience confirmed all they believed, but Cornuke and Williams took little pleasure in what they saw. The tacky commercialism, the utter disregard, struck them as depressingly vulgar, if not sacrilegious. They hurried back to Cairo, eager to get to London and on to their mountain, the real mountain of God.

26

London, England: June 1988

ALL is forgiven, Nikoli. No hard feelings.

On the plane back to London, Williams rehearsed the words. He repeated them to himself so many times that when the plane came down for a landing, they were echoing through his head like a mantra. It was important to sound sincere. He wanted Nikoli to believe he was a worldly sort, willing to shrug off the Turk's mischief. And, above all, he wanted to keep his temper in check. Because, regardless of the genial and understanding script he had prepared, he was livid.

In the solitude of his bunk in the dark hold of Abu's tug, the rocking of the sea proving a gentle stimulus, Williams had replayed the strange days in London until a logic fit them. The break-in, the hookers with their patently laughable interest in the Book of Exodus, the bearded motorcyclist on his back—all these, he had come to realize, were Nikoli's handiwork. He was on a boat in the Strait of Tiran, but in his mind he pictured the scene that must have been played out in Warren's Belgravia office.

Nikoli: Williams is not fooling anybody with that Mount Sinai story.

Warren: Certainly not this kid from Indianapolis.

Nikoli: He's going off to Saudi to take down a score.

Warren: And the trouble he's going to, it's got to be one big payday.

Nikoli: Well, I'm going to have to find out just what he has up his sleeve.

Drifting around the Red Sea, Williams had worked it all out. It was the only explanation that made any sense. Who else would be interested in what he was up to? But now Williams wanted Nikoli to know he was ready to forgive and forget. He was, in fact, prepared if necessary to cut the Turk in on a hundred deals. There was only one thing that mattered. Nikoli had to come through on his promise. He had to deliver the Saudi travel visas.

And so, after impatiently creeping through the traffic jam in Heathrow's customs hall, Williams sprang into action. He told Cornuke to stand guard over the bags while he went to the nearest phone. He got through at once and listened as an officious secretary explained that it would take a minute, please, to hunt down Nikoli. Williams, shuffling back and forth in the tiny booth, used the time to once again practice his lines. He had settled on a tone that, he felt, had a convincing ring of sincerity. But before he could even get out a single word, Nikoli brought the curtain down on his performance with a crash.

"Larry," he announced mournfully, "I've got to admit I'm having a problem. Things are sort of complicated with my Saudi friends."

"But you promised!" Williams shouted, throwing out his script in an instant.

"I know. I know. But I've got another idea. A plan. Foolproof, maybe. You're going to love it. Trust me. Everything's going to work out. Now when you can get here?"

"I'm on my way," Williams said, and hung up without saying good-bye.

So, given his charged-up state and what was at stake, when he saw a familiar figure in a long black leather coat and a blue cap on his curly head standing next to Cornuke, Williams put off making an issue of it. All that mattered was getting to Warren's office and hearing the plan.

NIKOLI was playing the magician. In one hand, he announced to Cornuke and Williams, he had a blank piece of paper. He held it high and made a show of displaying both sides so they could verify his claim. In the other hand, he continued, he had a letter faxed by a genuine Saudi prince. He passed it to Williams for closer scrutiny and explained that it had been sent by His Royal Highness regarding his participation in an oil deal that, unfortunately, had not come to fruition. Williams studied the letterhead embossed with the crossed swords of the Al-Faisal clan and the scrawled but apparently royal signature. Satisfied, he returned the document to Nikoli.

Now here's the trick, Nikoli said, continuing to play Houdini. I will use the blank sheet to create a fax that looks exactly like the real McCoy—with one crucial difference. It will not say a single word about such a mundane concern as the price of oil. It will, instead, be a request by the noble prince to the lackeys in the Saudi embassy here in London to grant his good friends, Misters Cornuke and Williams, travel visas posthaste or feel the sharp sting of his royal wrath.

"You're nuts," Cornuke decided rudely.

But Nikoli was not insulted. "Watch me," he said with undisguised relish, "pull the rabbit from the hat."

His "first trick," he declared, would be "to wave my magic wand" over a fax machine. As Cornuke and Williams looked on with mute fascination, Nikoli went to work on Warren's machine. It took him some time to work out the differences in the time zones, but when he was done he had reprogrammed the machine so that, he claimed, it would automatically print a sender ID line on the top of each transmission that was identical to the one that had come from the royal palace.

To demonstrate this to his obviously skeptical audience, Nikoli pressed a button, waited a quick moment, and then, to the accompanying shout of "Presto!" pulled the test sheet from the machine. He was so confident that he did not even look at the paper before handing it to Williams. But Williams was suspicious. With Cornuke peering over his shoulder, he took his time studying the small line at the top of the page: "SENT BY: HRH PR. M. A. AL-FAISAL . . ." The phone number, too, was the same as the one on the genuine fax. And as best as Cornuke and Williams could figure, the printed time was precisely what it was at that moment in Riyadh.

Williams, however, was still not persuaded. He said the only true test would be an actual transmission. "Be my guest," Nikoli offered gallantly. So Williams quickly scrawled a note to his office in California, asking his secretary to stand by for his call, and sent it from Warren's machine. And while he waited for the fax to be received, he explained his fear. The telephone company would have its own tricks; a London area code would automatically be included in the ID line.

"We'll see soon enough," said Nikoli, unruffled, as Williams placed his call. But for all his bravado, the Turk, as well as Cornuke, fell into a tense silence when Williams instructed his secretary to read off what had been printed at the top of the fax she had just received. He thanked her and rang off.

"Well?" demanded Cornuke.

"It worked. Exact ID as on the test run," Williams admitted, still a bit amazed.

That gave them something to think about. For the first time, the two friends began seriously considering the possibility that Nikoli's magic might be real. And they were also coming to terms with the fact that it was their one last hope.

Williams, without consulting his friend, announced their decision. "How can we help?" he asked Nikoli.

Now that they were in it together, they split up the remaining tasks. Nikoli volunteered to fabricate a ream of royal stationery. This was easy enough: cut the prince's letterhead off the genuine fax, paste it to a piece of blank paper, then run this makeshift counterfeit through a photocopier, and, presto! a seamless copy perfect for faxing emerged.

Cornuke, meanwhile, was busy composing the text of the letter that would be sent to the Saudi embassy. He did his artful best to mimic the elaborately cumbersome prose in the original: "Every courtesy you are able to extend to them on my behalf will be greatly appreciated with reference to the granting of a visa." And he obediently followed the royal tendency to capitalize any noun at will.

But it was Williams who proved the most inventive, and the most painstaking. His job was to copy the prince's self-important scribble of a signature. He had minored in art in college and tried for a while doing it freehand, but he wasn't able to come up with anything that raced across the page with the casual smugness of the real thing. Then, in a moment of inspiration, he decided on a new strategy. He enlarged the original with the photocopier until it was nearly a foot across and went to work using a pencil to trace each character. When he was satisfied that he gotten it right, he went over this faint signature with black ink. After that it was simply a matter of going back to the copier and reducing his creation to normal size. He looked at the page that slid out of the machine and was pleased. This was the royal signature.

Now the three men moved quickly to see if all the pieces would fit together. Nikoli filled the tray in the laser-jet printer with royal stationery. On the computer screen was the letter requesting travel visas for Mr. Robert Gary Cornuke and Mr. Larry Richard Williams. Cornuke pressed "Print," and the page that spewed out looked convincing enough. It was up to Williams to add the final touch. He pasted a two-inch strip—his inked tracing of the prince's signature—to the bottom of the page and placed the composite document in the photocopier. The letter that came out was perfect.

Nikoli insisted that he should have the honor of doing the actual faxing. He pushed the Send button, and when the transmission was completed everyone suddenly felt drained. Not that it mattered, for it had been agreed that since it was late, after business hours, they wouldn't try to contact the embassy until the morning. Now all they could do was wait; and, as Cornuke couldn't help pointing out, worry.

Williams asked Nikoli to join them for dinner. He was grateful, and at the time it had seemed like a small gesture. But it proved to be a mistake. He took no pleasure in the Turk's bombastic company, and he used it as an excuse to drink too much. So things were already going downhill when Cornuke, during a lull, casually mentioned something that had been troubling him. "You know," he threw out to the table, "what we did today was a crime. We forged someone's signature."

"Not just someone," said Nikoli jovially. "A prince." Either he had missed the point, or, just as likely, it was beyond him.

"What choice did we have?" Williams asked. "Getting into Saudi—that's all that matters."

"I guess," Cornuke agreed.

But now that it had been spoken, it was impossible to get it out of their minds. Perhaps even more than the waiting and the worrying, it helped to give them quite a night.

IT worked. They had faxed a counterfeit letter across London, a distance of not more than eight city blocks, but the Royal Consulate of Saudi Arabia was apparently convinced it had received a genuine transmission from a royal palace in Riyadh. When Williams picked up the phone that morning at precisely 10:00 to call the embassy, there was a moment's panic and he had to struggle not to slam down the receiver. But then he reminded himself of what was at stake, and how far they had come, and what they had learned in the Strait of Tiran. And he knew that, regardless of what the forgery might cost them, there was no giving up. He made the call.

When the official at the other end told him with great politeness that if he and Mr. Cornuke would be so kind as to come to the embassy with their passports at their earliest convenience, they would be expected, Williams was too stunned to mutter anything but a perfunctory "Sure" and "Thanks." But in another moment the realization of what they had pulled off set in, and he was slapping Cornuke on the back and they were trading high fives like schoolyard champions. On the way to the embassy, even Peter seemed to be caught up in their mood. "This is great. I'm really happy for you," he kept repeating. By now they had given up trying to figure out why or even how Peter always managed to be around. Williams suspected the driver was part of Nikoli's scheming, and if Peter was, he persuaded himself, it really didn't matter. He had nothing to hide. And besides, Peter and his car did come in handy.

There was a small crisis, or at least it seemed that way, when just before they entered the consulate Cornuke whispered a warning to Williams. "You know, this could be a trap. There could be police, Scotland Yard maybe, waiting for us." But all that was waiting was a diligent and accommodating visa official in a three-piece suit and a clipped Oxford accent. He insisted on personally filling out the many forms for them; as friends of His Royal Highness they were apparently too important to waste their time on such a trivial exercise. When he was done, he gave them red receipts that they would be able to exchange at the consulate for their passports and newly issued visas. Everything, he promised, would be ready on Monday morning.

It was only as they walked out into the bright summer sunshine of Belgrave Square that Williams had another worry. It was Thursday. If they waited until Monday—four more days—anything could happen. What if someone in the embassy happened to talk to the prince? What if the fax was discovered to be a forgery? Williams, still on the steps of the consulate, had a sudden realization—the sooner they could leave, the better. And then immediately he made an irrevocable decision. They had to leave tomorrow, he told Cornuke. The success of their entire expedition depended on it.

He was desperate, and with nowhere else to turn, they went back to Nikoli. "*This* I can handle," Nikoli guaranteed. "Let me make a call."

Cornuke and Williams paced across the thick carpet in his office until the Turk returned. He was smiling like a conqueror. "No problem. Meet me here at ten tomorrow morning and we'll go on over to the consulate together. We'll see my friend and pick up your papers. You'll have plenty of time to make the one o'clock flight for Jeddah."

At ten the next morning, they were in Nikoli's office. Peter, with their bags loaded in the trunk of his car, was parked in the street. Cornuke felt comfortable, not on edge but up, the way he had before a big game. Williams' mood was more self-contained as he tried to keep all his emotions under control. But Nikoli wasn't there, and when there was still no sign of him at 10:30, they began to panic. They managed to track him down on his cellular phone, and he told them he'd be there in two minutes. "Relax," he said convincingly. Fifteen minutes later he had still not arrived and was no longer answering his cell phone. By eleven, Williams realized "We're on our own." The two men raced out of the office.

Peter drove them to the embassy. Their last-ditch plan, pieced together in the car, was to intimidate an official and simply insist that they needed their passports immediately. But once they saw a line of perhaps 150 people snaking around the building, all presumably waiting for visas, their expectations of success nose-dived. "Our plane leaves in an hour and forty-five minutes," Williams said. "I don't see how we're going to make it."

"Maybe I can help out," Peter said from the front seat.

"Unless you're really a Saudi prince, I don't see how," Cornuke replied testily.

But Peter would not be put off. "Look," he said, "you want to make your plane or not? Now give me the receipts for your passports," he ordered. After only the slightest hesitation, they obeyed.

He returned in twelve minutes and without a word started the engine and moved into traffic.

"Now where the hell are we going?" Williams snapped.

"I thought you had a plane to catch," Peter answered. With one hand still on the wheel, he reached into his leather coat and extracted one and then the other passport. Inside each passport, the two men immediately discovered, were their travel visas.

"How did you do that?" Cornuke demanded.

Peter smiled. "Friend of my barber. He works in the embassy. He owed me a favor."

At the time it seemed like a plausible explanation. But then again it was hard to think too clearly. They were trapped in the backseat as Peter, a determined smile on his face, drove them across London with a recklessness that filled them with pure terror. Still, they made it to the departure gate with four minutes to spare.

"YOU steal something, they cut off your hand," the Arab sitting next to Cornuke on the plane to Jeddah explained with a philosophical nonchalance. He was quite fat, and as he spoke, Cornuke saw his belly rise and fall with each breath. "That's why there's no crime in the kingdom. None. I know you people think we're barbaric. Medieval. Well, how about this? We're experimenting with a laser that will cut off the thief's hand and cauterize the wound at the same time. We're not cruel."

Why is he telling me this? Cornuke worried. Does he know something? It was irrational, he realized, but he couldn't help feeling anxious. Finally, he had to ask. "So what if they catch someone doing something else? I don't know, another crime, say, like forgery?"

"Oh, for that," the Arab said happily, "they cut off your head. Definitely the head."

Part Four

INTO THE WILDERNESS

27

The Royal Palace, Riyadh, Saudi Arabia: Spring, 1988

THE playboy king was no longer interested in having fun. The rumor that spread through the court, and quickly made its way to the CIA, was that he was impotent. And as the months passed, King Fahd grew even more sulky and depressed. His worried advisors suggested his spirits (and, they perhaps hoped, his potency) might be restored by the remedies available on a trip to his estate in Marbella, or his palace in Geneva, or his vast farm outside the capital, or even a cruise on his yacht anchored off Jeddah. But the king, after decades crammed with an indefatigable hedonism, was no longer interested. Instead, he insisted on remaining in the palace. He spent his days alone in the royal bedchamber playing Nintendo and munching Cheez Doodles served up in solid gold punch bowls. Two huge guards, armed like executioners with gleaming scimitars, were stationed outside his door at all times. They were very effective in discouraging any intrusions.

As the king, never industrious, became further estranged from the affairs of state, his half brother Crown Prince Abdullah took on more and more responsibilities with mounting assertiveness. The monarch's advisors realized they had little choice but to seek medical help. Their search, a mission conducted with understandable discretion, led them to Israel. In Tel Aviv they located a team of urologists who by all accounts had had spectacular success in curing conditions similar to the king's. The doctors demanded an outrageous fee, which only helped to convince the Saudis they had come to the right men, and they were hired. These doctors, accompanied by several nurses, began making frequent trips to Riyadh, and soon their treatment, which included a series of injections administered to the royal testicles, proved effective. The king's isolated and detached mood seemed to lift, and his advisors were cheered.

So was the Mossad. The doctors, whom deskmen in Tel Aviv and Jerusalem immediately took to calling "The Custodians of the Two Holy Places," were unwitting yet surprisingly adept spies. After every trip to Riyadh, they just happened to find themselves sharing their eyewitness gossip about the king and the excesses of palace life with a fascinated colleague. And without the doctors' knowledge (but perhaps with a few of their suspicions), their colleague passed summaries of these conversations on to the Mossad. His reports soon acquired a reputation far beyond their pure intelligence value, and each installment was widely distributed throughout a curious, and frequently titillated, secret service.

In the spring of 1988, then, when the CIA made a seemingly offhanded approach to the Mossad for help in updating their backgrounder on King Fahd, the Israelis, with only minor deletions, obligingly passed on a stack of the doctors' reports. In the strained aftermath of the Jonathan Pollard fiasco, the Mossad was eager for any opportunity to score a few collegial points with the agency; and, no doubt, there was a streak of professional pride in showing off the unique perspectives their sources could provide on the king. This small decision to share the intelligence briefs based on the doctors' observations, however, had unforeseen consequences.

Perhaps the initial error was the Americans'. For despite their back-channel approach to the Mossad and the deliberate casualness of their request, there was a genuine urgency in their need to know. The Saudis, the intelligence analysts at the CIA and the National Security Council were beginning to suspect, were up to something. The covert purchase of Chinese ballistic missiles was the first dramatic clue. But with the weapons already stockpiled throughout the kingdom there was little that could be done about that—except, it was agreed, to make sure the wealthy Saudis were not secretly pursuing grander and more provocative strategic ambitions. Therefore, President Reagan, on the recommendation of the National Security Council, decided to send a special envoy to the palace to confront King Fahd. The United States wanted assurances that the East Wind missiles would have conventional warheads. The possibility that Saudi Arabia might arm its intermediate-range CSS-3s with chemical-biological or perhaps even nuclear payloads was suddenly very real, and very chilling.

The importance of this mission was emphasized by the State Department's choice of envoy. It was decided that the U.S. ambassador to the kingdom, the crusty longtime Arabist Hume Horan, would, on his own, not be sufficiently impressive. A "star" personage was necessary and, fresh from his heralded diplomatic troubleshooting in Lebanon, Philip Habib was recruited. In preparation for the meeting with the king, the burrowers at the State Department's Office of Intelligence and Research worked through files of reports. But it was the briefs based on the conversations with the chatty urologists that, according to a chagrined CIA analyst, received the most attention. Perhaps it was their immediacy or their authentic insider's familiarity that made these observations so valued by State's I and R division.

However, the CIA intel owls, the State Department's rivals, it must in fairness be noted, and also working with the cushion of hindsight, were less generous. They insisted that the fascination with the observations passed on by the Mossad was largely puri-ent, and this "voyeurism"—*their* loaded word—resulted in a back-grounder that placed a naive and disproportionate emphasis on the king's pursuit of pleasure. The reality, at least according to the sub-tler CIA perspective, was that King Fahd, like so many others of lesser station, was able to pledge allegiance simultaneously and with equal conviction to totally contradictory ideals. The king could be resolute in his sacred responsibility to defend the holy sites of Mecca and Medina, and at the same time be one hell of a party animal.

But regardless of what prompted their conclusions, the briefing paper prepared by the State Department for the two ambassadors contained an escalating series of monumental misjudgments. With unflinching certainty, it began by asserting that King Fahd must have had little, if any, role in the decision to arm the kingdom with intermediate-range ballistic missiles. Such innovative strategic think-ing, the backgrounder argued, could only have been the brainchild of Prince Abdullah. The stuttering, anti-American brother, the pa-per asserted, must have taken it upon himself to change the balance of power in the Middle East while King Fahd was locked in his room playing Nintendo and eating Cheez Doodles. But now that the king, thanks to the ministrations of his Israeli specialists, was in effect reborn, the I and R analysts urged the two ambassadors to take advantage of his return to absolute power. King Fahd, after all, was no Prince Abdullah. Push Fahd, the backgrounder urged, and he would meekly say, "*Shahih, shahih*"—"OK, OK." Talk tough, growl with unseemly insistence, and the playboy king would cave. He would unconditionally guarantee that the missiles would be conventional weapons. In fact, the paper suggested, if the two men summoned up enough indignant fury, while at the same time emphasizing America's firm commitment to Saudi security, it was a possibility that the hapless monarch, eager to head off to more relaxing activities, might throw up his hands and agree to the removal of the CSS-3s.

• • •

AFTERWARD, Ambassador Horan came in for the most criticism, and with reason. It was the ambassador who, while Habib was sharing an amusing, yet meandering anecdote about Lebanon with the king, pointedly passed a note to his colleague reminding him that time was short and that they should focus on their mission. Still, it was Habib who after reading the note abruptly concluded his story and, returning to the State Department script, went on to address the monarch with an unseemly directness. But then again, it was Horan who, even after the monarch's shaken interpreter took it upon himself to soften Habib's undiplomatic language, would not let things be. He interrupted, and translated Habib's words with stinging exactitude. And when the king, who at this point in the discussion was clearly agitated, struck back by asserting that every country had the right to defend itself, Horan still did not back off.

In fact, when Fahd asked for assurances that Israel would not attack its missile installations, it was Horan who couldn't wait to go toe to toe. "But you said every country had a right to defend itself," the ambassador countered boldly. "Doesn't that include Israel?" So perhaps Horan deserved the blame. Nevertheless, it was clear that both men—and the State Department—had been led to misjudge the steel that could on occasion fortify the royal temperament. And that the U.S. government had been unaware that King Fahd had personally initiated, blessed, and continued to encourage Project Falcon.

After the audience with the king, the State Department was officially informed that the missiles would be deployed throughout Saudi Arabia. Further, the weapons would not be subjected to inspection by American or any other international agencies, including those monitoring nuclear proliferation. And, finally, Ambassador Horan was no longer welcome in the kingdom.

• • •

BUT it did not end there. King Fahd, still seething at such imperious diplomatic behavior, instructed Prince Sultan to move quickly to establish full diplomatic relations with the People's Republic of China. On the face of it, this was simply one more public tweak of the haughty Americans. However, the monarch's motivation was more subtle. The discussions over an impending diplomatic agreement between the two countries were the perfect cover for more secret negotiations. Prince Abdel Rahman bin Mohammed, the monarch's nephew, had been sent to China to buy a nuclear reactor. Price, the prince was instructed, was of no consequence. The king's meeting with the rude Americans—and their provocative reference to Israel—had reinforced the monarch's commitment to his grand strategy. The kingdom must have a superweapon.

On a related front, immediately following the audience with Horan and Habib, the king summoned another nephew, Prince Khaled bin Sultan, to the palace. Why were the missile delivery systems still not functional? the king demanded. What was the delay? The kingdom had contracted, he pointed out with barely controlled fury, according to a conversation the chagrined prince later had with his American advisors, to pay billions of dollars to Litton Industries and the Boeing Corporation. Yet nothing was in place. Why?

The prince began to mumble about problems with the command and control software. He even summoned a major, an expert who quickly plunged into the technological thicket of "anomalous propagation," how the radars on the Red Sea coast were having trouble defining their targets. But King Fahd summarily cut the major off and turned to his nephew. The prince was ordered to go to America and reiterate that the contracts must be satisfactorily fulfilled. His instructions were succinct. If Boeing was unable to design an integrated offensive missile delivery system, he was immediately to stop all payments, void the contract, and find a defense contractor who would get the job done.

In the weeks that followed, despite the prospect of long and complicated negotiations with the Chinese and the daunting technical delays, Project Falcon moved forward. Missiles were being assembled in fortified, blast-proof underground bunkers. Launch crews were being trained. Scientists at the secret compound at Al Sulayyil worked on creating a nuclear device. And as these preparations escalated, the Higher Officers' Committee, the group of princes and generals in charge of Project Falcon, issued new orders. Barbed-wire fences would be erected at the prospective command and control sites throughout the kingdom. Guardhouses, to be staffed by regular army soldiers, would be built. The patrols by the militia would also continue. And preliminary excavation at the sites for radars, microwave relays, and underground control centers would begin.

Above all, as the plan proceeded on its many fronts, the Higher Officers' Committee remained convinced that secrecy must be maintained. Somehow, mystifyingly, Washington and Tel Aviv had learned about the missiles. But that, fortunately, was all they knew. It was vital to the future and security of the kingdom that Project Falcon—an integrated missile system capable of delivering a first-strike nuclear attack anywhere in the Middle East—be in place and fully operational. After this superweapon was armed, the Americans could send all the hostile envoys they wanted to make their imperious protests. And if Israeli jets came, they would be blown out of the sky.

28

ON a scorching hot summer's day not long after Ambassador Horan had been ordered home, as the intrigues of kings, generals, and even urologists were still being played out, Larry Williams and Bob Cornuke illegally—and in total ignorance of these worldly affairs—entered the kingdom on their own secret mission. Yet from the start their trip seemed destined to be as ill-fated as that of the two presidential envoys. For as their plane approached the lights of Tabuk, it suddenly began dropping from the sky with the suddenness of an elevator whose cable had snapped.

As the plane continued to fall, it started to rain. *Rain? In the desert?* A corner of Williams' mind managed to register this despite his panic. But almost in the same moment, his sense of astonishment gave way to a terrible despair. It wasn't rain. It was gasoline. They were dumping fuel, he realized—standard procedure when a plane's about to go belly up. It reduces the risk of the fuselage becoming a colossal ball of fire. On impact. With the earth. Thousands of feet below.

What a bad joke, he nearly moaned out loud. Just when they had outsmarted the Saudis. Just when they were starting to believe nothing could stop them.

Only hours ago the seven-hour flight from London, the first leg of their journey, had touched down expertly in Jeddah. While the jet taxied toward the gate, Williams had leaned toward his friend and shared what he assumed would be their one big worry. "Here's where things might get a little dicey," he said. "But if we get through this, we're home free."

Soon they were making their way toward the head of the line at immigration. Williams darted furtive looks at the impassive face of the uniformed soldier who was stamping passports and his equally grim sidekick with the machine gun cradled in his arms. All at once he cursed himself for listening to Nikoli. A phony fax! A forged royal signature! And, one more craziness, a visa somehow stamped by a friend of a London cabdriver! When he handed his passport to the soldier, a boy he now realized, certainly not more than nineteen, and the soldier began tapping into his computer with a look of earnest concentration that in itself was unsettling, Williams tried not to tremble. But in the next instant, with not even a change of expression, the soldier stamped his passport and Williams was silently blessing Nikoli and Peter. They had pulled it off. They had conned their way into the kingdom of Saudi Arabia.

Or maybe not. Just after Cornuke, too, was waved through and Williams was beginning to get the strength back in his legs, something totally unanticipated happened. The customs inspector who had been rummaging through Williams' luggage pulled out the cassette that was in his video camera.

"It's blank," Williams spoke up quickly. And in an attempt to convey his utter harmlessness, he added, "Oh, maybe there are some shots of my wife and daughters, playing their harps."

"*Women?*"

"No," Williams argued with what to him seemed like perfectly reasonable logic, "not women. My wife. My daughters."

"You will come with me," the customs inspector ordered.

Williams was led to a closet-sized room where another grim man in a uniform sat at a metal desk that stretched nearly from one narrow wall to the other. And for the next two hours, he was forced to watch as this censor diligently played and replayed the entire tape. It was blank except for a brief interlude of Carla and the girls at their harps in the big living room with its southwestern furniture and the view toward the Pacific. Finally, the censor rose, walked over to Williams, and with a Solomonic gravity announced his decision. He could enter the kingdom, but the videotape would have to be confiscated. As Williams left the room, he turned to see the censor putting his tape on a shelf filled with other apparently offensive videos—*Alice in Wonderland, Rocky,* and *The Sound of Music.*

It was, he explained when he caught up with Cornuke and they hurried to catch the connecting night flight to Tabuk, a good first lesson in the ways of the strange land they had entered. "File it away," he told his friend. "Things are done differently here. Still, we're in nice and official."

"Nothing can stop us now," Cornuke agreed. But then this, too, had turned out to be little more than wishful thinking. Only two hours later, their plane was falling from the sky.

In a matter of seconds, the plane had been jolted from its cruising altitude and now, rocking unsteadily, was struggling to make its way to the airport. It was nighttime, but the sky over Tabuk was lit in bright streaks by a forest of tall, glowing streetlamps. The plane dipped even lower, and Cornuke saw rooftops glittering with turquoise stones in this illuminated night. Somewhere he had read that it meant the occupants had been to Mecca, and as the plane started to rattle ominously, he began to have thoughts about his own immortal soul. He remembered his wife's good-bye speech, about his walking away from any crash, and he hoped that for once at least she knew what she was talking about. And then there was a bang that resounded like a cannon blast, and the plane bounced once, then twice, and went into a screeching skid as the rim of its flat tire scratched against the asphalt. This sharp, grinding noise continued until the plane jerked to a stop at the very end of the runway.

The two friends, after a long, unexplained wait that only served to feed new fears, at last were led to the rear of the plane. A rubber slide stretched to the tarmac. Arms crisscrossed over their chests, they began to coast down when all at once they were hit by a furnace blast of heat. The plane is on fire, Williams thought. But in the next instant he realized it was only the hot, intense desert air. And as firemen in white protective suits and with, curiously, sandals on their feet rushed forward to spray the plane with a prophylactic foam, the two men, for the moment at least convinced of their invincibility, walked confidently off. They had arrived.

THE pool at the Tabuk Sahara was long and a perfect blue, and sitting there in the late afternoon sun in their trunks with glasses of icy orange juice in their hands, Williams and Cornuke might have been mistaken for complacent tourists. But this was not the case. It was the afternoon before the dawn when they would go off into the desert. Suddenly a long and challenging year had been compressed into just a few hours' wait.

Despite having checked into the hotel some time after 2 A.M., they had risen early. Too eager for sleep, they woke up full of heady optimism. And it was over breakfast, while they were still fresh with that strong mix of confidence and ambition, that they made a decision. It was Williams who proposed the new plan, but that was only because he beat Cornuke to the punch. The truth was, the idea had been taking shape in both men's minds ever since they stood on the land bridge stretching across the Strait of Tiran toward Saudi Arabia.

Before his first sip of the strong, sweet coffee that had been placed in front of him by the Filipino waiter, Williams announced that he wanted to change their itinerary. He no longer wanted to go straight from Tabuk to Jabal al Lawz. Instead, he wanted—"needed" would have been more accurate, considering his intensity—to follow the entire course of the Israelites' journey through the land of Midian to the mountain of Moses. His hope was to stand on the sandy Saudi Arabian beach he had seen in the distance from the waters of the Gulf of Aqaba, and then follow in the ancient footsteps of Moses and the twelve tribes across the biblical Wilderness of Sin. They would re-create the true path of the Exodus as they made their way to the true Mount Sinai. "We'll make history," Williams said with an offhanded confidence that left him embarrassed after he spoke the words.

"Mount Sinai is not going anywhere. It can wait for us a little longer," Cornuke agreed.

"Same for the gold," Williams said. But he also couldn't help adding, "I hope."

So it was decided. They would leave Tabuk and with the Bible as their guide backtrack across the desert to the site of the Red Sea crossing. Then they would return to Tabuk and, following the route that Fasold had mapped out in his letter, head straight to Jabal al Lawz. But that adventure, their exodus, would not begin until tomorrow. Meanwhile, as Williams reminded his friend, there were still plenty of things to be done today.

After finishing breakfast, they went into the town of Tabuk. Williams on his own had put together a shopping list, but that seemed fair enough to Cornuke since after all it was his money. They wandered through a maze of twisting streets so hot that the pavement, or, as was more often the case, the packed dusty dirt, seemed to burn through the soles of their shoes. Tabuk was, they discovered, a faded, sleepy little town. The sky above was a soft, tepid blue, and the buildings were mostly concrete, painted in a washed-out shade of white. Many stores were shut, but whether this was for prayers or simply out of a commercial lethargy, they could only guess. Nevertheless, by the time they returned to the hotel they had been able, after searching about with some determination, to find most of the things on Williams' list. They were loaded down with flashlights, shovels, brooms for sweeping off the artifacts, plenty of water, and baskets of outrageously expensive fresh fruits and vegetables. And in a transaction that proved to be much less complicated than they expected, they had rented a white, not too bedraggled Datsun pickup. Cornuke had driven it out of the lot, and, after putting it through its paces over a stretch of flat highway, announced with some satisfaction, "Would've been a whole lot easier for Moses if he'd had a fleet of these."

There was one last purchase. It was not on Williams' list but rather came to him as a sudden inspiration. Why not, he suggested to his own amazement, go native? And so they wound up buying checkered headdresses, which proved annoyingly complicated to first fold and then keep in place despite the braided *agal* cords that were supposed to do the job, and long white *thobe*s, which were remarkably cool and comfortable in the desert sun. "What do you think?" Williams asked his friend as he modeled his sheik's garb. "Real Lawrence of Arabia."

"Definitely," Cornuke agreed. But he was also thinking that you never could tell when a disguise might come in handy.

And then it was late afternoon and they were back at the hotel pool, hoping to relax with a mile or two of laps and a gallon of the delicious ice-cold orange juice the Filipino kept on serving. But as the shadows got longer and the day shorter, and tomorrow moved almost tangibly closer, there was no hope, or for that matter any real desire, to relax. Cornuke was well acquainted with this sort of edgy restlessness. How many times, he asked himself, had he sat encased in body armor with a loaded shotgun on his lap, waiting in the back of a police van for the inevitable call to action? His mood, as the sky became striped with the last bold colors of the setting desert sun, was climbing to that familiar sharp peak. And he realized there was something else they needed to do.

When he was on the force, he told Williams, it was standard procedure to "what if" any situation from top to bottom. Before the SWAT guys went rushing with their guns drawn through any closed doors, they would give a whole lot of serious thought to what could be on the other side. Consider all the possibilities, expect the unexpected, and determine in advance how you're going to handle it—that, Cornuke explained, was the only safe way to head off into the unknown. For the remainder of that afternoon and, to Cornuke's surprise, over dinner and well into the night, the two men threw themselves into this exercise. What if they dug up a cache of ancient jewels? What if they needed to store artifacts in Tabuk until they could be smuggled out of the kingdom? What if they were arrested like Fasold? What if they wound up on trial, or in jail? For each new scenario, they plotted out a suitable response. By the time they were done, jet lag was finally beginning to catch up to them. Drained as much as exhausted, they headed off for what they knew would be their last night for a while in a soft bed. Yet they were pleased. They went to their rooms certain they had anticipated anything that could possibly be waiting for them out in the desert.

THE launch was postponed. The Ofek—Hebrew for "horizon"—satellite had been scheduled to be propelled into orbit by a Shavit rocket during the first week in June 1988. But now Israel's entry into the space age would have to be delayed. Yuval Ne'eman, the head of the country's fledgling space agency, assured the prime minister that the remaining technical problems were minor and that Ofek would soon be in orbit above the Middle East, certainly by the end of September. The Mossad, however, was not placated. It could not wait that long.

Ofek was to be the harbinger of a fleet of Israeli spy satellites. Following the successful journey into space of this prototype, the goal was to launch a series of Ofeks equipped with sophisticated cameras. They would lift off from a secret coastal base south of Tel Aviv and then go into orbit in an ellipse ranging from 155 to 620 miles above the planet. Every ninety minutes these eyes-in-the-sky would pass over the Middle East. Only now this ambitious program was delayed.

In the spring of 1988, as the Mossad continued to review with growing concern the puzzling reports of new military construction in isolated areas throughout the Kingdom of Saudi Arabia, this postponement, however brief, was treated as a major crisis. The Israeli Secret Service had been eagerly anticipating the definitive intelligence that satellite surveillance of the kingdom would provide. Its field agents were convinced it would be very difficult to penetrate the many new and well-guarded installations sprouting up in remote parts of the kingdom. The risk of capture and the international incident that would certainly follow was high. Yet the United States continued to refuse to share its overhead Keyhole satellite shots, and Jonathan Pollard was no longer in a position to steal them. All this left the Mossad with little choice. Until Israel had its own spy birds in orbit, the Mossad would have to use whatever inventive means it could to find out precisely what was happening deep in the Saudi desert.

29

WILLIAMS and Cornuke left Tabuk not long after dawn. They drove off into the desert in their pickup when the day's new light was shining like a beacon across the packed gray sand. Cornuke was at the wheel, and he had his dog-eared Bible with its faded red leather cover resting in his lap. Williams, leaning forward in the passenger's seat, struggled to keep a map of the kingdom spread across the dashboard. Back in London, he had used the French infrared satellite photographs as a guide to trace an imprecise trail that started at the crossing point on the Saudi side of the Strait of Tiran, Ra's ash Shaykh Humayd, and weaved across the desert to the highest point in the region, the mountain of Jabal al Lawz. The plan, and both men were ready to acknowledge it was a fairly loose one, was to keep to this route as best they could. If it was the true path of the Exodus, they were convinced they would be able to find confirming evidence in the Bible.

Unfortunately, and this was the part they were more reluctant to acknowledge, the task was complicated by a couple of very large problems. First, the names of biblical sites mentioned in the Book of Exodus, and later listed with authoritative specificity in Numbers, had no relation to contemporary or even documented ancient geography. And second, if they stuck *precisely* to the twisting black trail Williams had inked across the map, they would be taking their pickup off the main roads and into regions that their map warned remained uncharted to this day. Still, as they followed the road out of Tabuk before turning west toward the coast, Cornuke was undaunted. They were driving under the full glow of the morning sun, and this was to his susceptible mind an encouraging piece of symbolism. "The children of Israel were shown the way across the wilderness by a cloud during the day and a pillar of fire at night," he told Williams. Was it too much of a leap of faith to believe that their journey, too, was being similarly blessed? he suggested.

But after several long hot hours in the bouncing truck, after keeping to an elliptical route that took them through mile after mile of the same flat, velvet sand, the vividness of their expectations had given way to the monotony of their vague hunt. For Williams, the desert would always be remembered as he experienced it in those first hours: so vast that you were certain it was endless, a world unto itself; so eerily quiet, empty, that you felt you could travel for a lifetime in any direction and not see another person; and yet so filled with a nascent danger that you were always listening for the cocking of a gun, afraid that someone out there had you in his sights.

They stopped the truck finally in the middle of nowhere when Cornuke announced he had to pee. As Williams rummaged through the back of the cab for a bottle of grapefruit juice, his friend traipsed across the sand, hoping that even a modest distance would give him the pretense of privacy. He stopped when he found a big brown rock and began relieving himself against this handy target. The stream of pee was splashing against the rock when suddenly it began to move, rose up in stages in front of Cornuke's stunned eyes, and, as if a miracle, turned into a camel. It took him a moment before he realized what had happened, but by then, still unzipped, he was running back to the truck with the snorting beast in pursuit. Williams had finished the last swallow of warm juice only to look up and see the bewildering sight of his friend being chased across the desert by an angry camel.

Cornuke scrambled back into the truck, and when he looked in the rearview mirror, he was certain the animal was spitting at them. He pressed his foot to the accelerator, the tires began spinning in the loose sand, and for a frantic moment he thought they might be stuck. But the truck jerked forward, and while the camel continued to bay a chorus of insulting noises in the background, they were on their way. Only after they had gone some distance did Cornuke, by now more exhilarated than embarrassed, tell Williams what had happened. He did not seem amused, and when he finally spoke his voice had an uncharacteristic edge. "Next time," he suggested with what he later would insist was an unintentional irony, "try not to piss off any camels. OK?"

As they continued on through the perpetual sun and sand, Williams, already drained to the point of exhaustion, found himself beginning to sort through a list of previously discarded doubts. There really weren't any clues, any tangible evidence out here, he told himself. Sand *was* sand. How could he expect to prove that Moses had led his flock along this very route? All at once he felt defeated, and his mind wandered off to an unexpected memory. When he had studied the Book of Exodus in preparation for this trip, he had been troubled by the almost constant whining complaints of the Israelites. God had generously offered up so many full-blown miracles—the parting of the Red Sea, manna to eat, and even water from a rock—and still the twelve tribes were not satisfied. "And the people murmured against Moses . . ." was a phrase that riled him each time it was repeated. Back in the air-conditioned comfort of southern California, in his big house on the hill, it was difficult, incomprehensible really, to understand such colossal ingratitude. After everything the Hebrews had witnessed, after all they had overcome, where was their faith? But now that he, too, was out in the wilderness, he knew how the Israelites had felt.

. . .

THEY nearly drove straight through the town of Al Bad. The boldfaced dot next to the Arabic name on their map had given the two men hope that they were at last heading toward an established bit of civilization. But they had gone down a dusty, deserted stretch of road lined by a distant ridge of ancient hills, the dirt burned by the sun to a sour, caking yellow. They had passed a tin-roofed hut and then another, and there was a plume of gray smoke rising from a cluster of striped tents, and a skinny dog raised itself up to give a brief, halfhearted chase after their truck before they realized they had arrived. Cornuke stopped the Datsun in the middle of the road.

"What do you think?" he asked.

"Got to be the place," Williams said.

It was disappointing. Back in Tabuk, and even before, back in London, Al Bad had figured prominently in their plans. From the very first days they had spent hunched over a map of the kingdom, the town had taken on in both men's imaginations a significance that was far larger than might have been expected from the tiny block letters that spelled out its name. Not only did the infrared photographs show that the ancient path that led to Jabal al Lawz went straight through this town, but an older map of the kingdom in the professor's library also revealed a further tantalizing promise—there was an officially designated archaeological site there, too. Cornuke and Williams had added these two facts together and, a simple sum by their logic, had come up with the conclusion that Moses and his flock must have camped at the town of Al Bad on their journey to Mount Sinai. Even better, they decided, the archaeological proof needed to confirm their theory was waiting for their inspection, thoughtfully preserved by the royal commission on antiquities. But now the sorrowful actuality—a dusty cluster of tents and huts, a stooped Bedouin minding a small, passive flock of sheep, and not a ruin in sight—left them feeling close to ridiculous.

"Now what?" Williams asked.

Cornuke, however, had the capacity to bring enthusiasm to any catastrophe. "I say we find the ruins. They're on the map, so they have to be somewhere nearby."

They drove south, but they might have just as easily chosen another direction. There was no logic to their hunt, and, they would later confess, only the smallest of hopes. But within minutes, Cornuke was shouting. "Larry, do you see what I see?"

Williams looked all around. He had no idea what Cornuke was talking about.

"The trees," Cornuke said and suddenly stopped the truck. "*Palm* trees. They're all over the place. Everywhere."

Cornuke jumped out of the truck, and Williams, still mystified, followed after him. Then Williams saw it—the desert had changed completely. A small, green forest of graceful palms was spread out in front of them. With Cornuke charging ahead, Williams walked slowly through the surprisingly cool sand until he caught up with his friend under the shaded canopy formed by these tall trees. Cornuke, full of excitement, was standing by a well. Tentatively, Williams cupped his hands together, reached into the bucket Cornuke had already raised, and tasted the water. The first drop was ice on his tongue. Immediately refreshed, he started drinking greedily, taking big, thick gulps from his hands. The liquid had a purity, a sweetness, he had never experienced before. Each swallow was a surprise, and it began to wash away his crankiness. And yet he was still confused. He realized they had stumbled on an oasis. But was that really cause enough for such excitement?

Cornuke, however, must have guessed his thoughts. He went back to the truck and returned with his Bible. He held it open in his hands like a minister at a wedding. And the rays of light filtering down on him through the lattice of green fronds also gave the moment a sense of sanctity. In his soft, precise voice he read: "'And they came to Elim, where there were twelve springs and seventy palm trees: and they camped near the waters.'"

"Don't you get it?" Cornuke demanded, slamming the red

leather covers shut. His smile, Williams will always remember, was exuberant. "This is Elim. The springs, the seventy palm trees—it's all here. And the location's right, too. According to the Book of Exodus, Elim was more or less halfway between the crossing site and Mount Sinai. Well, Al Bad, or Elim, or whatever you want to call this place, is midway between the coast and Jabal al Lawz. It all fits. We're standing on the very spot where Moses and the twelve tribes stood, where they camped. We're drinking water from the same well they drank from on their way to the mountain of God."

Williams thought about that for a moment. It made sense, and still it was overwhelming. "Yes," he said finally, "I think you're right."

30

THEY were determined to find the ruins of Al Bad. More than ever, Cornuke and Williams were convinced the site held secrets, secrets they needed to know. Reason, of course, might have tempered their confidence. After all, it was just as logical that waiting out in the desert was simply just some ancient monument reverentially preserved because of the part it had played in the long and noble history of the Al Saud family. However, that possibility was not even considered. In their hearts, they knew without even the remotest of evidence that the site was part of *their* mystery. The ruins at Al Bad would help to prove that Moses had led the children of Israel through the Saudi wilderness. For something else, unspoken yet of great consequence, had occurred that afternoon out in the desert. The miracle of finding the oasis at Elim had restored their faith.

The two men remained at the oasis only long enough to take a series of photographs. *Then they came to Elim, where there were twelve springs and seventy palm trees: and they camped near the waters.* It had been these trees, this very water. Study our photos, they would tell the skeptics. In their minds, they were already standing behind lecterns, talking of their adventure to large and attentive audiences. Now that they had found a campground, they knew they were on the trail to the true Mount Sinai. Wildly encouraged, Williams and Cornuke went back to the truck. The next piece of evidence was, they knew, waiting for them somewhere nearby.

Only they could not find it. The archaeological site was definitively marked on their map. An unmistakable diamond-shaped symbol—code for a location designated in the kingdom's official archaeological survey—was directly adjacent to the black dot signifying the town of Al Bad. But when they scoured the desert, searching the flat horizon in all directions from the front seat of their truck, they couldn't find a clue. Not an official sign. A plaque. Or a monument. They drove around the outskirts of the town in a small, clockwise circle, and then, increasingly frustrated, repeated the dull exercise by going off in the reverse direction. They found nothing.

After several futile hours they were at a total loss, yet they were also unwilling to concede defeat. Cornuke, still trying to sound confident, suggested they could ask for directions in the village. He realized there wasn't much likelihood that anyone in Al Bad would be able to make sense of their Arabic, a makeshift lingo that consisted of a few mispronounced guidebook phrases and a lot of sign language. And there was even less chance of their happening on a Bedouin who spoke English. Still, Cornuke, always optimistic, tried to be encouraging. He reminded Williams that finding an oasis was supposed to be a harbinger of further good luck.

In town, they split up. Cornuke volunteered to try knocking on doors and, he added only partly joking, "the flaps of tents." So Williams gamely went off to check out the staggered row of huts, hoping one of them would be a store. The wooden door of the first shanty he approached was propped open with a stone, and, tentatively, he walked in. A sewing machine that looked as if it could have seen duty stitching up uniforms for World War I doughboys was on a worn wooden table in the middle of the almost airless room. And beneath it, curled up in a fetal position on a dusty carpet, was a man—a tailor? he wondered—fast asleep. Williams retreated quickly. The next door was locked, or at least it didn't open when he gave it a push. But the third hut had a screen door that he was able to pull open on the first try, and inside was what appeared to be a general store. When Williams, by now emboldened, gave its sleeping owner a gentle shove, the man awoke instantly and seemed ready to do business.

"Do you speak English?" Williams asked.

The man nodded happily, but Williams had his doubts. He grabbed a couple of anemic-looking lemons and put them on the scale that sat on the counter. Might as well let the poor guy make a sale, he reasoned with a businessman's practicality, before I even try asking him for some free information.

The shopkeeper looked at the two small lemons on the scale and, with the same happy expression on his face, announced, "One kilo."

That was a kilo more lemons than Williams had any need for in the middle of the Saudi desert. But he also realized it was a small price to pay for learning the location of the town's archaeological site. For the shopkeeper's two succinct words were a revelation: He really did speak English.

Williams quickly grabbed another handful of lemons and dumped them on the scale.

At once the merchant merrily announced, "Two kilos."

Williams wanted to laugh. Even in the middle of nowhere someone was trying to hustle him. It wasn't the most ingenious of scams he had ever run up against, but there was no getting around the fact that this gap-toothed shopkeeper was out to sell him the town's entire inventory of lemons. Still, Williams reasoned to himself, what was the cost of a few more lemons in the scheme of things if he got the information he wanted? So once again he gathered up a handful of lemons, but this time, before dropping them on the scale and with the prospect of his purchase still a tantalizing possibility, he asked his question. Perhaps the gentleman knew the location of the town's famous ruins? He would be most grateful, very generous in fact, if the man would be kind enough to show him the way.

The old man seemed suddenly confused. He opened his mouth to speak, then he stopped. The intensity of concentration reminded Williams of someone who was trying to add up a long and difficult sum. At last the man found the words. With a now familiar, happy smile animating his face, he said, "Three kilos?"

That was when Williams finally got it: The man didn't speak English at all. Except for the word "kilo" and probably enough numbers to count off the fingers on one hand. Feeling more bemused than cheated, he handed over a handful of coins. And as he left the store, balancing a pile of lemons awkwardly against his chest, he heard the man calling after him, "Four kilos?"

Williams was making his way carefully to the white Datsun, doing his best not to lose another lemon from his unsteady pyramid, when he heard Cornuke call out, "Where have you been? I've been looking all over for you."

Cornuke trotted over. "What's with all these lemons? You going to make lemonade or something? It doesn't matter. I've got someone I want you to meet. Right away. You're not going to believe this."

Williams dumped the lemons into the back of the truck; and then, with Cornuke leading the way, they headed to a green-striped tent. On Cornuke's instructions, Williams waited while his friend disappeared inside. Across from him a small fire was burning, warming a coffeepot. Williams could smell the cardamom. He also couldn't help noticing that a roll of paper towels, similar to the ones in his own kitchen, hung by a rope from the side of the tent.

In a moment, Cornuke reappeared. And with him was an Arab, perhaps a weathered 40, in a pristinely white *thobe*. The man had a teacher's thoughtful, almost solemn, face, Williams immediately decided. Without bothering to make introductions, Cornuke instructed, "Please tell my friend what you just told me. He would like to hear it."

The Arab turned and looked directly at Williams. He made a

sour expression as if he was annoyed at having to go through this one more time. But finally in a somewhat impatient voice he said, "Yes, I know the ruins you mentioned. They are on the outskirts of town, just south of here."

His English, Williams realized, was not only fluent but also barely accented. And no sooner had that registered than he heard the Arab's next words. "Those are the caves of Moses," he said.

"What did I tell you, Larry?" Cornuke said exuberantly, pounding the Arab on the back and completely oblivious to the suddenly wary look the Arab shot back at him. "We're onto something all right. The caves of Moses."

But Williams could only wonder, what caves? As far as he knew, there was no mention anywhere in the Bible of "the caves of Moses."

THEY were sitting on a coarse rug inside the tent, and coffee was being poured from a brass pot. A boy of about eight had reached into an aluminum tin surrounded by buzzing flies and shyly offered Williams a sticky date. Williams took a bite of the sweet and chewed it with what he hoped was an ingratiating relish. After both Williams and Cornuke had taken a few sips of the pale green coffee, the protocols of desert hospitality must have been satisfied because, as if on command, their host began to speak.

The man had been born in Syria, he said, and had learned his English as a boy. When Williams complimented him on his proficiency and went on to admit his genuine surprise at finding someone so remarkably skilled in remote Al Bad, the man's only response was a small, controlled shrug. It was another typically Arab gesture, Williams was learning. It was not so much self-effacing, he decided, as philosophical. The way he deciphered it, the man was saying that the ways of the world are often strange.

Perhaps that was why Williams and Cornuke, although both their minds raced with questions, were persuaded to sit there pleasantly, models of gracious patience, as the Arab rambled on. They heard a long-winded and increasingly mournful account of the life, ill-fated in their host's own view, that had led to his becoming, after all else had failed, a novice shepherd. But just as both men were beginning to feel their calves start to tingle from having sat for so long cross-legged, the man returned to more relevant matters. And his suddenly weary, almost bored tone was, to Williams' ears, the equivalent of his earlier shrug: This is the way things are; how could you not know?

Moses, he began, had always been part of the history of this village. It was common knowledge among the people of the surrounding desert that he had camped in Al Bad on his way to Mount Sinai. In fact, the people in the village were proud of this heritage, their association with Moses.

"Proud?" Williams wondered skeptically.

"Moses," the shepherd reminded his guests, "was also a Muslim prophet."

"And the caves?" Williams asked. "Just where do they fit in?"

In the same complaisant tone, as if this, too, were readily apparent, the man explained that Jethro, Moses' father-in-law, the priest of Midian, had lived in the caves.

"Then they must be the caves where Moses lived with his wife, Zipporah, Jethro's daughter, and their two sons," Cornuke said, working things out in his mind as he spoke. "They were Moses' home for the forty years he spent in Midian, before God appeared to him in the burning bush and ordered him to return to Egypt."

"Yes," the man said, "that is the tradition."

"And," Cornuke continued, "Jethro was still living in the caves when Moses, leading the twelve tribes, came back to Midian from Egypt. According to the Bible, Jethro lived just a hop, skip, and a jump from Mount Sinai." Cornuke could hardly control his excitement. The prospect of what was waiting for them outside of town gave him immense satisfaction.

Their host, however, simply nodded as if, again, to say, of course.

"We've got to see them," Cornuke announced.

"Impossible," the man said. He spoke the word swiftly and forcefully. "You can't go there. It's not safe." Williams noticed the expression on the man's face had also changed. He was scared.

"Not safe?" Williams asked. "I don't understand. We're talking about an archaeological dig, right? We're not going to take anything. We're just going to look. What's the problem?"

"There's a fence around the caves," the man explained.

"I see," Williams said.

"There's barbed wire," the man went on, now turning to Cornuke as if to appeal to his greater wisdom. "People are ordered to stay away. That is the law."

"Right," said Cornuke.

"You must listen to me," the man insisted. He paused for a moment, and when he spoke again it was with obvious reluctance, as if this last piece of information were being pulled from him. "There are soldiers at the caves," he warned.

31

CORNUKE and Williams were lying in the slope of a wadi, flat on their stomachs against the warm sand. With their heads raised, they were able to look past a single-lane asphalt road, through a steel mesh fence topped with three rows of barbed wire, and across to a guardhouse. And beyond the flat-roofed, cinder-block building, silhouetted against a crown of smooth blue sky, was a long, rolling bank of mustard-colored hills riddled with dozens of dark, narrow apertures—the caves of Moses.

From their hiding place, the two men had quickly decided that cutting a hole in a back stretch of fence, a few hundred yards or so from the guardhouse, would not be too much of a problem. But, as Cornuke pointed out, getting in was one thing. Getting out would be another. They needed to know, he insisted with the caution of a man who actually had made a few mad dashes through enemy territory, how many soldiers were in that guardhouse. They needed to know what sort of force they would be up against, if there was even a chance they could make their way undetected to the caves. So they lay there as if immersed, the sand hot and coarse and seeping over them, as they watched and they waited.

Yesterday, after finally persuading the Syrian shepherd first to accept the small handful of bills Williams had offered as a gesture of thanks for his hospitality, and then, after considerably more effort, to give them directions to the caves, the two men had immediately headed out back into the desert. Their plan was to drive straight to the site. They were not at all deterred by the shepherd's warning about soldiers. It did not make any sense, they reassured each other as soon as they were back in the Datsun. Sure, there very well could be a guard or two to watch over things and maybe pick up the tourists' candy wrappers. But an armed battalion bivouacked in the middle of nowhere to guard a bunch of old caves? "Gimme a break," Cornuke complained. And Williams for once did not want to find a reason to disagree. Therefore, after leaving the shepherd's tent, they found themselves driving out of Al Bad as the final sliver of sun was beginning to descend like a bright red blade on a perfect stretch of horizon. During the day, Williams was coming to learn, the desert was unfriendly. At night, empty yet alive with small, anonymous sounds, it was hostile. When Cornuke suggested they camp for the night at the oasis at Elim, he quickly agreed.

Dinner was a couple of plastic bags of dehydrated beef Stroganoff that Williams had greatly improved, or so he would boast, with a sprinkle of the tart juice from one of the lemons he had purchased in Al Bad. Afterward they sat by a fire Cornuke had built and watched in a deep, thoughtful silence as its flame shot up through the heavy darkness. They remained this way for a long while, as mute and pensive as Quakers at a meeting. When Cornuke finally began thumbing through his Bible, the fire had been burning for so long that its light had become weak; and even when he moved in closer, its glow barely illuminated the minuscule black print on the thin pages. But he managed to find the chapter of Exodus he was looking for and, taking his time, he read aloud: "'Now Jethro, the priest of Midian, Moses' father-in-law, heard of all that God had done for Moses, and for Israel His people, how that the Lord had brought Israel out of Egypt. . . . And Jethro, Moses' father-in-law, came with his sons and his wife unto Moses into the wilderness where he was encamped, at the mount of God.'"

"You know what that tells me?" Cornuke asked Williams. "It tells me that the twelve tribes must have camped by Jethro's home. That's how he heard about what had gone down in Egypt. His home was close to their campground, and not that far at all from Mount Sinai."

"It all fits, doesn't it?" Williams agreed. "Elim, the caves, and Jabal al Lawz. They're all pieces of the same puzzle."

The fire had burned down to only a faint glow by the time they decided to go to bed. Cornuke, who had a deep, perhaps even, he acknowledged with some embarrassment, neurotic fear of snakes, bunked down on an air mattress wedged into the back of the truck. It was close quarters, but he fell asleep quickly. Williams was not so fortunate. He lay in a sleeping bag spread across the sand and, although exhausted, felt he needed, for some vague yet anxious reason, to stay on guard.

At first he told himself there were ghosts out there, the spirits of the ancient Israelites still murmuring in the soft, high whine of the desert wind. But then, listening keenly, he knew he heard a noise—the sound of tires rubbing against sand. And in the next moment, for just an instant, there was a light, and it was distinct and worldly: a pair of headlights shining from out of the darkness straight into their camp. But immediately the desert was once again a thick, impenetrable black. As he slipped into a restless sleep, he was almost able to convince himself that it had been a mean trick played by his susceptible imagination, and that the only things out there were sand and spirits.

In the morning after that fitful night Williams slept late, and it was nearly noon before they reached the caves. At first look they were, Williams felt, both less and more than he had anticipated. When seen from the distance, with the high fence preventing him from making a closer inspection, the caves struck him as simply dark, narrow, inhospitable holes. A man would have to stoop, perhaps even crawl, to enter. It did not, at least to his measured way of looking at the world, seem an appropriate sort of home for Moses. But he also found himself thinking, if these barren caves had indeed been his home—for forty years—then for the first time he had a sense of Moses as a man. He began to contemplate what a profound and courageous act of will, what pure faith, would have been required for a shepherd to leave an anonymous life in these empty, arid hills and go into Egypt to confront the mighty Pharaoh in the grandeur of his own court.

Imagine, he told himself, a man coming from *this,* this nothingness, and finding within himself the talent and wisdom to lead and to command; to take a slave people and, through the force of his discipline and the power of his beliefs, transform them into a great nation. As Williams looked across to those bleak, sandy hills, the texture of Moses' internal struggles, the fears and doubts of a humble shepherd forced without warning to become a great man, to step into world history, were suddenly very real to Williams. And he was awed.

He wanted to tell all this to Cornuke, but his friend was completely focused in his study of the guardhouse. And Cornuke was not happy with what he saw. It was a more substantial structure than he had expected. Perhaps the Syrian was correct. It didn't make any sense, but maybe there were soldiers out here. "We'd better hunker down someplace," he told Williams. "Take the lay of the land before we do anything foolish."

They had been hiding in the wadi, spies in the desert, for a couple of long, hot hours when there was a quick, high-pitched whine like an infant's muffled cry. But it was only the squeaking sound of a tired set of hinges as the door to the guardhouse was flung open and a soldier came out. He was dressed in fatigues and had a carbine slung over his shoulder. They watched as he took a few steps, placed his weapon down so gently on the sand that Cornuke wondered if he was afraid the rifle would go off, and then, without further ceremony, dropped to his knees. He was facing east, toward Mecca, and he began to pray.

Williams was about to say something, but Cornuke raised an admonishing finger. The two men continued to wait in this careful silence for what seemed to Williams like another hour but, as clocked by the minute hand of Cornuke's watch, was precisely ten full minutes. Then, his voice a conspiratorial whisper, Cornuke spoke. "This is looking good. Very good. If there were any more soldiers in there, they'd have come out for prayers."

"Of course there's only one guy," Williams said. "You don't need an army to guard a bunch of empty caves."

When the soldier finished his prayers and returned to the guardhouse, the two men scrambled from their hiding place and made it back to the truck. The plan was to circle around to the rear of the caves and look for a secluded spot where, under the cover of night, they would cut their hole. Perhaps with a little luck, they might even find a gap in the fence. The one risk was that they would have to take some care since they would be trudging up the narrow path to the caves in the dark. Still, Williams reminded his friend, Jethro and Moses couldn't have relied on flashlights either when they came home at night.

After their long wait, they both were eager to get going, but Cornuke was at the wheel and he made sure not to get back onto the asphalt strip of road until the guardhouse was nearly out of sight. He followed the road as it twisted around hills. Williams would usually complain that he "drove that damn truck like it was the pace car in the Indy 500." But this afternoon Cornuke took his time. He drove slowly, almost at a crawl, so that Williams from his front-seat perch would be able to scan the fence. It was this rare occurrence, both men would later decide, that undoubtedly saved them from spending some time in a Saudi jail—and perhaps it also saved their lives. For Cornuke, without burning rubber, without smashing down on the brakes with the uncontrolled panic of a man heading off the edge of a cliff, was able to bring the truck to a sudden, yet still discreet, halt. Just in time.

"Now what?" Williams wondered, at once annoyed. He had been concentrating on the fence line off to his right and didn't appreciate being interrupted.

"Look," Cornuke instructed, pointing straight ahead.

About one hundred yards off, where the road began to twist around to the rear shaded portion of the hillside, there was a gate.

And on either side of the gate were soldiers in battle dress and armed with submachine guns. And beyond the gate were more soldiers—dozens of men and trucks and bulldozers and derricks. At the foot of the caves of Moses, in the midst of a remote and empty desert, they had stumbled on a busy and well-guarded Saudi military base.

"What's going on?" Williams asked.

But Cornuke didn't think it would be wise to wait around guessing. He immediately made a U-turn and, driving as if his life depended upon it, a possibility that he instinctively realized might very well be the case, he sped away in the opposite direction.

"We still could go back. Same plan as before, except we go in the front. We know there's only one soldier in that guardhouse. What are the odds of his stopping us before we make it to the caves?"

They had parked their truck off in the desert about ten kilometers from the caves, and Williams was doing the talking. But by the halfhearted way he was going on, Cornuke could tell he had not really made up his mind. He was simply tossing a scheme out, seeing if it made sense.

"Sure," Williams continued, "it's a risk, all right. But suppose we get to the caves. It'd be worth it."

Cornuke decided he should step in before things got too out of hand. "What do you think all those soldiers were doing out there?" he asked.

"I don't know," Williams admitted.

"Neither do I. But it sure looks like it's something mighty important. Must be at battalion strength. Armed to the teeth."

Williams nodded evenly. He could see where this was leading, and he was glad to let Cornuke take him there.

"Now," Cornuke continued, "let's say those soldiers happen to patrol the caves at night. Let's say they're poking around with dogs and searchlights and they come across a couple of Americans. With forged visas. In a military compound. You think they're going to let us go? You think they'll say this is really fascinating? 'Hey, guys,' I can hear some lieutenant yelling to his men, 'You know Moses lived here?' And then they'll send us off to Jabal al Lawz to see what else we can find? They catch us and you can forget about getting your hands on the gold of Exodus. Hell, you can forget about the next twenty years."

"Priorities," Williams glumly conceded. "Nothing's more important than you and me getting to Mount Sinai. The two of us standing on the top of the mountain of God—that's what it's all about. Let's head to the coast."

"On to Ra's ash Shaykh Humayd," Cornuke agreed. He started up the truck and they were on their way.

BUT the way out of the desert took them back to the single-lane road and they found themselves, to their surprise, once again passing by another corner of the military compound. It was Williams' idea, a sudden whim, really, that perhaps they should take a photograph or two of the detachment of soldiers who were camped out in the caves of Moses. It would be part of their record, more solid proof of what they had seen. "We'll put it in the scrapbook. Right after the shots from the Strait of Tiran and the oasis at Elim," he said lightly enough.

"But from a distance," Cornuke warned. "Strictly long-range lens stuff. Last thing we want is the Saudis thinking we're spies."

They parked the Datsun off the road, and the two men walked side by side deeper into the desert. They went only about ten feet before Williams announced he had found an angle that gave him a full shot of the cliffs but also kept them out of the sightline of the soldiers. He was snapping away when he heard Cornuke mutter one woeful word—"Damn."

Williams looked up to see a blue truck coming down the road straight toward them. And it was moving very fast.

"Soldiers?" he asked.

"Good chance," Cornuke said. His voice was calm, even softer than usual, but his mind was sorting through possibilities.

"Should we run?" Williams asked.

"Nowhere to go."

The blue truck had swung off the road and now was heading into the desert. Right at them. With a good throw, they could have hit it with a rock. It was that close. In a minute it would be even closer.

"Here's how we play it," Cornuke quickly instructed, his voice still flat and steady. "We're tourists. We're Americans. We've got nothing to hide. Remember that."

And then the truck was right on top of them and, to their relief, a Bedouin got out. He wore a *thobe* and, Williams noticed, hiking boots.

"You can't take pictures here," he threatened. "You could be arrested."

"Sorry," said Williams.

"Our mistake," Cornuke said apologetically. But he made sure to keep his hands at his sides, and he clenched them into hard fists.

"You'd better go. Get out of here," ordered the Bedouin.

The two men quickly obeyed. They were so relieved it was some arrogant Bedouin giving the commands and not a squad of Saudi soldiers that only later did they think about how it was odd to come across an Arab driving a truck through the desert who spoke perfect English. But, they asked themselves, was that really any odder than finding a sprawling military base being constructed around the caves that had been home to God's chosen prophet?

32

AFTER they broke camp the next morning, Cornuke turned the trip odometer on the truck back to zero.

Williams wondered what that was all about as he settled into the passenger's seat. The vinyl was already hot to his touch. It was going to be another broiling day. Last night Cornuke had taken off his watch and shown him that the sun had even squeezed through the holes in the band and left a pattern of tiny brown dots on his wrist. Williams was glad they were on the way to the coast. According to their map, Ra's ash Shaykh Humayd was about 65 kilometers to the southwest if they stuck to the main road. If they traveled a more meandering route across the desert, it still couldn't be more than about 120 kilometers. Either way, an easy trip, he decided. In his mind he began washing out days of sand and sun in the cool water of the Gulf of Aqaba.

Cornuke started the engine, and they drove back out into the desert. He still had not bothered to say a word about the trip odometer, but by now Williams had gotten used to Cornuke's taciturn, often pensive way. In fact, after the encounter with the truck-driving Bedouin, Williams had congratulated himself on having chosen the perfect companion for this adventure. The man was a rock. Even the heat did not seem to bother him; or if it did, he never complained. And while Williams was well aware of how wildly his own mood swung with each new success or disappointment, he also could not help marveling at how steady—"grounded" was the admiring word he would still use years later—Cornuke had been from the moment they had touched down in Saudi Arabia. He had even stopped reminiscing in his hangdog way about his unsatisfying life with his wife. Out in the field, Williams was discovering, Cornuke was pure function.

So Williams did not make anything out of it when Cornuke failed to explain about the trip odometer. And when, instead, he launched into a seemingly unconnected biblical story, Williams gave him his complete attention.

"After Moses led the children of Israel across the Red Sea," Cornuke said, "they went off into the vast wilderness of Shur. For three long days they wandered through the desert without a drop of water to drink. Then, on the third day, they came to a spring. At last, the tribes rejoiced. But when they went to drink the water, it was so bitter that they could not even swallow it. And the people began to speak out against Moses, saying, 'What shall we drink? Why has he led us here to Marah?' which was what they named the spring since that is the Hebrew word for bitter. Moses, desperate and anxious, cried to the Lord for help, and God showed him a tree. Moses understood. He threw it into the waters, and the waters were made sweet."

"Not a bad trick," Williams interrupted, only to be embarrassed by how unintentionally glib, if not sacrilegious, his words sounded.

But if Cornuke was offended, he did not reveal it. With a sudden fluency that left Williams genuinely impressed, he said that what happened after the miracle was an even more significant event. At the Springs of Marah, God issued what the Book of Exodus referred to, in a rare instance of almost legalistic precision, as "a statute and an ordinance." "The Lord," Cornuke said, "made what boiled down to a terrific deal with the children of Israel: If they kept their faith, if they would do what was right in God's eyes, He would always protect them."

Williams waited; presumably Cornuke was not finished. But he showed no signs of any willingness to take things further. He continued to drive along in a very comfortable silence until, finally, Williams decided he would have to pry the rest out. "And this, this story about the bitter water, has something to do with your turning the trip counter back to zero?" he asked, pointing toward the dashboard.

"Of course," Cornuke said. "Isn't it obvious?"

When Williams, as pleasantly as his frustration would allow, assured him that it was not, Cornuke shrugged and then patiently went on. It was, he said, once again simply a question of mathematics. "The Bible clearly states that the sweetening of the waters occurred three days after the crossing of the Red Sea. Now we've already determined, and most scholars agree, that the twelve tribes probably covered at best maybe fifteen kilometers a day as they headed to Mount Sinai. That would mean that the Springs of Marah were approximately forty-five kilometers from the coast. Therefore, since we know Ra's ash Shaykh Humayd is about, oh, sixty-five kilometers southwest from where we shoved off this morning, and . . ."

Williams, suddenly excited by the possibility promised by Cornuke's math, interrupted. "You're saying that when we see the mileage counter hit twenty, we look up and right in front of us there should be the very site where God performed the miracle that sweetened the bitter waters—the Springs of Marah."

"Give or take a kilometer," Cornuke said without the least bit of irony.

THERE were, Williams had come to decide, three distinct types of sand in the Saudi desert. There was the fine, silky sand that crested in high dunes and glowed a blood red in the sun; you could pick up a warm handful and it would seep through your fingers like so much soft, vanishing time. Then there was the packed gray sand of the plains, blasted by the heat until it was as strong and as dense as asphalt. And, a true misery, there were the brownish pellets of sand that were swept up in sudden rushes of burning desert wind and would come raining down with rock-hard force. That morning, as they followed their meandering route to the coast, they had, by Williams' observant eye, passed through all three subtle varieties of desert sand. Cataloguing such things was how he had trained himself to pass the time during the long, sticky, and too often bouncing rides in their little truck. But this morning these careful observations were also a prelude, an exercise in sharpening his senses for what would be coming.

When the numbers on the trip odometer slowly turned from 10 to 15, there was an immediate heightening of the tension in the truck. Nothing was said, and this reserve was deliberate; any announcement, they both intuitively felt, would have been a jinx. But both men's attention was rigid. They were now on the lookout for the Springs of Marah.

The next four kilometers might just as well have been a hundred. That was how it felt to both men. Everything was slowed, each moment was in itself an adventure. Cornuke drove at a turtle's pace, and both men scrutinized nearly every inch of the surrounding desert. But they did not find what they were looking for. When the numbers 2 and 0 fell into place on the counter, once again there was only a guarded silence to mark the occasion. At that precise moment Cornuke and Williams both felt such a profound sense of disappointment that it would not have surprised either of them if they had let loose with an agonized moan. To their credit, however, they suffered in disciplined silence.

As 21, 22, and, almost painfully, 23 fell into place, things only got worse. They realized they would have to acknowledge that they had failed. Perhaps their theories about the route of the Exodus through the Saudi desert would need to be reviewed, even revised. But without warning, before there could be any reconsideration or apologies, in the small instant before the next number could drop down like a final curtain, Cornuke pointed into the distance. And in a tone of genuine wonder he asked, "Do you see what I see?"

He did not wait for an answer. Cornuke immediately swung the truck westward. He slammed down hard on the accelerator, and the truck began kicking up comets of sand as it sped into the flat, gray heart of the desert. He came to a stop in what appeared to be, to a skeptical Williams, nothing more than the very center of a large sunbaked plain. It was pockmarked with deep, scorched craters, and its surface was rutted with an intricate network of cracks that spread in all directions like tendrils. In its topography, this land was, Williams imagined, closer to a bleak, ruined portion of moonscape than anything he had previously encountered in the desert.

He followed Cornuke out of the truck more to stretch his legs than with any real expectations. But as soon as he took his first steps, he realized it was not sand beneath his boots. It was clay, a hard, sun-bleached, whitish clay. With a little effort, he managed to dig up a handful and crumbled it into small, stiff shards with his fingers. Then he understood. He was walking through a dried-up lake bed. In his mind he abruptly traveled back to the Montana of his youth: a landscape marked with dry alkaline flats. He was on the other side of the world, but he was standing in nearly a mirror image of those dried-up Montana lake beds that, with the spring rains, filled each year with a fresh yet bitter water.

Whatever remaining doubts he had were erased after he hurried over to inspect a nearby crater. It was a man-made well. On its slope, there was an indentation cut by a rope where a bucket, or some sort of container, had been lowered. The Arabs, he quickly deduced, still continued to dig for water in the depths of this parched lake bed. But it was Cornuke who pointed out the most indisputable part of the case Williams was already building. He gave a yell and Williams looked up. Not more than twenty yards off stood his friend—leaning against a tree. A tree that was adjacent to a dry, alkaline lake bed that was approximately forty kilometers from the Saudi coast and the Strait of Tiran. *Then Moses led Israel from the Red Sea and they went into the Desert of Shur. For three days they traveled into the desert without finding water. When they came to Marah they could not drink its water because it was bitter. . . . And the Lord showed him a tree, and he cast it into the waters, and the waters were made sweet.*

Yes, Williams told himself, it all fit.

WEEKS ago, standing on a land bridge in the Strait of Tiran, Williams had looked across to the distant coast and wondered if he would ever get an opportunity to set foot in Saudi Arabia. It all had seemed next to impossible. So it was with a sense of personal triumph that later that afternoon he walked on the pebbled beach at Ra's ash Shaykh Humayd and looked across the Gulf of Aqaba *toward* Egypt. But whatever pride he felt at that moment was, he would have quickly conceded, nothing more than a footnote, and a decidedly private one, when measured against what Cornuke and he had already accomplished. They were on their way to documenting the true route of the Exodus. They had already followed in Moses' footsteps across the Red Sea to the Springs of Marah, to the oasis at Elim, and then to the caves outside the modern-day village of Al Bad where Moses had lived with his family. They were on a historic journey. With a certainty that was nurtured, if not inflated, by these successes, Williams had no doubt that when they broke camp tomorrow they would be on their way to their greatest triumph—the site of the true mountain of God.

Williams stripped down to his underwear and ran out into the cool, cleansing water of the gulf. It was, in his contented mind, a celebration. He was enjoying his reward for what he had accomplished; just as he was relishing the monumental discovery he would soon make. He swam for a bit with big, powerful strokes, and then when he was completely spent, he turned to float on his back. It felt incredibly good just to drift, to let the water soak over him as it washed away the heat and sand and smell of the desert.

He stayed like that for a while, floating indolently. His eyes were shut, yet he knew he was drifting closer to the shore so he was unconcerned.

All at once Cornuke's voice pierced his sleepy mood. "A lionfish! Get out quick!" He opened his eyes to see Cornuke close enough so he could reach out to touch him, except he was swimming like a dynamo, arms churning, legs splashing, each stroke wild and desperate, a man hell-bent on escaping. That was enough to fill Williams with panic. He chased after his friend. Williams was an expert swimmer, vain about his stroke, but now he was suddenly formless, simply a body determined to reach the safety of the beach. It was only after both men were on the beach, nearly doubled over and still panting, that Williams asked what exactly a lionfish was. Cornuke was succinct. It was a large, puffy fish covered with tentacles that ended in barbed hooks. You bump up against it and you die. A lionfish had been swimming along less than a yard from where Williams was floating. If Cornuke had not happened to swim by when he did, Williams would very likely at this moment be lapsing into a coma that would lead to a quick death.

Williams could not speak. It seemed to take all his energy, all his remaining stamina, to hide from his friend the sharp, debilitating fear that was rushing through him. For the first time he understood the unpredictability of each new moment in this foreign land, and it left him feeling as woozy as if he had, in fact, been pierced by a lionfish. He found himself contemplating how unexpectedly his ambitions could be undermined. All his bold plans, all that he still hoped to accomplish, could have been destroyed by . . . a fish. Jabal al Lawz now seemed very far off in the desert. And he was ready to sink to his knees from the weight of all the uncertainty that lay ahead.

WILLIAMS slept on the beach that night, his mind a conflicting clutter of doubts and certainties. He thought of what they had seen out in the desert earlier that day, and as he drifted, half asleep, back to a vision of the Springs of Marah, he pondered something Cornuke had said. "A statute and an ordinance," God had decreed at that very spot, a blessing that would from that moment on forever protect the Israelites. In this almost dreamlike state, Williams began to persuade himself that his mission was similarly blessed. How else could he explain their getting even this far? Content, he drifted deeper into sleep, a real sleep, and he saw himself once again at Marah. But now the lake beds were overflowing with a sweet, cool water. And he was swimming in it, luxuriating, until he was suddenly swimming madly to the shore—but not fast enough. A lionfish caught up with him, and at the moment of contact there was, oddly, no pain, merely a sense of leaving. Yet he knew he was dying. He called out to Carla and the girls, and he saw them in the big room overlooking the Pacific, playing their harps. But worst of all, they could not hear him.

And then he saw before him the mountain of God. It was ringed in a glorious white light, but he could not approach it. Like Moses, he realized, he was being shown the Promised Land but denied this final reward. He woke up with a shudder, only to see that the light *was* real. It was coming from out of the desert, two perfect circles of amber light, headlights he knew at once, shining into their camp. Someone was watching them just like the night before. He sat up, instantly alert. And as if in response to his movement, the desert went black. The headlights had been extinguished. Before he could rouse Cornuke, he heard the distinct sound of a vehicle speeding off over the sand, and he kept listening until the noise disappeared into the faraway darkness.

So he let Cornuke sleep, but he remained awake for hours trying to sort it all through. The more he thought about it, the more he considered everything that had happened to them, in Saudi Arabia *and* in London, the more he failed to make any rational connections. There was a pattern, he decided, but he could not find a logic that held it all together. Finally, he gave up on reason. It was impossible to make sense of things. He would just have to accept them. In this new mood he found himself, to his surprise, praying for a statute and ordinance that would protect them from evil as they went off to the mountain. But he could not find in himself that pure faith. And by the time dawn came and lit up the Strait of Tiran, he was still wide awake and scared far beyond any previous dream.

33

IT was a long knife, the blade was easily eight inches, and it had one serrated edge that had been designed as a saw and another straight edge that, after some effort, had been honed as sharp as a razor. In the morning, when a still shaky Williams reported that their camp had been spied on again, Cornuke went hunting through his duffel for the knife. It was where he had packed it, beneath the metal detector. He examined the blade and, pleased, returned it to its sheath. Then he rolled up his chinos until they were just below his knee and tied the sheath around the thick muscle of his calf. When he lowered his pants leg, there was a small bulge above the top of his boot, but he felt no one would notice unless he was looking for something; and, as he matter-of-factly remarked to Williams, if that was the case, "a concealed weapon might very well be the least of our problems."

While Williams watched in intrigued silence, Cornuke executed a few practice draws, satisfying himself that the pants leg was loose enough that he could reach down and extract the knife in one nearly fluid motion. Then he pointed to the humpbacked shape of a large brown rock in the distance and, with the same tone he might have used to inquire about the weather, asked Williams how far off he thought it was. Twenty-five yards or so, Williams judged. Like a gunslinger drawing on his man, Cornuke suddenly reached down, and the next thing Williams saw was the long knife flying end over end in the air until it landed point down in the sand directly in front of the rock. "I'm ready. Anybody comes calling tonight, I'll be waiting," Cornuke said as he went off to retrieve his knife. And Williams could not help noting that there was not even a trace of a self-congratulatory smile across his stolid face.

But Williams was less confident. They had one knife. Who knew how many were out there watching, waiting to make their move? The potential odds were not very comforting at all, he decided. Cornuke, however, must have picked up on his worries and tried to be reassuring. "The Amalekites thought the children of Israel would be easy pickings when they saw them wandering through the desert," he said. "Well, they were in for a surprise. Same if anyone tries to mess with us. Like Joshua on the plains near Mount Sinai, I'll 'discomfit them with the edge of my sword.'" And as if to illustrate, he cut a couple of manly slices through the air with his big knife before returning it to its sheath.

Williams still had his doubts. Yet as he put his sleeping bag in the back of the white truck, he thought, yes, this is how it must have been back then, too. At the start of each new day was the daunting prospect of going off deeper into the unknown. The Israelites were also constantly surrounded by intimations of unseen yet powerful enemies. Of course, they were scared. Of course, they would be murmuring. And yet for them, too, there was the incredible prospect of God's mountain and all its glory waiting at the end of the journey. In the desert, he told himself, there was no such thing as ancient history.

MINUTES later they were on the road, heading away from the coast and on their way at last to Mount Sinai. They were flying.

Traveling east, they stuck to the roads drawn on their map with bright orange double lines, and they were happy to discover that they were, except for a few disconcertingly bumpy stretches, paved as promised. Encouraged, they pushed the little truck as fast as it would go and headed toward Tabuk. It had taken Moses, the Book of Exodus said, three arduous months to lead the tribes to the mountain. Cornuke and Williams were determined to get there as quickly as possible.

The time for thoughtful wandering, for searching for the traces of the Israelites' journey, was over. On their way to the Strait of Tiran they had already backtracked, or so they genuinely believed, over much of the path of the original Exodus. Now they wanted to get to the heart of their adventure. As Williams had pointed out before the pair broke camp, if they had indeed been following the Exodus, if the clues in the Bible were only more proof that they were on the right path, then it was likely, very likely, that at the end of trail, where X finally marked the spot, their grand theory would also be confirmed. They would find the gold of Exodus. And so, like sprinters heading into the homestretch, they pushed on toward the mountain. The Datsun offered no resistance, speeding along the road at a steady 60 miles an hour and letting off what sounded like a contented hum.

They were optimistic that this stage of the journey, at least, would be uneventful. Getting back to the outskirts of Tabuk would be no problem, and once they were near the city, they would have the best possible guide for the remainder of the expedition—David Fasold's handwritten, painstakingly precise instructions. He had been to Jabal al Lawz not once, but twice. And more reason to be encouraged, not even two years had passed since he had made his trip. In the desert, change rarely intruded; time was measured in the steady, repetitive beat of centuries. Fasold's carefully designated landmarks would, presumably, still be standing.

When sometime shortly after lunch they passed, just as Fasold had promised, the single, squat pump of the Al Kan gas station rising from the sand like a totem pole, the two men let out an unrestrained cheer. Exactly four kilometers down the road, by Fasold's count, was a turnoff. If they took that road a quick eight kilometers farther to a large rock outcropping, then, according to his instructions, they would be on a fairly direct path to the mountain. It would be, he had said, easy.

It wasn't. Despite an attentive and careful search, they could not for the life of them find the first turnoff. They drove back and forth over the dusty stretch of asphalt parallel to the gas station, counted off first ten, then twenty kilometers in both directions (on the unlikely possibility that Fasold had actually meant the turnoff was *before* the station), and still they could not find anything resembling, however vaguely, a road, or even a trail. Finally, when they had run out of alternatives, Cornuke continued on precisely four kilometers from the location of the gas pump, and then promptly executed his turn. All at once they were off the paved road, and they found themselves bouncing along the sand.

It was slow, deliberate going. Fasold had instructed them to look for the first rock pile at 8 kilometers, then another at precisely 16.8 kilometers, and, finally, a huge, pyramidal assemblage of rocks would be on their left when the trip odometer registered an exact 22.4 kilometers. Yet while they measured out each leg of the journey with meticulous precision, they could not find anything resembling Fasold's promised rock piles. Worse, each kilometer they drove away from the main road took them deeper and deeper into, they feared, a remote terrain that was full of lurking dangers.

One moment the Datsun would be in first gear, plowing with considerable effort through a thick, gray ocean of sand. Next, the little truck would be bouncing wildly over a kidney-jarring bed of rocks. The heat was an additional torture, continually assaulting them with its relentless force. It was as if, Williams would forever remember, a hair dryer had been aimed at their faces. Yet they continued on. After all they had been through, after their many unanticipated successes, they could not help feeling that they would look up and suddenly see the summit of a mountain, the mountain of God and Moses, rising before them. But it did not happen. They simply drove deeper and deeper into the vast, inhospitable Saudi desert. They were, Cornuke and Williams felt with an almost tangible uneasiness, all alone.

At last, Cornuke decided that beyond the distant horizon there would only be another flat, sandy horizon. "We're lost," he announced.

"Smack dab in the middle of nowhere," Williams agreed. "We'd better try to get back to the main road. Start over again from there."

Cornuke nodded. He swung the steering wheel in a broad circle, pressed his foot down hard on the accelerator, and began to execute a wide U-turn. But as the truck was completing its turn, the wheels started slipping, then spinning, and it sank deep into the soft sand until it could barely move forward at all. In his frustration, Cornuke gave the truck more gas, hoping to power it out of its hole. It was the worst possible strategy. As the truck shook futilely, walls of sand collapsed about the wheels until it was buried up to its axles. When he stepped on the accelerator again, there was no movement at all; the wheels might just as well have been locked in place.

They had no choice but to get out and try somehow to extricate the truck. Cornuke, embarrassed, attempted to atone for his error by coming up with all sorts of desperately inventive techniques. He wedged rocks under the wheels, then improvised a pillow of sagebrush, and when those efforts failed to give the vehicle any traction, he let out a roar of despair that, Williams was certain, must have echoed across the entire desert.

"Now what do we do?" Williams said. In his mind he was already rationing the food. They had enough to stretch for three days, perhaps even four if they were not greedy. Water, however, he knew would be another problem entirely, and it would have to be dealt with a lot sooner.

Cornuke refused to give up. "I'll show you what we can do," he said. He approached the back of the truck. Slowly, taking great care, he set his two strong legs comfortably apart, wrapped his callused hands tightly over the rear bumper of the truck, and then, his body straining from his calves to his shoulders, pushed straight ahead with every bit of his ferocious, frustrated might. The truck would not budge, but Cornuke still would not surrender. His entire body arched into this great effort, straining against itself as it defiantly challenged an immovable object. He pushed mightily. He would not quit. And then something gave—his body broke. The wave of pain started in the small of his back, but in an instant it had traveled like a red-hot speeding laser to every nerve ending in his brain, and he collapsed in a heap, wild with pain. He felt for a moment as if he could not breathe. When this passed, there was another sobering realization: the slightest movement was excruciating. His football injuries had returned, he knew at once, to defeat him. The scarred and herniated discs were once again thrown out of kilter, only now it was worse than ever.

Williams found the courage not to panic. Instead, while Cornuke lay there with his eyes shut as tightly as if he were already dead, he forced himself to take stock of the situation. His partner—the colossus he counted on—was prostrate on the ground, and even the smallest movement caused him to clench his teeth and made his eyes tear up from the agony. Their truck was buried in a tomb of sand. Food and water were not a problem yet, but they would be since they were tens or maybe hundreds of kilometers from the nearest village or camp or even person. And in hours night would descend upon them while they waited helplessly in the middle of nowhere.

Williams thought up a dozen plans and just as quickly abandoned each of them as rash, or senseless, or impossible. But just as he was trying to come up with something, a strategy that would let them both live to tell about this day, he thought he heard something. A distinct noise . . . like an engine. He looked up, and not that far off were two small trucks leading a train of camels. He waved and shouted to them wildly, calling for help at the top of his lungs, and they must have noticed him because the procession suddenly switched directions. They were now coming straight toward him. And while he waited for their arrival, he knew, despite the enthusiasm he tried to convey to Cornuke, that these Bedouins moving across the hot desert sand would be either their salvation or something a lot worse.

THERE were three men and perhaps twice that many boys, and they quickly went to work like a small, well-organized army. They did not speak any English, but apparently the problem was obvious. Without any discussion, one man hitched up his frayed *thobe* and got behind the wheel. As he gunned the motor, the other two Bedouins positioned themselves by the front and rear bumpers and methodically rocked the truck back and forth. When at last it slowly started to move, the gaggle of boys joined in, pushing the truck steadily forward with a high-spirited, giggling energy. The men worked without comment for perhaps twenty full minutes. When they were done, the truck roared out of its pit and settled onto flat, level sand. And another miracle, Cornuke could by this point stand. With considerable effort he even managed, to both his and Williams' surprise, to take a few tentative steps.

To celebrate, a buoyant Williams searched his belongings for an appropriate reward and wound up distributing fresh oranges to his saviors. At that happy moment he would have, if they had been able to ask, just as readily bought each of the Bedouins a new truck, or camel, or even, he later joked, a new wife. But as it turned out, the oranges were the perfect gift. The children particularly relished the sweet juice, and they held the fruit high above their heads and let it drip slowly into their parched mouths. The men, Cornuke and Williams observed, took an even greater pleasure in the boys' delight.

It was only as the Bedouins were preparing to leave that Williams realized he would have to ask for more help or else it quickly would be too late. He huddled first, however, with Cornuke, and the two men quietly discussed their options. "We're still lost," Williams began. "Maybe we should try to get them to lead us back to the main road."

"Lot of good that'll do," Cornuke said sourly. Every word, Williams noted, seemed to take a great deal of effort. "It would make more sense to ask them to take us to Jabal al Lawz," Cornuke finally suggested in a thin, brittle voice.

Williams disagreed. Wyatt and Fasold, he pointed out, had been arrested simply for going to the mountain. He didn't think it would be very wise to announce Jabal al Lawz as their destination. Who knew what kind of trouble that could get them in? But he had an idea. While Cornuke had been flat on his back, the truck buried, Williams had scoured his mind, searching for possible ways out of their predicament. One plan he had played with was to head off on foot to search for the camp of a shepherd Fasold had mentioned who lived in the vicinity of the mountain, a Bedouin by the name of Ibrahim Frich. Perhaps, he told Cornuke, we could try to persuade these Arabs to lead us to Frich. After a night's sleep at that camp, we might be able to find the mountain on our own.

"I'm game," Cornuke said. But he later would admit that, in his weakened condition, it was the prospect of a night's restorative sleep that was the most promising part of the proposal.

It took some complicated and energetic negotiations before Williams, waving his hands quickly and talking slowly in his pidgin Arabic, managed to convey to the Bedouins that they wanted to be led to the camp of Ibrahim Frich. Even then, he had to volunteer another dozen oranges to clinch the deal. It was not until nearly four in the afternoon, when mercifully the heat was finally starting to break, that the convoy of three trucks and a line of baying camels headed once again on into the desert.

THEY turned eastward up a large, flat ravine, nearly three-quarters of a mile wide, and drove for what seemed days but, when Cornuke checked his watch, turned out to have been only forty minutes. He was still in pain, but at this level it was manageable, even, he felt, oddly familiar. Williams, who was now at the wheel, tried as they slowed down to find their position on the map, but it was useless. There were no landmarks he could use as reference points. He found Tabuk on the map, and he saw a mustard-colored sea of desert surrounding it in all directions. They were somewhere in the desert outside Tabuk, on their way to the camp of a shepherd called Ibrahim Frich. That was the best he could do.

At last they drove into a campsite, or at least that was what Williams supposed it was since there were crowds of scurrying children, barking dogs, and a corral full of camels. The lead truck came to a stop, and when the Bedouin in the frayed *thobe* got out, Williams followed him. He walked purposefully toward a red-striped tent beyond the corral, and Williams did his best to keep up. When they got to the tent, the Bedouin called out in a harsh, rude-sounding Arabic. There was no response, but without any hesitation, he lifted the flap and entered. Williams decided to go in after him.

At first Williams thought the tent was empty. Then, as his eyes grew accustomed to the darkness, he saw an old man, his wizened skin the color of mahogany, sleeping peacefully in a corner. The Bedouin, with what struck Williams as great tenderness, managed to rouse the old man to a sort of wheezing wakefulness. The two Arabs spoke for only a few moments. When the old man returned once again to his prone position, the Bedouin marched out of the tent.

He was waiting for Williams by the camel corral. "Ibrahim Frich. Tabuk," the Bedouin said.

"How long?" Williams asked, and he spread his hands apart, a gesture that he hoped conveyed the passing of time.

The Bedouin seemed to understand. But the best answer he could come up with was a large, perplexed shrug.

It was then that Williams, desperate, made a sudden decision. "Jabal al Lawz," he said, and he motioned imploringly with his hand toward the Arab. The implication, he hoped, was clear: I want you to take me there.

The Arab began to shake his head emphatically. No, no, he was clearly trying to say. He shook an admonishing finger at Williams.

But Williams was insistent. He had come too far to be put off.

"Jabal al Lawz," he said once more, and again motioned with his hand to indicate he wanted the Arab to take him there.

This time the Arab did not answer. His brown eyes gazed downward toward Williams' shoes. He clearly wanted to end the conversation. It occurred to Williams that the Arab was scared. Yet he was determined and repeated his request, summoning up an officious snarl that had served well in the past. But it did not have the desired effect. The Bedouin simply turned and walked very quickly toward his truck.

IT took every orange Cornuke and Williams had, and still they had to throw in a pouch of the dehydrated Stroganoff before one of the Bedouins, despite the vociferous protests of his friends, agreed to take them to Jabal al Lawz. He led the way in a blue pickup, and they followed in their Datsun. Williams drove and neither of the men spoke. The possibility that at last, after all their efforts, they would finally see the mountain to which Moses had led the Israelites, where God had descended, had them on edge. The impending moment was too great. They concentrated on keeping up with the Bedouin's truck as it slowly made its way across a flat piece of desert, and then began to weave around a small brown hill. But just as it was rounding the hill, before it emerged onto an open plain, the truck came to a stop.

The driver got out, and Cornuke and Williams joined him. He had a small toylike telescope in his hand, and he kept his body pressed against the base of the hill as if he was trying to hide.

"Jabal al Lawz?" Williams asked. He still did not understand.

The Bedouin handed Williams the telescope and pointed beyond the corner of the hill where they were concealed.

Williams went out into the open and raised the telescope to his eye. And there it was—a mountain rising majestically up into the sky just as Fasold had described it. There were two sharp peaks and a large, graceful tree growing between the twin summits. It was the mountain of God.

Williams was trembling. The thrill had been anticipated, and yet it still was overwhelming. Slowly, with great care, he began to lower the telescope, scanning toward the base of the mountain. He wanted to study it. But then he saw something that struck him with the force of a blow to the chest. There, surrounding the holiest spot on earth, the mountain he had traveled halfway around the world to climb, was a fifteen-foot-high chain-link fence topped with barbed wire. And inside the fence, at the foot of the mountain, was a guardhouse that he knew at once had to be filled with soldiers.

34

THEY were stunned. In all of their imagined scenarios, Cornuke and Williams had never conceived one even remotely as unlikely as this: the mountain of God had been transformed into a military fortress. They now used Williams' binoculars and took turns staring at the peak in the distance. They were still unsettled, but right from the start they realized what was at stake and what had to be decided.

They could stay. Or they could go. It was that simple. Then again, as Williams acknowledged to Cornuke with complete seriousness, it was also that complicated. There are decisions that have the power to change, to transform, the course of an entire life. Both men fully understood this was one of them.

They could stand outside the barbed-wire fence and take one more long look at the mountain, then return to Tabuk and get on a plane that would take them, and their theories and expectations, back home. Or they could attempt to penetrate a remote Saudi military installation, try to sneak past the watchful guards, avoid the inevitable patrols, and, under the cover of darkness, make history by climbing to the summit of the mountain where God had given His law to Moses. And if both their luck and the nighttime shadows held, they could furtively dig at the base of the mountain for its treasure—the long-buried gold of Exodus. Of course, they first had to work their way up an 8,465-foot mountain in the dead of night without taking a wrong step—a narrow ledge? an unseen rock?—and falling hundreds of feet. If they were not shot without warning by an alert Saudi marksman. Or if they were not apprehended by a patrol of soldiers and handed over to a royal court to face the inevitable death sentence for espionage. For what other logical explanation could there be for two foreigners with phony travel documents sneaking into a restricted military compound in the middle of the desert?

Nearly two years of intense effort, education, intrigue, and precious dreams. It was as if they had spent the time in training for a larger, monumental life. Now if they were ever to fulfill this grand promise, they would first have to make a simple decision. They could go. Or they could stay.

They continued to stare at the mountain as if immobilized. The Bedouin, his job done, had left, but neither of the men seemed to notice. Soon it began to turn cool, and with the evening a small, rustling wind slowly began to pick up. To Cornuke's sensitive ears, it wailed across the desert like the steady, high-pitched keen of a flock of Arab women in mourning.

"We can't spend the night here," he said abruptly. "The last thing we need is for some soldier to spot us." Williams agreed, and in a moment they were back in the truck.

Williams was once again at the wheel and drove away from the mountain, heading, quite arbitrarily, south. He did not go far before they discovered there was a dusty trail that led away from the desert valley, and, shifting to low, he followed it as it climbed upwards. In time, the narrow, twisting trail leveled out into what appeared to be a vast, flat plain. They drove until the twin peaks of the mountain were out of sight, and then, for good measure, they drove farther. When they came to a wide and deep bowl-shaped gully, an indentation that seemed as if it could have been a footprint made in the soft sand by a passing giant, Williams brought the truck to a halt. They pitched their camp in the very center of this sandy bowl and ate their dehydrated meal as thousands of bright stars shone down on them.

During the long, eerie desert night, feeling as alone as if they were stranded on another planet, they discussed their dilemma. They went at it from every angle: what was at stake, how much they had to win, how much they had to lose. They started out analyzing the situation with a cool logic, and when they discovered that could take them only so far, they tried a more romantic sort of wishful thinking. Faith, too, played a part in many of the equations they were constructing; they wanted to believe in their ultimate success. Naturally, they tried to make sense of what they had seen, and both agreed there seemed to be only one possible explanation. Fasold's expedition, or perhaps it was his trial, had inadvertently alerted the Saudis to what Jabal al Lawz really was. The troops must have been deployed not long after that to secure the sacred mountain.

But in all their long night of talk, never once did either man complain or even hint that it had been a mistake to come across the world to Saudi Arabia, to have gone this far. For even if they were ultimately to decide that the odds stacked against them were too great, that for safety's sake their expedition must end immediately, both men believed that they had already seen things few other men had ever seen, and that their lives had been blessed.

Did they sleep that night? Neither Williams or Cornuke would remember actually dozing off, but they both would admit that they must have. For suddenly a closed-eyed Williams was brought around to an unexpected consciousness. A strong light was shining straight at him from out in the desert. In an instant, he was alert. Headlights, he realized, no doubt from the same vehicle whose unknown occupants had been spying on them for days. He needed, unobtrusively, to wake Cornuke. But when he looked closely, he saw that although Cornuke was lying on his side as if still asleep, one hand was resting behind his back, in the shadows. In it he held his long knife by the handle, ready to throw.

Without a word, they waited for something to happen. In Williams' fired-up mind, he could see Bedouin marauders preparing to charge down into their gully. Cornuke did not bother to give the enemy a name or a face. He simply planned to throw his knife without hesitation into the chest of the first man who came into their camp. The wait lasted forever, and each moment was excruciating. But finally there was the distinct sound of a vehicle turning around, and then its lights swung away from the gully and it drove off, disappearing quickly behind the wall of night.

It was not long before they were once again totally alone. The intruder had vanished without a trace; it might as well have been another of the desert's tricks, a mirage. Only the stars and the bright moon remained. With a strong sense of relief, Cornuke replaced the knife in its sheath and soon closed his eyes. But Williams was beyond any peace. It was not just speculation about who might be out there that made it impossible for him to sleep. There were other things goading him on. Even after all their talk, nothing had been resolved. Tomorrow was getting closer, yet it remained a mystery of possibilities. And it was these conflicting alternatives that continued to perplex him, confusing his mind with dangerous choices and exorbitant hopes until the bright desert dawn.

THE morning began with a new disaster. Back in California, a life that now seemed so irrelevant that it might as well have been part of a previous incarnation, Williams had purchased a state-of-the-art metal detector. Fasold in his letter had bragged about the immediate success he had had with his machine, and Williams, always looking for an edge, had paid close attention. From the moment he had started making serious plans to go to Mount Sinai, he had been determined to bring along the sort of technology that could lead him to the gold.

He had packed up his new, highly touted purchase with great

care and taken it on each leg of their journey. It was with them in London. When they headed off on the spur of the moment to Egypt, he decided to carry it along too; the mysterious break-in to his hotel room was, he instinctively felt, a warning. And how many anxious hours had he spent putting together a story involving oil prospecting for his royal sponsor that, while patently absurd, he nevertheless hoped would get the machine past customs in Jeddah? And how grateful he was when, remarkably, the metal detector did not even provoke a raised eyebrow from the Saudi officials. Only now, this of all mornings, the damn machine did not work.

The day had begun just as the night before had ended. They still had not reached a decision. But by the time the strong, warm glow from this first light was promising once again to turn the desert into a cauldron, Cornuke took charge. Without even proposing the matter as open for discussion, he announced an agenda, or at least an interim one. They would return to the area surrounding the mountain and, as he put it, doing his best to sound offhanded and relaxed, "feel things out." "For the time being," he advised, "we forget about even approaching the fence. We keep our distance. At the first rumble from the guardhouse, we're in our truck and hightailing it back to Tabuk." He insisted there was still a great deal that could be discovered. The Bible was full of clues about what they should find near the mountain if Jabal al Lawz was Mount Sinai.

And he had an additional argument. Once again trying to keep things casual, Cornuke said that if they got lucky, they might even stumble across a back door, a hole in the barbed-wire perimeter far from the prying eyes and ears of the soldiers. Of course, the last time they had gone off to take the scent of a place was at Elim, and they had run into a heavily armed battalion. But he chose not to bring that up.

Williams said he was game, but Cornuke thought he looked far away in his mind. He might as well have been contemplating a doctor's grim diagnosis. After another moment, however, Williams began hunting through his duffel for the metal detector. The Bible, he reminded Cornuke as he started to assemble the machine, said there had been as many as a million Israelites camped in the valley around Sinai. "There's got to be something buried out there. A piece of pottery? Maybe even some coin? Hell, there must be graves at least." But just as Williams seemed to be coming around, as the burden of their still unresolved decision seemed to be lifting, he made his discovery. The damn machine would not work. Williams tried everything. Showing impressive patience, he reassembled it from scratch. He played with the dials. He twisted the knobs in all kinds of combinations. But no matter what he did, he could not get a reading. Finally, it was Cornuke who after only a cursory inspection zeroed in on the problem—there were no batteries.

"Impossible!" Williams shouted. He was so intent on making sure that this sort of disaster would never happen that he had bought a new set of batteries the first afternoon he had gone shopping in London. He had found them in the same store that had sold him the night-vision binoculars. And as soon as he had returned to the hotel, he had loaded them. The machine had worked like a charm. "Impossible," he repeated. But when he checked the battery case, he saw that Cornuke was right: It was empty.

And that, he realized, made sense only if someone had gone to the trouble of deliberately removing the batteries. But that was impossible, too. And then he remembered when he had tested the machine. It was the evening before they had gone gambling. And that night someone had broken into his room. It had never occurred to him that someone would have left the machine yet taken the batteries. But now Williams realized that was precisely what had happened. He just could not understand why.

IT was not a mystery that would be solved standing around in the desert, the two men finally realized. It made sense only as one more piece in a pattern of curious and unexplained events. Occurrences, they were now starting to suspect but still could not begin to prove or even comprehend, that were somehow tied to their decision to go to Saudi Arabia. And to Jabal al Lawz.

So they did their best to steady their increasing fears and tried not to brood over their latest suspicions. Instead, they decided to follow the morning's original plan and return to the mountain. It was the only choice that made any sense. Besides, Cornuke pointed out when they were back in the truck, the metal detector would have done them little good. There was a fence and soldiers separating them from the treasure.

"Perhaps you're right," Williams said. "Even if we used it outside the fence, the machine might have attracted attention." He was driving, and, with some concentration, he managed to retrace the route to the hill where they had parked yesterday. They got out of the truck and walked toward the open plain. And at once all other mysteries receded.

The mountain overwhelmed them. It stood there majestic in the clear morning light, a strong, dark tower reaching up into the sky. But they felt even more than they saw. It was not rational, yet it was very real. The mountain was *radiant.* It was, they knew at once, the mountain of God. The moment was beyond words, so all they could do was stand there staring into the distance until Cornuke opened his Bible and, without prelude, began to read. His voice, Williams said he will always remember, was gentle, yet the words he read struck with a force that left him shaken.

"'On the third day, as morning dawned, there was thunder, and lightning, and a dense cloud upon the mountain, and a very loud blast of the horn; and all the people who were in the camp trembled. Moses led the people out of the camp, and they took their places at the foot of the mountain.

"'Now Mount Sinai was all in smoke, for the Lord had come down upon it in fire; the smoke rose like the smoke of a furnace, and the whole mountain trembled violently. The blare of the horn grew louder and louder. As Moses spoke, God answered him in thunder. The Lord came down upon Mount Sinai, on the top of the mountain; and the Lord called Moses to the top of the mountain; and Moses went up. . . .'"

Did Williams, looking up at that moment toward the summit as if he might have been one of the ancient Israelites, *really* hear the blast of heavenly horns? The thunder? Did he see the supernal fire, taste the celestial smoke? Perhaps not. But while listening to Cornuke read, with Jabal al Lawz as the momentous backdrop for each resonating verse, he felt as if he might have. The Old Testament, and its raging, all-powerful God, seemed very real.

Then this mood exploded and another reality intruded. In the distance, from somewhere behind the fence, there was the noise of a dog's angry bark. A watchdog, Williams thought in a panic. But Cornuke remained calm. "A sheepdog getting his flock in line," he suggested reasonably. But before Williams had a chance to accept that, there was something else: the unmistakably clear, loud crack of a far-off rifle shot. All at once he took off for the truck, with Cornuke, his back muscles strained to the point of agony, hobbling after him.

By the time the Datsun was moving across the desert, it seemed easier to believe that neither the dog's anger nor the subsequent shot had been provoked by their presence. They had been too far off to have been noticed, they reassured themselves. So instead of returning immediately to Tabuk as they had earlier agreed, they decided to continue to hunt around the mountain. It was not the final decision. That was a reckoning that was still waiting; but like any easily broken vow, it took them one step closer.

THEY returned to their mission, and soon it was the only thing on their minds. At first, as they started to explore the desert that stretched beyond the perimeter of the mountain, they made sure to keep their distance, staying out of sight of the guardhouse. Yet after a while the activity and the heat worked to dull their fears. They even stopped worrying about the Saudi soldiers. Under the full blast of the midday sun, they were completely caught up in the search for a battlefield.

"'Then came Amalek'"—as the Amalekites, a fierce tribe of desert nomads, were known—"'and fought with Israel at Rephidim. And Moses said to Joshua, Choose us out men, and go out, fight with Amalek. Tomorrow I will stand on the top of the hill with the rod of God in my hand.'"

Cornuke, once again, had worked it all out, he said when he had finished reading. To his mind, several truths were revealed in that chapter. First, that Rephidim, the site of battle, had to be very near Sinai. He deduced this, he told Williams, because when the tribes first camped at Rephidim, they began, the Bible said, to murmur that there was no water for them to drink. So what did God instruct Moses to do? "'Behold, I will stand before thee there upon the rock in Horeb; and thou shalt smite the rock, and there shall come water out of it, that the people may drink.'"

Now, Cornuke continued, Horeb was used interchangeably in the Bible for Sinai. In fact, biblical scholars believe this was the same rock where God had first spoken to Moses when he was a shepherd tending his flock at the foot of the mountain. Therefore, if the battlefield was near the rock that miraculously gushed water, then the actual site, as he breezily put it, "can't be more than a hop, skip, and a jump" from Mount Sinai. His second deduction was also pure common sense. The conflict was not merely a raid by marauding nomads, but a huge, ferocious battle fought by large armies. It had lasted from sunup to sundown: "'But Moses' hands were heavy; and they took a stone, and put it under him, and he sat thereon; and Aaron and Hur stayed up his hands, the one on the one side, and the other on the other side; and his hands were steady until the going down of the sun.'" And if the battle had raged on for quite possibly twelve full hours, Cornuke continued, it must have involved sizable forces. The Israelis had a potential army, it said in the Book of Numbers, of 603,000 men. Since the battle went on for a full day, since it was so fiercely contested, it was logical to assume that the Amalekites had brought a comparably sized force, a genuine army, onto the field. "We're looking for one big plain," he said, "a site vast enough for two large armies to go at it tooth and nail for hours."

And, he concluded, there was still another revealing detail in the text. Moses, the rod of God in his hand, had followed the course of the battle from a hilltop. If they found the battlefield, there would be a nearby hill, or at the very least some sort of promontory, that offered a commanding view over the vast plain below.

They had their clues—proximity to Jabal al Lawz, a wide, open space, and a telltale hilltop—and they threw themselves into the hunt. They drove north from the mountain, but only for a short time. Williams, on a whim, turned south, and then they found themselves entering a wide, flat expanse.

It was a level plain the size, he guessed, of maybe a dozen football fields placed end to end. The Datsun crossed it as easily as if it were a stretch of blacktop. And when Williams stopped the truck and pointed to the brown camel's hump of a hill that sat at one end, to the east and close to Jabal al Lawz, neither of the men was surprised. They had known they would find it. It had to be. This was the wilderness of Exodus, and it was a desert full of miracles.

THERE are certain moments when the shock of recognition can fill the mind with a sudden clarity that is the foundation of a pure, confident knowledge. That was how Cornuke and Williams felt that day. The Bible was no longer simply a story, it was history: It all had happened. As they drove around the mountain, they knew they were crossing over the very land where the twelve tribes had been gathered. They saw a city of tents stretching for miles. Cooking fires lit up the desert sky, flocks of children scampered mischievously about. They could hear an ancient nation calling out across time, fearful, yet exhilarated with the wonder, the momentousness of it all: We have come to this mountain to be anointed by God.

Emboldened by their discovery, now almost reckless, they moved closer and closer to the mountain. The guardhouse was soon in view, but they were no longer cautious. They were caught up in other concerns. And effortlessly, without even the pretense of detective work, more pieces of the puzzle began to slide into place.

Now Moses kept the flock of Jethro his father-in-law, the priest of Midian; and he led the flock to the back or west side of the wilderness, and came to Horeb or Sinai, the mountain of God. And there it was, a mountain with vegetation on its back side where sheep could graze. A mountain not far from the caves of Elim, where Jethro lived. A mountain surrounded not by desolation, the oceans of sand or inhospitable rock of the desert, but a mountain that faced a relatively verdant valley, a suitable home to the Israelites for the eleven months they camped at Sinai. It all fit, but further evidence was no longer necessary. The case was closed. They believed.

And yet they still could be surprised. Fasold had mentioned that there were petroglyphs drawn on a pile of large rocks not too far from the base of the mountain, and they decided to hunt for them. It would be, they realized, an expedition that would take them even closer to the soldiers, but they were so charged up by what they had already found that they were willing to take the risk. They parked the truck behind a small rise they hoped would prevent its being seen from the guardhouse and went off on foot.

As they got closer to the fence, they decided to separate. They could cover more ground that way, but it was also Cornuke's small strategic concession to the danger that was nearby. If soldiers happened to be patrolling outside the fence, one man would strike them as less threatening than two, or so he tried to convince himself. Williams took the higher route, climbing up toward the summit of some stubby, rocky cliffs. Cornuke, his back still a constant, throbbing pain, stuck to an examination of the tall rocks gathered near their base.

It took Williams an exhausting hour to make his way up one side of the cliff, but he found nothing. He had started to work his way down the other slope when he heard his name being excitedly called. Hell, Bob, he thought, why don't you just go up to the guardhouse and knock on the door? He quickly responded with a sharp whistle, and it was an effective reprimand. It seemed to quiet his friend. It took Williams about fifteen minutes to make his way down to where Cornuke was standing. As he approached, he could see Cornuke was giving him a triumphant two thumbs up. Now Williams became excited too.

But he was not prepared for what he saw a moment later. There was another fifteen-foot fence topped by barbed wire. And on the fence was a blue and white sign in Arabic and English. The English warned: "THIS IS AN ARCHAEOLOGICAL SITE, DO NOT ENTER." And behind the fence were two large rocks, boulders really. The stone at its thick base was, he estimated, ten feet long and perhaps twice as high. On top of it was another smaller, yet still huge rock with a flat, almost smooth surface *as if it were an altar.* And painted on these rocks were distinct drawings of cows—not sheep, not animals that were native to the desert, but cattle. In a land where there were no cattle. And these were cattle drawn with large, graceful horns, cattle that even to Williams' untrained eye looked Egyptian, the very image of the Apis and Hathor bulls he had seen in books. But, he realized when he looked closer, there was more. The stick figures in the petroglyphs were not hunting. They were holding a cow above their heads—*as if they were worshiping it.*

"And Aaron said unto them: 'Break off the golden rings, which are in the ears of your wives, of your sons, and of your daughters, and bring them unto me.' . . . And he received it at their hand, and fashioned it with a graving tool, and made it a molten calf; and they said: 'This is thy god, O Israel, which brought thee up out of the land of Egypt.' And when Aaron saw this, he built an altar before it."

Williams looked with astonishment at Cornuke. His friend simply answered with a mute but confirming nod. Yes, he was saying, this is what you think it is. We are standing in front of the altar of the golden calf.

BUT they had not been to the mountain. Like Moses—and at once Williams remembered his own dream—he was being allowed to see the Promised Land, but he could not enter it. Unless he crossed the fence.

It was still light when they returned to the gully to make camp. The two men had scrupulously avoided speaking at any point in the course of their long day about the large decision that still remained. It was as if they felt that articulating the problem would hasten a resolution; and, they knew, there was an equal chance that they could make the wrong one as easily as the right one. They could go. Or they could stay. But the decision could no longer be deferred.

Ultimately, it would be Cornuke's choice. He was their tactician, their strategist, the professional with the steely nerves. That was why Williams had recruited him. If they were going to sneak into a military compound, it would have to be Cornuke's call. When they returned to camp, he went off by himself to sort things out.

His back was still a misery, and he found a stick to help him hobble around. He used it as a staff, and perhaps that was why he found himself thinking of Moses. Moses, he remembered, had once been a simple shepherd who had tended his flock in this very desert. For all Cornuke knew, Moses had rested on the spot where he now seated himself. He sat for a while in a deep silence, hardly moving, trying to make things work in his mind. But, as if he no longer had control of his thoughts, all his introspection led back to the example of Moses. Moses had been uncertain at first, daunted by the challenges and the obstacles in his way. Moses' adult life had been a forty-year lull, a seemingly inconsequential exile that led up to a defining moment: his decision to return, against all rational odds, to Egypt. Moses had been tested, and he did not back down. Moses had stepped forward, and into history.

The familiar desert wind, high-pitched and abrasive, had picked up by the time he returned to the campsite. His friend had started a fire, and Cornuke approached it. But his intention was not to warm himself. Instead, he cast his crutch into the flames. He had made up his mind that he would not need it anymore.

And he said, "More than anything else, I want to stand on the top of Mount Sinai. Let's do it."

35

IT was after midnight when they left the gully, but a full moon lit up the desert as boldly as if it were a stage. They went on foot, two men in black, and the unexpected light, Cornuke and Williams realized at once, was a mixed blessing. They would be able to see where they were going; at the same time, it would also be easier for anyone to see them. But they had made their decision and there was no talk of turning back.

The hours before they had moved out of the camp had been busy. Williams had anxiously checked and then rechecked the infrared night-vision binoculars he had bought in London, and, to his relief, they worked perfectly. He went over the length of the thick rope he had bought in Tabuk, satisfying himself that there were no frayed spots before placing it in his backpack. Finally, using a smooth stick he had found as a pointer, Cornuke drew a crude map in the sand. His plan, as he succinctly explained it to Williams, was that they should cross the plain at the base of the mountain from the west and head straight to the fence. That angle of attack should take them far enough away from the guardhouse so that, he hoped, the sleeping soldiers would not hear them climbing over, or, if it seemed easier, cutting a hole. Once they were inside, it was simply a matter of finding a trail that would lead them up the mountain.

It was, he knew, a flexible, almost extemporaneous plan. But he also understood that once they were inside the fence anything could happen. They had no idea what was waiting for them on the other side. There really was no point in working things out in any detail. "You do what you can, and then you improvise," his SWAT team leader had lectured, and he had learned to respect that rule. But Cornuke had also been in enough tight spots to know that ultimately luck would decide things. And, he told himself, he was feeling lucky tonight. He did, however, take one precaution. He asked Williams to help him gather up a few sticks and some sagebrush, which he then piled onto their air mattresses in the shape of two figures. With the blankets pulled up, they looked, at least from a distance, like sleeping forms.

"Anyone comes around tonight, they'll see we're tucked in safe and sound. Same as usual," he said. "Nothing for them to worry about."

"Unless this is the night they decide to wake us up for a chat," Williams replied, only to regret it instantly. But Cornuke acted as if he had not even heard. They had decided to go. There was no longer any point in worrying about what they could not control.

"Got your climbing gloves?" he asked Williams. "The rope?" Williams nodded.

"Then what are we waiting for?" Cornuke said. Without looking back, he took the first step away from the gully and toward the mountain.

It was Williams who first spotted the sentry. Up until that moment, as they had made their way across the plain and then down the steep trail that led to Jabal al Lawz, he had convinced himself that he was no longer afraid. The steady activity of walking miles in the moonlight and the unspoken discipline of keeping a brisk pace while also making sure to muffle his footsteps into a soft tattoo against the hard sand required him to focus entirely on the mission. His commitment was complete. Had he ever known another life? He would never have believed it. There was only now. Williams congratulated himself that he had become like Cornuke. He, too, was a rock.

They had made their way after about half an hour to the tall cliff where only two days ago the Bedouin had shown them Jabal al Lawz for the first time. On Cornuke's signal, they would leave this cover and go out into the broad, open valley that spread in front of the mountain and head for the fence. Williams was coiled in a half crouch, ready to make his dash, when at the last possible instant Cornuke dropped a heavy, restraining hand on his shoulder. Silence was the rule, so he pointed to the mountain and then to the night-vision binoculars around Williams' neck.

Williams understood. He pulled himself up and began to scan the mountainside. That was when he saw the telltale glow from what he knew must be a cigarette. He adjusted the range on the binoculars until he had a clear picture. Illuminated in the lurid green light of the device, the cigarette, he could now see, was dangling from the hand of a Bedouin. He had a rifle slung over his shoulder, and a bandolier filled with bullets crisscrossed his chest. But what spooked Williams most of all were the man's eyes. The Arab, a model of disciplined attention, was staring out into the moonlit desert—watching. And at that moment Williams knew his fate. They would never make it up the mountain, but they would still try. He was a condemned man.

He handed the binoculars to Cornuke, who began his own methodical survey of the mountain. Why bother? Williams felt like shouting. Let's do it! The truth was, he wanted to go while he still had the will. If he did not have the courage, he still had the adrenaline. "What are we waiting for?" he finally whispered in frustration. Cornuke, however, only raised an admonishing finger. He would not be rushed. At last, his survey finally completed, he motioned for Williams to follow him.

Cornuke walked away from the cliff, back into the desert, and covered a good twenty yards before he came to a stop. Now they could talk. He laid it all out quickly; this was not the time for theories, only facts. There was not just a single sentry, he said. There were three. He drew an X in the sand and told Williams to think of it as the guardhouse. About the X, in a small semicircle, he used a finger to make three distinct dots. Each dot, he explained, was a guard. They were spread out across the face of the mountain in a curving row directly above the concrete structure.

"Protecting their sleeping buddies?" Williams asked.

"Doesn't matter," Cornuke said. "We take what we know and use it. Tomorrow we can talk about the 'whys.'"

Another time Williams might have disagreed. He enjoyed taking things apart, looking at them from all angles. But tonight, standing in the moonlit Saudi desert as they prepared to sneak into a military compound, he just wanted to get on with it. "So you got an idea?" he asked.

Cornuke nodded. There was, Williams can still recall, a moment's hesitation. And in that silence Williams had time to wonder if his friend, too, was having his doubts. But then he heard Cornuke's voice and it was confident. "Here's what we do," he said.

It was, by necessity, a simple plan. Since the watchers were, for whatever reason, congregated above the guardhouse, the two men would now enter the plain from the east, circling wider than they had originally planned, toward the far side of the mountain. They needed to rush the fence at a point where the soldiers in the guardhouse would not hear them and the sentries would have no chance of seeing them. Both men were aware that these tactics were not radically different from the ones that had been previously worked out. In fact, it was not much of a plan at all. But they had come too far not to give it a try just the same.

. . .

It's a shooting gallery and I'm the wooden duck, Williams thought. On Cornuke's silent signal, he ran in a crouch across the open plain in front of the mountain. The full moon, he felt, was a spotlight focused directly on him. Worse, there was nowhere to hide. The plain seemed as vast and as empty as an ocean. He kept his head down, but that was more because he was afraid to see what was happening than because he was worried about stumbling. He wondered what would come first, if he would hear the shot or feel the bullet smacking into his back, and he made a wild promise to himself to learn some physics if he ever got out of this alive. But as Cornuke had instructed, he did not stop. He was determined to keep on going no matter what.

It was the longest marathon he had ever run, the most grueling race of his life, and if anyone had pointed out to him that the distance was barely a half mile, he would never have believed it. When he saw the dome-shaped rock Cornuke had designated as their cover, he dived headfirst for it. No ballplayer had ever been more hell-bent on coming home. Drained, breathless, he lay there. He did not raise his head. He could not find the strength to move. And when, still facedown, he heard—the question answered!—what he knew was the inevitable bullet that would explode his head like a melon, all he could do was grimace. There was nowhere else to run.

But it was not a bullet. It was only Cornuke pounding across the hard sand until he, too, was huddled beside the rock. "I'm going to check out the fence," he said after he caught his breath. And when he added, "You stay put," Williams was about to tell his friend not to worry. There was not much chance of his finding either the energy or the desire to move from this rock ever again. But before he could get the words out, Cornuke was off and running.

How long was he gone? Crouched behind a rock in the Saudi desert, more alone than he had ever imagined possible, Williams measured time by the feverish beating of his heart. When Cornuke was gone for what, by a more conventional calculation, must only have been a full fifteen minutes, Williams began to believe that he had been captured. There could be no other explanation. For all

Williams knew, the soldiers had already left the compound and were coming across the plain in his direction. Summing all his remaining courage, he raised his head and looked out toward the fence.

That was when he saw it. But it was neither advancing soldiers nor Cornuke's being held at gunpoint. It was Jabal al Lawz, and it completely captured his attention. In all the long night's journey, in his mad run across the valley, in his cowering wait behind the rock, he had not dared to steal a glance at the mountain. But now, as if by accident, it was in front of him, and it was a powerful sight. The full moon played across it, bathing the entire mountain in a splendid blue light. It was not like any blue he had ever seen before. Not the blue of the desert sky or of the sea in the Strait of Tiran. Rather, he decided, it was a blue that was so luminous, so shimmering in its soft, pale intensity, that it must have been filtered through heaven itself: a holy light.

Williams was so caught up in this spectacle that he did not hear Cornuke approaching until his friend was nearly beside him. Without taking a moment's rest, Cornuke whispered to him, "Time to move out. Stay close to me." A moment later, Williams found himself once again running across the desert. But this time he was all eagerness.

THERE was no need to climb over or to cut a hole. Cornuke had found a spot where the fence stretched across a soft, siltlike bed of sand. Using his knife and then his hands, he had dug a crawl space that was at least ten inches deep. It had been easy work, the sand was that soft, more like gravel than the hard, packed dirt they had just run across. It was the tail of an old, dried-out stream that had once run twisting down the mountain.

Moses had said: *I took your sin, the calf which you had made, and burned it with fire and crushed it, grinding it very small, until it was as fine as dust; and I cast the dust of it into the brook that came down out of the mountain.*

Cornuke grabbed the fence with both hands and pulled up, and Williams wriggled under. Then it was Cornuke's turn, with Williams raising the fence. And suddenly both men were inside the compound, running to hide in the deep blue shadows cast by the mountain of God.

36

FROM the fence, it was perhaps fifty yards to the base of the mountain. It was open land—a sniper hidden up in the foothills would not even need an infrared scope on a night like this—so Cornuke had decided that they should go the distance on their stomachs, crawling across the sand. At least that way the bastard would have to work for his shot. But as soon as they were inside the fence, before he had a chance to give any instructions, Williams took off, an erect figure perfectly illuminated in the weird blue light. Damn, damn, damn, Cornuke quietly groaned. But in the next instant he, too, was running for all he was worth to the mountain.

The two men, Williams still in the lead, had covered about twenty yards when the dogs began to bark. The noise seemed to be coming from the other side of the mountain, but that was only a guess, or maybe a hope. Wherever it was coming from, it was a malicious and persistent whine, and it was very easy for Cornuke to imagine the foaming mouths, the bared teeth. Watchdogs, he knew. And the animals had their scent. But it was too late to turn back. All Cornuke and Williams could do was to keep on running.

They were nearly halfway there when Williams went down. He fell headfirst, like a man diving into a pool, and Cornuke, who was behind him when it happened, had no doubt that his friend had been shot. Williams thought so too, and he lay there motionless for a moment, waiting to feel the pain. When it did not come, he started to search for the wound, preparing himself for the shock of feeling his hands grow warm and sticky with his own blood. But he could not find a trace of any injury, and when he got to his feet everything felt all right. Cornuke was standing next to him.

"I must've tripped," Williams said sheepishly, kicking at the pile of rocks he had fallen over. "But I'm OK. Let's get going."

This time Cornuke managed to grab him before he took off, and Williams figured his friend was still annoyed that he had cut loose back at the fence.

"You got any idea . . . ?" Cornuke began, only to leave his thoughts unfinished.

"Rocks, damn it. Come on, we're almost there."

But Cornuke would not move. He was pointing at something off in the distance, to his right. He no longer cared if he was a target or not. "There. Don't you see it?" he asked Williams.

The only thing Williams saw was another pile of rocks. They were a good way off; he figured he would need a four iron to drive a ball that far. But from where he was, the rocks looked pretty much like the pile he had tripped over—but maybe four feet high and eight or so feet in diameter. Cornuke started jogging toward it, so Williams, baffled, decided he had no choice but to go after him.

When Cornuke got to the mound, he asked Williams for his binoculars. By now the dogs had stopped barking, or their handlers had quieted them. Either way, the silence gave Williams little comfort. Cornuke, putting all his training aside, stood as tall as a statue on the mound of rocks and searched into the distance. "I knew it," he announced when he lowered the glasses. "They seem to go around the entire front of the mountain. Pretty evenly spaced, too. It's got to be."

"Got to be what?" Williams asked.

"The boundary markers," Cornuke said, jumping down from the pile.

And you shall set bounds for the people round about, saying, Take heed that you do go not up into the mountain or touch the border of it.

"God ordered Moses to come up with something that would keep the Israelites a safe distance away from Mount Sinai," Cornuke said. "And here they are—stone boundary markers. Right where you'd expect them to be."

Their discovery was more encouragement. But Williams was beginning to feel the night's strain. He was winded, and when he suggested they start to pace themselves, that perhaps they should cover the rest of the way to the mountain in a walk, Cornuke agreed. If there were a sniper on the mountain, he told Williams, the guy would have nailed them by now. That immediately seemed to ease Williams' taut mood. So Cornuke figured there was little point in telling his friend what the Book of Exodus had warned would happen to anyone who went past the boundary markers:

Whoever touches the mountain shall be surely put to death.

THEY had no trouble finding a path that went up Jabal al Lawz. The problem was deciding which one to take. They had walked in a more or less straight line from the boundary marker where Williams had stumbled, which led them to a wide, apparently well-trod piece of ground at the foot of the mountain. Three distinct paths branched off from this juncture like limbs from a tree trunk. It would be a guess, and a completely arbitrary one, as to which one led to the summit, or back to the guardhouse, or to a wandering patrol. It was impossible to tell whether a particular path had been trod by soldiers or shepherds or, no less likely a possibility, they sincerely believed, Moses himself. So Williams, whose luck had already earned him fortunes, quickly made a choice, and Cornuke, satisfied to be going up the mountain at last, followed without giving too much thought to the odds.

It was an easy climb for a while. The grade rose steadily but gradually. Although they took care to use the night-vision binoculars to scan each new stretch of the route before they proceeded, this precaution proved unnecessary. There were no obstacles, no boulders blocking their path, no fallen trees, not even a rut or two to make the footing precarious. They walked two abreast like a pair of hikers, and Cornuke had no trouble imagining Moses, a man of 80, the Bible said, when he took his last journey to the top of Sinai, making this climb.

But after the initial, almost effortless half hour, things started to fall apart. The light was the first to go. All at once the moon was extinguished, or so it seemed. One moment they were walking across a brightly lit stage; the next they might as well have been in a pitch-black closet. They did not know whether it was a passing wall of clouds, or simply that the moon was played out for the night. All they knew was that it was growing ominously dark just as the path began to narrow. Without the infrared binoculars, it would have been too risky to continue. A careless step and they would go straight over the edge.

As they climbed higher, the wind, always mercurial in the desert, started to moan. It attacked them, slapping hard at their faces and wailing, Cornuke thought, like a loud heavenly trumpet signaling the end of the world. But it was only the end of the trail. They were only halfway up the mountain, and their path had led them straight to a high, craggy wall of solid rock.

So they backtracked, returning to a spot not too far below where the trail, they had seen, sprouted another branch. They took this new path, but it soon appeared that they were circling the mountain rather than heading toward the peak. If they continued, it would lead them directly to the sentries stationed above the guardhouse. Once again, they reversed directions. The wind was howling and the darkness was intense. The dogs had started in again, too, and this time they seemed closer. Their only hope was to try to find another trail. When they came to a wide plateau where a huge, craggy tower of rock leaned out across their path, Cornuke suggested they climb over it and see what was on the other side.

Even with the wind assaulting them, it was an easy climb. The surface of the tall rock had been so battered by time and the elements that it was studded with crevices. It might as well have been the climbing wall Williams had practiced on in the gym in La Jolla. When he got to the top, making sure to keep himself hidden behind a ledge, he raised his binoculars and saw a patrol truck parked by the side of a road that went up the mountain. Soldiers, he knew, could not be far off. Perhaps they were already in place, waiting in the darkness for the signal to attack. "We've had it," he whispered to Cornuke, passing him the glasses.

Cornuke peered over the ledge and studied the scene below. Then he returned the binoculars to Williams and, betraying nothing, tersely ordered, "Follow me." To Williams' utter disbelief, he climbed over the ledge and headed down toward the truck. At that moment, Williams decided it was very likely that all the pressure had brought his friend to the breaking point. Yet just as quickly he realized that was impossible. Bob would never break. The man was a rock. So Williams followed him, but that did not stop him from being scared stiff the whole way down.

When he caught up with Cornuke, his friend was smiling and Williams at once understood the reason. The truck he had been so worried about was a rusted hulk. There were no tires on the rims of the wheels. The front window was a spiderweb of cracked glass. And then beyond the wreck they saw another trail. Cornuke took the lead, and Williams stayed right behind, telling himself with every step to get a grip. It was going to be a long night.

This trail led them higher up the mountain, and as they climbed toward the summit, the wind died down. It gave way to a chill that, after their days in the desert, felt almost arctic. They kept going, not certain of where they were on the mountain's face, or if they were east or west of the guardhouse. All they knew for sure was that they were getting closer to the twin peaks of Jabal al Lawz. They could see them without using the binoculars. They looked as black as coal.

The two men were still hoping to find a route that would lead them straight to the summit, and when the trail branched again, it was Cornuke's turn to choose. He decided to give the westerly path a try. It took them even higher, and when they stopped for a moment to rest, looking through the binoculars they could see the plain spread out below them. It was a long way down. After only a few, too brief minutes, Cornuke said it was time to continue. Williams, weary, exhausted nearly to the point of collapse, went on.

They were lost, all their reserves of energy were close to being spent, yet they continued climbing higher with every new step. In time they came to a huge, concave rock, so tall that a man could stand in its hollow without bumping his head. It was like no other rock outcropping they had encountered on the face of the mountain. Williams was curious, and when he inspected it, he saw that the sheltered surface of the rock was covered with petroglyphs. The form looked similar to what they had seen on the rock outside the fence: stick figures worshiping a cow. But why they were etched into this particular rock near the summit of Jabal al Lawz, was, both men had to concede, a mystery.

That night they had other concerns that took up all their energy and concentration. They continued climbing upward. And that was when they heard the voices. Williams wanted to believe it was his imagination playing another trick, just as it had transformed an abandoned truck into a military vehicle. But when Cornuke raised a silencing finger to his mouth and then hit the dirt, he knew the voices were real.

The two men lay there flat on their stomachs in the darkness. They did not dare look to see who was out there. The voices, however, carried in the night, coming from farther up the trail. Williams heard two men speaking in a soft, conversational Arabic, and that gave him some comfort. If there were only two of them, they would have a fighting chance. But when he heard a third voice break in, arguing, or so it seemed by the belligerent tone, he knew things would be a lot tougher.

Cornuke had his knife out, thinking that the first one who raised his rifle would be his target. After that, it would be a battle. But for now the two men just lay there, waiting, until at last the voices seemed to grow fainter. Cornuke raised himself up slowly. Looking through the binoculars, he had a good view. There were three Bedouins, and they were all armed. The way they were strolling up the trail in the middle of the night, it seemed a pretty good bet that they were on patrol. And if there was one patrol, then there were probably others combing the mountain. But all he told Williams was, "We've lucked out. They're heading away from us."

The two men lay there until they could no longer hear the Arabs' voices. When they finally got up, Cornuke said they would have to find another route to the top. Williams realized he was right. If they continued on this path, they could run into the Arabs again. Or worse, the Arabs might run into them.

So once again they searched for a trail to the top of the mountain, but they could not find one. Each new direction they tried led them to a dark wall of stone. The choice was clear: They could go back down, or they could climb up the mountainside.

Cornuke led the way, and in the night every move was a guess, full of its own high adventure. Each time Cornuke spread his arms wide across the broad face of the mountain, the tips of his fingers anxiously exploring the wall of stone, his body stretched to its limits, the ledge supporting his feet threatening to crumble at any moment, he never knew if he would find the new crevice he needed, or just sheer, solid rock. Directly below them as they climbed was a sharp precipice that protruded from the side of the mountain like a lance. It was a thirty-foot drop. Williams followed Cornuke's lead, but every move he made was preceded by his fear that it would be his last, and that in the next instant he would be free-falling through space to the stone ledge that would be his final resting place.

But they persevered. In one strong burst of focused energy, Cornuke pulled himself over the crest of the mountain and then reached down to give his friend a strong, helping hand. In an instant, Williams was next to him. They were standing on the summit of the mountain of God.

37

ALL along, from their very first speculative discussions back in California, they had known that if they succeeded their journey would take them to the holiest place on Earth. The site where Moses had received the Ten Commandments. A piece of this planet that God had touched with His presence. But nothing in any of their books, or discussions, or for that matter their imaginations, had prepared them for the force of this moment.

They were more than eight thousand feet above the desert, closer to the sky, they intensely felt, than the earth below, and in their minds it might just as well have been another world. The air they breathed, the dirt they stood on, had a texture and a fragrance; and it was all unique. They were on holy ground.

Yet they felt no sense of triumph. In fact, they felt daunted. Standing there on the top of Mount Sinai, they knew there was a God and that He had made the heavens and the earth and all the universe. They believed this with a certainty and a passion that would not have been possible before.

Their experience had moved to a higher level, and they did not know how to deal with it. Yet there was a clarity to the moment that was reassuring and calming. They stood there transfixed, immobilized without even realizing it until later.

But the moment could not last. In time things eased, and the experience eased into a reality they could begin to comprehend. Cornuke would remember with wonder "how suddenly, without warning, we fell from one level to another. It was like being on an emotional roller coaster."

They were once again explorers, and when they looked around them, they saw that the mountain had two snub-nosed peaks. And between them lay a wide, rock-strewn plain sloping down from each summit like the inside of a barrel. It was a natural amphitheater at the top of the world, and they knew it was the stage on which the most momentous drama in the history of the world had been played out.

And the Lord came down upon Mount Sinai, to the top of the mount; and the Lord called Moses to the top of the mount; and Moses went up. . . .

And God spake all these words saying: I am the Lord thy God who brought you out of the land of Egypt. . . .

Cornuke and Williams explored the entire summit, walking methodically in one direction and then another. Intent on following every sacred footstep, they wanted to experience it all.

The ground they walked on was colored a deep, unnatural black. Going up the mountain, making their way over the many paths and trails, they had walked on dirt that was the stuff of desert sand, darker in spots but always familiar. But the dirt at the summit of Jabal al Lawz was as black as obsidian. The rocks were like lumps of coal. There was no reason it should be that way. Unless . . .

Mount Sinai was wrapped in smoke, for the Lord descended it in fire . . . and when you heard the voice out of the midst of the darkness while the mountain was burning with fire . . .

The earth beneath them had been blackened by heavenly flames. It had been scorched by God.

As they made their way across the mountaintop, they did not

know what they might find, or even precisely what they were looking for, and this uncertainty heightened the drama of each moment. Their sense of anticipation was explosive. They were making history. And when Cornuke saw, just beneath the pinnacle of the mountain, two huge rocks fused together in a V, the cleft between them wide enough for a man to hide in, he understood at once.

And the Lord continued, See, there is a place by me where you shall stand on the rock; and while my glory passes by I will put you in a cleft of the rock, and I will cover you with my hand until I have passed by; then, I will take away my hand, and you shall see my back; but my face shall not be seen.

This was, Cornuke believed, the very rock where God had revealed a portion of His mystery to Moses, an event of incredible intimacy. Moses had earned God's favor, and his reward was to be bound to God with a closeness that was like no one else's. This was the rock where God had sealed His personal relationship with Moses.

Cornuke thought about climbing up the rock. He wanted to stand in the cleft where Moses had hidden, where God had passed. But he did not dare.

THE two men were tired, but their exhaustion was now caused as much by a draining, all-encompassing awe as it was by their climb up the mountain. They needed to regain control. In two hours it would be dawn, and they still had to get down the mountain and through the fence.

They went to the edge of the mountaintop and sat there for a while. They did not speak, and there was no wind, no sounds in the night. Their only company was their thoughts, and they began, each in his own way, to come to terms with the experience.

Cornuke took up the binoculars, and when he looked out he felt as if he could see beyond the plain, across the desert, and all the way to the Red Sea. It was as if the entire Book of Exodus were spread out before him. And he knew every word was true.

But Williams' thoughts led him in another direction, and he began to focus on what had really brought him to Saudi Arabia and to this mountain. He thought about the gold of Exodus and what he would have to do to get it. In the course of this long night, he had already outsmarted the Saudi soldiers. He had sneaked through their fence, climbed their mountain, dodged their patrols. He would challenge them one more time tonight. There was a treasure buried at the base of this mountain, and his mind was made up. He would not leave the desert without his share.

This rush of thoughts was interrupted by one whispered yet instantly frightening word. "Listen!" Cornuke warned. And when Williams did, he too could hear the voices. Men were talking in Arabic. There were too many to count, but one thing was certain. They were slowly coming up the one trail that led to the top of the mountain.

Williams and Cornuke looked at each other and realized they were trapped. There was no place to hide.

38

CORNUKE'S mind was racing. He could hear the voices getting closer as the patrol made its way to the top of the mountain, and he could almost feel how intently Williams was counting on him. However, Cornuke knew he had to shut everything out. Discipline must prevail. He was a professional, schooled to deal with sudden, unexpected events. But what kind of training can prepare a man for being stranded on the summit of the mountain of God? Finally, with the patrol so close that he was already imagining the face that belonged to each distinct voice, it was, appropriately, the Bible that offered him some hope.

On the way up, while they had been scaling the cliff, his eye had wandered and he thought he saw the entrance to a cave. It was only a moment's glance. As they got closer to the summit, the night's shadows had a way of playing across the face of the mountain, manipulating and obscuring things. He could not be certain.

But this was Mount Sinai.

So he [the prophet Elijah] *arose, and ate and drank, and went in the strength of that food forty days and nights to Horeb* [as Sinai was also known] *the mount of God. There he came to a cave and lodged in it; and, behold, the word of the Lord came to him. . . . When Elijah heard the voice, he wrapped his face in his mantle and went out and stood in the entrance of the cave.*

It must have been a cave, Cornuke decided. The Book of Exodus also mentioned that Moses had found a cave on the mountain. Besides, there was nowhere else to hide. Either they took a chance on the veracity of the Bible, or they gambled on the mercy of a Saudi patrol.

"C'mon," he ordered suddenly. "We're getting out of here."

THEY rappelled their way down, and that was a lot quicker and easier than their climb up. Or perhaps it just seemed that way because they were too preoccupied to think about the danger. By the time they were dangling on the sheer face of the mountain, somewhere between the summit and the narrow ledge about twenty feet below, the patrol had reached the top of Jabal al Lawz. Cornuke and Williams could not see them, but they were so close that when one of the Arabs struck a match they could hear its hiss. It took all their concentration to control the sound of their feet hitting against the side of the mountain as they lowered themselves. And whatever energy was left was channeled into prayer: Please don't let them come this way. Don't let them see the rope. Don't let them look over the side.

They made it down to the ledge without an alarm being sounded, without a shot being fired. But they were still exposed. There was no cover. If one of the Arabs on the mountaintop decided to saunter over to admire the view, he could not fail to notice them. They would be trapped. Why had they even tried? Williams complained to himself. They were only postponing the inevitable and risking their necks in the futile process.

But Cornuke was pointing to something not more than twenty yards away, a short walk along the narrow ledge. Williams, however, was having difficulty making things out very precisely. A swirl of misty shadows, like thin plumes of smoke, obstructed his view. But when he raised his binoculars and took a careful look, he was certain it was a cave. "How did you know?" he asked Cornuke in a whisper. "Don't tell me. The Bible, right?" A thin smile was all the answer he got.

The ledge was not much wider than a broad bookshelf, and so they had to make their way single file. They were thousands of feet above the valley, and one look told them it would be certain death if they fell. But there was also reason to hurry. They could still hear the voices above them, and at any moment one of the Arabs might decide to glance over the edge. There was another concern, too. The dark trail they were following was becoming even narrower. Cornuke was in the lead, and he had to put one foot in front of the other like a man walking a tightrope. His right shoulder was pressed flat against the side of the mountain, and the pain was coming back. Perhaps that was why he did not see the gap. But whatever the reason, when he took his next step his foot found nothing but thin air. In his confusion, trying to keep his balance, he went down hard on one knee, and under the impact of his weight, a piece of the already crumbling ledge broke off. It was only Williams' quick forearm that shot out and locked onto his collar, steadying him, that prevented Cornuke from following the stone as it went crashing down to the promontory thirty feet below.

Neither man dared to move. The piece of ledge had landed with all the fury of an exploding bomb, and the noise, they were certain, would surely have the Arabs peering over the edge of the mountaintop to investigate. But if they heard anything, they did not care to look. When Cornuke was convinced it was safe and his galloping heartbeat had settled down to a mere trot, he got to his feet. He started off again, but this time he was careful to study the possibilities in each new step before he took it. Williams trailed close behind, progressing with equal caution.

In this halting fashion, they managed to reach the entrance to the cave. But now there was another problem. Williams refused to step inside. He was, at last, too afraid.

. . .

DECADES ago, when Williams was a dreamy-eyed kid living in the wilds of Montana, he had stumbled onto an Indian burial cave and it had been the first great adventure of his life. And in later years, too, he had gone off on digs and routinely, eagerly even, shimmied down the side of a well or foraged on his hands and knees through a long, dark tunnel. But this cave on the mountain of God, Williams believed with all his intuitive might, was different. He felt a presence.

"Come on, get inside," he heard Cornuke, standing right beside him, hiss.

Always a rational man, Williams tried to find a reason for his misgivings. It was just the shadows, he told himself, the way the weak, predawn light was framing the broad, oval mouth of the cave. In an act that was as brave as any in his life, he took one small step forward. He walked through the soft, dim light to the very entrance of the cave and felt it part for him as if it were a diaphanous curtain. But at the same time, he heard a sound from the depths of the cave. It was high-pitched, almost like a hum. It was not unpleasant but it would not stop—until he stepped back, out of the cave.

He told Cornuke he would not go back in. He did not want to violate a sacred place. It would go against the way things were meant to be. And yet even as Williams spoke the words, he was amazed because such emotions were not like him at all. But he would not budge.

How could Cornuke challenge what he could not see, or feel, or even completely understand? All he could do, he decided, was to take an uncomfortable seat next to his friend on the rocky plateau at the entrance to the cave, and hope that the overhang jutted out sufficiently to block the view from above.

JUST before daybreak, Cornuke decided they should leave. Either they went down the mountain while there was still some darkness, before the soldiers in the guardhouse emerged for morning prayers and while their night-vision binoculars gave them a small edge. Or they spent the day hidden in the cave of Elijah—as they both had taken to calling it—waiting for a new night and a new chance to make their escape. His vote was that they go now, while their luck still seemed to be strong. Either way, he said, it would be a risk.

"No problem," Williams said, his voice full of irony. But he was also genuinely eager to go. Cornuke had not been the only one working things out while they had sat by the cave. Williams had been thinking about the gold of Exodus, and now he had a plan.

Cornuke again took the lead, and once they got past the ledge they found a trail and made good progress. After a while Williams raised his binoculars and could see a section of the barbed-wire fence. He figured now was as good a time as any to let Cornuke in on what he intended to do. If his friend did not want to go along, he would not blame him. Taking a chance was one thing, but Williams knew the kind of risk he planned was sheer foolishness. He just could not help himself—all that gold, the chance to make history, it had a real pull on him. But before he could get a word out, he was pushed to the ground from behind and Cornuke had a hand wrapped tight across his mouth and was whispering, "Quiet!" When Williams finally dared to raise his head, he saw two silhouettes moving behind a boulder a hundred yards or so off, red-checkered *gutras* wrapped around their heads and Kalashnikovs strapped over their shoulders.

The two friends lay there, not speaking, all frozen control, until the two Arabs had moved from their sight. When they finally found the nerve to continue down the mountain, Williams decided it was not the right time to tell Cornuke what he had in mind. At the very least, he chided himself, it would probably sound a lot more feasible if he could lay it all out when he was not shaking.

It was a short distance down to the boulders that were bunched near the base of the mountain. They crouched behind a rock and looked toward the barbed-wire fence. The plain that stretched out in front of them was flat, without even a tree for cover. Still, Cornuke told himself, it was not quite light yet. If they made a dash, they might make it. "On three," he informed Williams.

"I'll meet you back at the truck," Williams said evenly. "I've got some things to do."

"What the hell are you talking about?" Cornuke was so surprised that he forgot to whisper. The words came out in a shout.

Williams told him that he was not leaving without at least trying to bring home a single piece of the treasure. He did not need the metal detector. He had worked it all out. Fasold's crew had dug near some pillars they had spotted at the base of the mountain, and straight off had found a piece of gold jewelry. Williams' plan was to find the pillars, pray that they were not anywhere near the guardhouse, and then see what might be waiting beneath the soft sand.

"What about the soldiers?" Cornuke asked.

"I've been ducking them all night."

"It's getting light," Cornuke warned.

"That's why I've got to hurry."

"You mean *we,*" Cornuke corrected.

There was no way he was going to leave his friend behind. And anyway, he had his own reasons for wanting to find the pillars.

THE tall rocks that clung to the base of the mountain gave them some protection, and they took advantage of it, keeping low and moving quickly. Still, they were heading farther away from the stretch of fence they had crawled under and, at the same time, coming closer to the guardhouse. Time was another worry—they did not have much left. They had awakened to enough desert sunrises to know that out here the sun hit with full blast at first light. And when that happened, they could forget about cover. They were dressed in black clothes, and the dash across the sand to the fence would be suicide. But Williams was determined. He kept his eyes focused on the broad plain around them, looking for anything that might resemble Fasold's pillars.

When they had worked their way almost halfway across the base of the mountain, Williams saw something that made him come to a stop. Two huge rocks, each one perhaps sixty feet long, had been wedged together to form a V. The point was aimed directly at the mountain, and in the middle, as if deliberately equidistant from each arm, was a flat stone mound. He pointed it out to Cornuke, who knew at once what this had to be.

And Moses wrote all the words of the Lord, and rose up early in the morning, and builded an altar under the mount . . .

"We should come across those pillars in a minute," he told Williams. "Should be twelve of them."

. . . *and twelve pillars, according to the twelve tribes of Israel.*

Williams was too excited to ask for chapter and verse. He stood up, scanning the plain with his binoculars, and he found them. They were sticking out from the sand, all in a row, each one perhaps eighteen feet in diameter and spaced about five feet apart. They were perilously near the guardhouse, but, a bit of luck, there was a long, deep wadi about the size of a soccer field that ran parallel to them.

He had no time to think things through, so he acted on pure instinct. Without pausing to say even a word to Cornuke, he sprinted from the cover of the rocks. His plan, such as it was, began to take shape in the course of this mad run. He would get to the wadi and, shielded by its high, sandy walls, crawl on his belly to a pillar, preferably the one farthest away from the guardhouse and the three guards stationed on the precipice above it. He would . . .

But all at once, as he was pounding across the sand, nearly in midstride, he came to an abrupt stop. He stood completely still, staring in utter disbelief. Now that he was closer, he saw that it was not a wadi. It was a pit, a deep pit. And it was crowded with excavation equipment.

And in that same terrible moment, he knew why the three armed guards were stationed on the mountainside. They were not there to protect the sleeping soldiers. They were there to guard the treasure, the treasure lying deep in the bottom of the pit. The bounty of ancient Egypt was being systematically unearthed from the plains of Mount Sinai—the gold of Exodus that should have been his.

It was a treasure hunter's worst fear—someone had beaten him to the gold. For an instant he thought about getting closer to the pit, perhaps taking a glimpse at what had already been dug up. But it was a colossal risk, and one without a promise of any tangible return. If he approached the excavation, the guards would spot him for sure. He would never get home. And with this despairing realization, he made an about-face and ran back to the safety of the rocks as if in a trance.

IT was time to leave. They had made their way back to the spot where the fence intersected with the dried-up creek bed just as the sun was beginning to rise in the desert sky. They could hear people stirring in the guardhouse, but it was a way off, and after the long, memorable night they were too drained to care.

"On three," Cornuke said.

But Williams interrupted. "How many were there? Did you count?"

Cornuke did not understand at first. Then he got it. "There were twelve. Twelve pillars in a row, just like the Bible said."

"It really is Mount Sinai," said Williams, genuinely astonished. But even as he felt this, part of him was also bitterly disappointed. He had failed. He had come so close, yet he was leaving without a single piece of the treasure.

Still, there no longer was any reason to delay. Without another word, they were off and running. It was the race of their lives. All that mattered was getting to the fence and crawling under. And they did it. Minutes later they were on the other side, heading away from the fence, the soldiers, and the mountain.

The walk back to their camp in the gully was long and hot. They were exhausted. But, even for Williams, it was impossible not to feel good.

The truck was sitting right where they had left it, and the blankets were still pulled up high on their air mattresses. Williams was already thinking about getting back to Tabuk and having a long, warm bath, and then, restored, trying to make some sense of all he had seen and felt. Cornuke, full of the occasion, stuck out his hand to congratulate his friend.

That was when the two Bedouins stepped out from behind a large bush where they had been waiting all along. The taller of the two leveled a 12-gauge shotgun at them.

Williams ignored the gun and took a step forward. A 12-gauge, he knew, was a single-shot. Maybe only one of them would have to die. Cornuke saw what his friend was up to, and he, too, began to inch his way toward the gunman. After all they had been through, after all they had seen, both of them were willing to risk dying if there was a chance for one of them to escape. The gunman yelled something harshly in Arabic, but they continued to close in on him slowly.

"Enough of that shit!" the shorter Bedouin suddenly shouted. He was holding a .45 in his hand, but it was his English that brought them to a halt. It took both men by surprise.

"I don't want you even thinking of getting cute on me," the Bedouin said as he rammed his weapon into Cornuke's belly. Then he led him to the other side of the gully where a truck was hidden. Williams was taken to the Datsun. That was the way professionals did it, Cornuke knew. They kept their prisoners separated. And when they drove off, one truck closely following the other across the desert, Cornuke tried not to think about where they were taking him. Or what the punishment would be for sneaking into a Saudi military compound.

39

IT was all over. In the course of one long, terrifying night, they had drawn on all their reserves of courage, ingenuity, and luck. And now, in the exhausted morning after, they found themselves left completely empty. Everything had been spent. Between the two of them, they could not raise even the smallest of hopes.

The two trucks drove across the desert at a mad speed. Both Cornuke and Williams soon gave up trying to figure out how far they had traveled, or even in what direction they were headed. For all they could tell, the trucks were turning in wide, repetitive circles. There were no landmarks, just the empty desert everywhere, endless sand baking in the bright, hot sun.

Williams tried to begin a conversation. His politician's instincts told him that if his captor got to know him, it might make things go easier. Besides, he had heard the man at the wheel speak English. "I'm an American. A geologist," he said, hoping his voice could hold on to a casual, conversational pitch. But the driver did not even look at him. Maybe the man was deaf, Williams tried to convince himself. Or maybe he really did not speak English. But

Williams could not sustain either of those fictions, and soon began to consider a long list of reasons why the Bedouin refused to acknowledge his existence. He did not enjoy where these led him at all.

The tall, gaunt Bedouin driving the Datsun was hunched over the wheel, the shotgun wedged between his knees. Cornuke did not try to make small talk; he knew there would be no point. After a while, he closed his eyes, hoping at least to rest, to find a space where he could settle and collect his thoughts. He knew what was coming would be as bad as it could get; he did not try to delude himself into thinking there might be a way out. He simply hoped he could find the strength to deal with it like a man.

The drive continued for at least an hour, and never once did they pass an asphalt road. Finally they came to a cluster of sun-bleached tents. Without slowing down, the two trucks went straight through the center of this encampment. A group of children followed their progress with a curiosity that struck Williams as both amused and oddly intense. He wanted to wave to them, to make contact with another living soul while he still had the chance, but he thought better of it. There was no predicting how the Bedouin at the wheel with the .45 in his holster would interpret the gesture.

About a five-minute drive beyond the encampment, the trucks came to a stop in front of a stucco hut. It stood at a slight angle, as if it had been built quickly and then had settled awkwardly into the sand. It had a roof of corrugated tin that hung over the four walls like an awning. The front door was made out of planks of unpainted wood, and a shiny new padlock held a steel bar in place. Williams took it all in, and his first thought was that the pickup he was sitting in had to be bigger than that whole damn hut.

But Cornuke was kicking around something else. Where were the soldiers? They had broken into a military installation and he had expected to be brought to a military jail, or at least a police station. But this was just a hut in the middle of the desert. There was nothing else around, unless, of course, you counted those mangy tents a mile or so back. There certainly was nothing official about this place—no one in uniform, no flag hanging limply from a pole, not even a sign. He did not know what to make of it. Unless . . . they had been kidnapped. A boldfaced headline jumped into his mind: AMERICANS HELD FOR RANSOM IN THE DESERT. If that was what these Bedouins were up to, he had to congratulate them. They sure had picked a damn good spot to keep a couple of guys hidden away. There was no chance of finding anyone out here. This was the end of the line, the place to lose people.

The two Bedouins ordered them out of the trucks, and then led them at gunpoint to the door of the shed. For only the second time since he had taken them prisoner, the short Arab spoke. In accented but perfect English, he told them to empty their pockets, and when they did, he took their money and their passports and threw them into a knapsack without examination. "Give me your shoes," he ordered.

Cornuke and Williams were startled by the order, and it was a moment before they responded. That was too long for the Bedouin with the shotgun. He shoved the long barrel of the weapon into Williams' chest as if it were a lance. The two men quickly started to take off their shoes, and that was when the Bedouins noticed the knife strapped to Cornuke's leg. They waited for him to hand it to them, and then took it without comment.

As Cornuke was undoing the laces of his hiking boots, he tried to figure out why they were taking their shoes. Maybe they wanted to compare them to footprints found at Jabal al Lawz. Maybe it was simply an elementary precaution. It would be pretty difficult for two hostages to escape across the desert in their bare feet. Or for all he knew, it was a religious custom, some deeply held Muslim belief about not wearing shoes indoors.

They stood in front of the hut in their stocking feet, and the sand was so hot that they felt as if they were walking on burning coals. But then the door was pulled open and they were shoved into a cool darkness. The door slammed shut, and they could hear the padlock being secured. And all at once Cornuke realized there was another reason why the Bedouins had taken their shoes. Dead men don't need shoes. It was only good sense not to let them go to waste.

THERE was a two-foot hole in one of the stucco walls of the hut with a piece of wire mesh covering it. It let in some light and, to their surprise, a bit of a breeze. When Cornuke gave the mesh a strong tug, it did not budge.

"Wouldn't happen to have a pair of wire cutters on you?" he asked.

"Left them in the hotel," Williams answered, and both men had a laugh. They made a lot more of the joke than it was worth, but it felt good and they did not know if they would ever get another chance to laugh.

Soon Williams got around to what was really on his mind. "What do we do now?" he asked.

Cornuke was sitting on one of the two dark-colored rugs that were lying parallel to each other on the dirt floor. "Nothing we can do," he said evenly. "It's all up to them."

It was not what Williams wanted to hear, but he could not come up with any reason to disagree.

"Might as well get some sleep while we can," Cornuke said. He lay down on the carpet, curled up in a fetal position, and shut his eyes.

Williams watched in pure amazement. Any of a world of grim possibilities could turn painfully real in the next moment, but Cornuke had put all that aside. He was sleeping. There was about as much likelihood of his finding that kind of calm, Williams thought, as there was his taking a pass on the anesthesia if they ever wheeled him in for open-heart. But when, utterly exhausted, he lay down on the adjoining rug, he immediately fell into a sleep so deep that he might as well have been anesthetized.

WILLIAMS awoke to find a circle of children starring curiously into his face, and for an instant he thought he was back home in California with the girls leaning over his bed on a lazy Sunday morning. But it was only the kids from the encampment. They had come with tea; and to stare at the two aliens from another planet who had landed in the middle of their desert.

Two boys, the older not more than seven, were in charge, and the others shyly stepped back to watch. With an intense concentration, as if spilling a single drop would be an unforgivable catastrophe, one boy, then the other, poured a pale green liquid from a bronze-colored pitcher into cups. Then, standing tall, their narrow backs erect, they marched forward as if on parade and with serious, unsmiling faces presented the cups to Cornuke and Williams.

Williams took a sip. "Delicious," he lied and made sure to smile broadly. Cornuke drained his cup in a single swallow and did his best to top Williams' grin.

The crowd of children giggled in delight, and the two boys quickly set out to repeat the entire process. Once again it was performed with such dignity, every move full of studious ceremony, that Cornuke and Williams almost felt as if they were guests, not prisoners. For the first time since their capture, a future seemed possible.

Genuinely grateful, Williams' first instinct was to repay the children for their kindness. But when he tried to think of a feasible reward, he was at a loss. At this dismal moment, he was a millionaire without means. He did not even have shoes. And then he hit on an idea. His traveling bag full of genuine made in the US of A lotions and potions was in the cab of the Datsun. Perhaps the guards would not begrudge his sharing something as innocuous as ChapStick with the kids. It was a triviality, he realized, but at that moment it seemed vitally important to repay their hospitality. If he could maintain the protocols of a social relationship, then maybe things were really not that bad. Maybe there would be a way out.

The immediate problem, however, was to get the kids to understand that he wanted them to bring him the bag from the truck. Williams threw himself into the task with an almost manic energy; and yet even as he was going at it, pantomiming, drawing stick pictures in the sand, talking in a pidgin Arabic that left the kids laughing uproariously, he knew all his efforts were a ludicrous diversion. But he kept on. It was the only thing holding his world together. Finally, after leading the older boy who had served the tea to the mesh window, he was able to point out the Datsun and the blue bag in the cab. The boy at last seemed to understand what Williams wanted. Except he refused. The boy made his case in a hesitant, clearly apologetic Arabic, and while Williams did not understand one single word, he got the message: It was impossible.

Cornuke, who had been taking in his friend's antics with a silent indulgence, now spoke up. "Doctors," he said, and pointed authoritatively to his own chest. "Physicians," he went on, and this time he included Williams. It was a moment's inspiration, a completely wild stab, but it worked. The children respectfully trooped out to retrieve the bag for the two "doctors."

Fifteen minutes later, when they still had not returned, the two friends were left wondering how effective a ploy it had been, or if the kids had even the slightest idea of what they had been trying to say. But then there was a knock on the door. Williams tried not to guess who was on the other side, or what he would want. Or if the formality of the knock was simply ironic. After a deep breath that had only a small effect on his conflicting emotions, he opened the door. The boy was standing there holding the blue bag. And behind him was an orderly line of a half-dozen or so Bedouins. They had come to be treated by the two American doctors.

In that initial moment, Cornuke was merely amused. The escape plan did not occur to him until later. After he had treated a festering wound on a wizened man's hand with the only thing he could find—Ban Roll-On—and after he had cured the vision problems of another grateful nomad with a few palliative drops of Visine, he realized he could prescribe anything and these people would take it. And that was when he fixed on the unopened bottle of sky-blue sleeping pills in his friend's bag.

For the next twenty minutes, Cornuke made sure that everyone had swallowed at least three of what he was hawking as "Dr. Bob's special little pills." He might just as well have been a barker in a traveling medicine show. Williams quickly realized what was up and enthusiastically joined in, walking around the small room with a pyramid of pills in his outstretched hand. The Bedouins grabbed at them eagerly. They could not get enough. For an unsteady moment, Williams felt a twinge of guilt. But he told himself the worst thing that was going to happen was that they were going to have a good, long sleep. If he did not get out of here, the sleep in store for him could be permanent.

The Arabs were greedy, but Cornuke made sure to save ten pills. And as they were filing out, he decided the time had come to offer "Dr. Bob's special little pills" to the guards. There were two of them stationed outside the hut on either side of the door, and they both had automatic rifles. He was optimistic that they would not turn down his generosity. The other Arabs hadn't. However, when he stuck an ingratiating smile on his face and launched into his speech about how he was a doctor and that these were magic pills, certain to cure a thousand ills from impotence to high blood pressure, they would not even turn to look at him. But when he casually took a step forward, his foot crossing the threshold of the hut, in an instant they both turned as if an alarm had sounded. Their weapons were raised and pointed straight at him. It was at that moment as he quickly stepped back into the hut that he realized his guards were a race apart from the people in the tents. It would be impossible to escape.

LYING on his rug that night and staring out through the iron mesh at the impenetrably dark desert, Williams felt the unsettling quiet in every pore of his skin. Unable to find the strength to summon a single memory from another time, he decided this was the loneliest night of his life, and that it would never end.

THERE was just one man, and he came at first light. He had a metal folding chair in his hand and a holster with a huge .357 Magnum strapped under his armpit. For a horrible second, Cornuke saw how it all would be played out. He would be forced to stand on the chair with a rope around his neck. Then it would be kicked away. If he did not want the rope, a bullet from the big revolver would do the trick just as nicely. But to his relief, the man opened the chair, put it down so that it faced them, and then settled into it as if he was about to watch a movie. The interrogation, Cornuke realized, was about to begin.

They had expected this. Last night Cornuke had led Williams to a corner of the hut, as far away as possible from the guards by the door, and whispered a strategy directly into his ear. Point one, he told his friend, we were not caught inside the fence. For all we know, they don't have any idea what we were up to, and they certainly don't have any proof. Two, we have valid visas. Three, we were invited to this kingdom by a crown prince. Four, we were looking for oil. That's our story and we stick to it. We don't do their work for them. We don't admit to anything. We never heard of Jabal al Lawz. And no matter what, no Mount Sinai, no gold of Exodus, and no talk about climbing to the top of the mountain in the middle of a military facility. Cornuke thought it would take a few days, maybe longer, while they checked out their stories. By the time their captors contacted the prince, by the time they discovered the tunnel dug beneath the fence, by the time they knew the two Americans were lying through their teeth, they might have lost interest. Or, another real long shot, he might be able to come up with something better.

The interrogator seemed in no hurry. Perhaps, Cornuke decided, that was part of his technique. Anyway, it gave him an opportunity to study the man. At first Cornuke thought he was near their age, but when he looked closely at the deeply tanned face and saw the small hoods of flesh beneath the sunken, tired eyes and the crevices in the neck that were as telltale as the rings on a tree trunk, he realized this was a man who could very well be a grandfather. He had a barrel chest to go with the belly that strained the buttons on his khaki shirt, but Cornuke, a bit of an authority, could tell it was the body of someone whose days of athletic grace were a distant memory. Still, there remained something military about him, a sense of command in the way he sat so erect, perfectly motionless, in the metal chair, expecting to be obeyed. His thin hair was brushed back neatly from his forehead, and it was more gray than black. All in all, Cornuke intuitively decided, this was not the worst captor they could have. If it came down to ransom, as soon as the money was paid, he would honor the deal and set them free.

But there was no talk of ransom. And all of Cornuke's careful strategizing proved worthless once the interrogation began. The man started in at precisely the point where Cornuke was hoping to end.

"Tell me," he asked, "did you succeed in climbing to the top of the mountain, all the way to the peak?"

Cornuke first and then Williams insisted they had no idea what he was talking about. They took turns explaining that they were in the kingdom at the invitation of a crown prince, that they were in the desert looking for oil when, for no apparent reason, they were taken at gunpoint to this hut where they were being held without an explanation. Wait until the prince hears about this. He'll have your job, if not your head. Wait until the American embassy finds out. It will be an international incident.

The interrogator let them rant. He did not interrupt. He simply sat there on the metal chair, his back as rigid as a surveyor's rod, and a tight smile that seemed to convey a great interest in their every word fixed on his face. When he finally spoke his voice was full of friendliness, and he used a discursive, almost chatty tone. His English was perfect, but he had an accent that to Cornuke's ear reminded him more of his Russian grandmother than any Arab. "Tell me," he repeated, "did you succeed in climbing to the top of the mountain, all the way to the peak?"

To their credit, both men once again tried to bluster their way out. But when Williams mentioned the prince, the interrogator cut him off. "Do you really want me to speak to His Royal Highness?" he asked.

Williams was saved the contrivance of an answer. The interrogator decided it was his turn to talk. *And he knew everything.* He knew about their trip to London, their journey to the Red Sea, their trip across the desert, and their theories about Mount Sinai. He even knew about the missing batteries in their metal detector. But he wanted to discuss only one subject: what they had found behind the fence at Jabal al Lawz.

"Tell me," he repeated for the third time but without a hint of impatience, "did you succeed in climbing to the top of the mountain, all the way to the peak?"

There was no longer any point in lying, and even if there had been, they were too shaken. So they told him everything. How they had, in fact, made it to the very summit of the mountain. How they had hidden from the patrols. How they had crawled under the fence. How they had found the pit and seen the excavating equipment.

When they were done, he had them go through it again. And this time they told the story with a great deal of pride, for no matter what was going to happen to them, they felt they had done a remarkable thing. Besides, the interrogator seemed to Williams to share their excitement in the adventure, and that worked to encourage him.

Finally, they were convinced there was nothing left to say, but the interrogator was not satisfied. With a bureaucratic meticulousness that was starting to take its toll on the two men, he insisted that they go through their adventure still one more time. But now, he would appreciate it, please, if they could be more exact. Precisely where was the pit? How deep was it? What sort of machines had they seen? What was the condition of the summit? Were there excavations? Equipment? How many guards had they seen? Where were they stationed? Which trail was the quickest to the peak? How many men were in the patrols? And on and on.

They answered truthfully, doing their best to cooperate, to fill in every detail. They no longer had anything to hide. But they could not understand why he was asking these questions, or even who he was.

The interrogation went on for hours, and then it was suddenly finished. The man rose from the metal chair, folded it, and turned to face Williams and Cornuke. "Thank you for your information," he said. "It was quite interesting." And then he left.

THEY waited for him to return, but he never did. They never saw him again. Instead, the short guard with the .45 came for them. He led them to their truck. "Get in," he ordered. By the time Williams had taken his place behind the wheel, a pickup with two Bedouins from the camp had parked in front of them, its motor running. "Follow them," the guard ordered. So they did. But whether the two Arabs were taking them out to the desert to dig their own graves or to some new prison was unknown to Cornuke and Williams. At this point they did not know what to expect, and nothing would have surprised them.

40

BUT it did not end with a bang. There was a rough moment when, after they had been following the Bedouins' pickup for about twenty minutes, it abruptly came to a halt in the middle of a panorama of flat, endless sand, and both Cornuke and Williams knew the time had come for them to get their bullets. But when the driver got out, marched over, and pointed his revolver at the speedometer, the only thing he seemed to have on his angry mind, at least as they understood it, was that they should speed up. They were lagging too far behind. For the next hour Williams did his best to keep the Datsun smack on the Bedouins' tail. Cornuke joked, "The Arabs must be worried we'll be late for our own funerals," but as soon as he said it, he realized it was not so much a joke as a distinct possibility. After that he just sat in the passenger's seat locked in a controlled, anxious silence. It lasted until they found themselves being led, to their great relief, back to the sleepy city of Tabuk.

What happened next was more farce than drama. Whether the Bedouins were following instructions or had gotten things muddled was one more mystery for Cornuke and Williams to pick over. All that they knew for sure was that the driver led them directly to a small police station, and that it was shut tight. The Bedouins pounded belligerently on the locked door, but it did not give an inch. They shouted until they were hoarse, but no one answered. Clearly exasperated, their authority sagging with each passing minute, they finally abandoned their efforts and fell into a huddle. They emerged only to instruct their two bewildered prisoners to get back in their truck and once again stay close. This time they led the two men to a walled compound in the heart of the city, and after a drive through several checkpoints, they arrived at an impressively active police station. However, these officers, whose fatigues suggested to Cornuke that they were members of a military rather than a civil force, were not interested in the two Americans. They refused to take them. It was, apparently, not their problem.

The Bedouins, however, were tenacious; and as far as Cornuke and Williams could tell, they did not know what else to do. So once again they led their prisoners back to the first police station. To the Arabs' immense delight, the door was open, and there was a spirited exchange with a bored-looking officer at the front desk. Cornuke and Williams could only observe in total ignorance, but at its conclusion the Bedouins looked pleased and marched out of the police station without even a look at the two men they had finally managed to deliver.

Now that he was certain he was not going to be shot, Williams played to the hilt the angry, put-upon American. He demanded to be taken back to his hotel. The officer mulled the request for an instant and then, to both men's surprise, agreed. At the hotel, the manager welcomed them back and, taking Williams off to a discreet corner, suggested a way out of their still unspecified predicament. And so, after being plied with a round of orange juice and a handful of bills, the policeman gave a polite nod that was almost a bow and left. They were free. The two friends celebrated by making reservations on the first plane out that night.

• • •

THEY were finally in the air, on their way home, and they could push their seats back and settle into a worry-free sleep. They were spent, and it was too soon for them to try to make sense of everything that had happened. There would be time later to celebrate and to solve puzzles. But even now, as he was on the verge of drifting off, Cornuke continued to feel the weight of his triumph. He had walked on the mountaintop where Moses had stood with God. Even more, he had proved that the Bible was true. These proud thoughts guided him into a deep, contented sleep.

Williams' stubborn mind, however, remained active. With only the night for company, he sorted through a long trail of coincidences that began with Peter's conveniently timed arrival at Heathrow and ended with the curious interrogation in the shack in the desert; and he knew he could no longer simply point an accusing finger at Nikoli and Warren. Forces more powerful than a couple of greedy brokers out to get the inside scoop on a business deal had been toying with them. Fasold had been tried by the Saudis and then expelled from the kingdom merely for visiting Jabal al Lawz. The mountain was now guarded by soldiers, but he and Cornuke had been released after only a few hours of questioning. It made no sense. He knew he was still disoriented, but he could not help feeling that they had been manipulated from the moment they arrived in London. More frustrating, he knew he was not even close to beginning to understand what role he and Cornuke had unsuspectingly been recruited to play, or who the other players were. But he no longer had any doubts that they had been caught up in someone else's mystery. That realization, he told himself, was his first small victory, and, he had decided by the time he finally fell asleep, the starting point for a new adventure.

Part Five

THE PROMISED LAND

41

The Royal Palace, Riyadh: August 1990

HIS Royal Highness King Fahd bin Abd al-Aziz could not sleep. At 2 A.M. on August 2, 1990, he was still awake playing Nintendo in his bedroom in the palace when a group of his advisors came to inform him that Iraqi commandos had taken control of Kuwait City. He refused to believe them.

Over the next several hours, there were more reports and more details. An invading force of three Iraqi Republican Guard divisions, armored and mechanized infantry troops, was marching through Kuwait. The king was still not convinced. He insisted on speaking directly to Saddam Hussein.

The palace had more than ten private telephone numbers for the Iraqi president in Baghdad. Calls were placed, but King Fahd received the same response at each number: The president was not available at this time. So be it, the king decided. Until he spoke directly to Saddam, he would not believe Iraq intended to maintain control over Kuwait. And he refused to consider seriously the possibility that his kingdom might be the Iraqi Army's next target.

It was not until ten the next morning that the king finally spoke with the Iraqi president. "What's this I hear?" he asked him. He might as well have been talking about a party he had missed.

"Don't worry about it," Saddam answered. He was in a jovial mood. "I am sending Izzat Ibrahim to explain it all to you."

At three the next afternoon, Izzat, the vice president of Iraq's Revolutionary Command Council, was received by King Fahd at the Riyadh palace. The Iraqi envoy began by relaying Saddam's assurance that the kingdom was safe. Saudi Arabia had nothing to fear from Iraq.

"I am discussing Kuwait, not the security of Saudi Arabia," the king said.

"I am not here to discuss Kuwait," Izzat countered. "The status of Kuwait has now been rectified. The clock cannot be turned back. I merely want to reassure you about the safety of Saudi Arabia."

By the time Izzat had left, the king firmly believed Iraq intended to occupy Kuwait permanently. But he also had decided there was little he could do about it. More important, he remained convinced that Saddam was still his ally. The $5 billion he had paid the Iraqis for their help in building a superweapon had not been a mistake. Project Falcon would soon be operational. And then the kingdom would not have to worry about Saddam Hussein. Or, for that matter, any of its neighbors.

AT approximately the same time as the king was meeting with the Iraqi envoy, satellite photographs of the invasion of Kuwait were being carefully studied at the National Photographic Interpretation Center in Washington. Six years earlier an industrious NPIC analyst had worked around the clock to uncover the first clues about what the Saudis were up to in their desert. Today, however, a photo intel team was working to cover up something, and they labored through the night to get this job done too.

Two days later, a large American delegation headed by Secretary of Defense Dick Cheney jetted to Saudi Arabia and met with King Fahd at the royal palace. The session began with a display of a series of satellite photographs. The detail in the shots was remarkable. They showed that Iraqi Republican Guard divisions were positioned just outside the northeastern corner of Saudi Arabia, with the kingdom's oil fields directly in their path. More ominously, the photos showed that the Iraqi troops were preparing to advance.

For the first time King Fahd believed his kingdom and his sovereignty were in danger. Saddam, he now knew, was his enemy. Iraq must be stopped. When the meeting ended, he asked the United States for its help in the defense of Saudi Arabia. The evidence presented by the American delegation had convinced him it had to be done.

The satellite photographs were genuine—in part. The Iraqi forces were, in fact, positioned in Kuwait within a two-day march of Saudi Arabia's oil-producing Eastern Province. However, the NPIC computers had very methodically erased all traces of an equally important actuality: The Iraqi forces were digging in. Every bulldozer, every trench, every fortification, and every latrine in the satellite shots had been effectively removed. The photographs had been edited to show an army that was preparing to move on, not one that had settled into a defensive position.

There was no confirming proof that the Iraqi forces were planning to invade Saudi Arabia, but the king did not know that. Nor, for that matter, did Secretary Cheney. The photographs had been doctored without his knowledge. In any case, it was quickly too late. That same day, just hours after the king's request, squadrons of American fighter-bombers took off for Saudi Arabia. Operation Desert Shield had begun. And Project Falcon was no longer a priority for King Fahd and his generals.

By January, a full-scale war had broken out. By March, Kuwait had been liberated and Iraq had been defeated. Yet in the aftermath of the Persian Gulf War, surprisingly little of strategic consequence had been changed in the region. Saddam was still in power. Israel still had to worry about its security. And Saudi Arabia still was a kingdom surrounded by enemies.

In fact, arguably the war's greatest legacy was the continuing grim contemplation of what did not occur. There was no germ warfare, no rockets filled with poison gas, no tactical nuclear strikes. But there could have been. During the war, Saddam had ranted about the "mother of all battles." And after the war, the threat continued to remain very real.

There was, therefore, a new urgency once the war was over for the men directing Project Falcon. Delays could no longer be tolerated. The entire plan, the king demanded, must become operational as soon as possible. If people would not cooperate, they would have to be replaced. If engineering contracts could not be fulfilled, new companies must be found.

In Israel, there was a renewed commitment by the intelligence service to find out precisely what the Saudis were planning. A total of 42 Iraqi Scud missiles had landed on Israel's cities during the Gulf War. Military intelligence could only guess at the location of their desert launch sites; and they could only pray that the next incoming missile did not carry a chemical-biological payload. It would be folly, the Ministry of Defense warned the prime minister in a confidential written assessment of the war, for the country ever again to be placed in such ignorance. "No," the prime minister reportedly responded, "it would be suicide." The order went out to the Mossad. It was imperative to discover precisely what the Saudis were building in the desert near Tabuk. If the Israeli Defense Forces could not intervene immediately to stop Project Falcon, the government wanted its forces prepared to strike if and when they had to.

Much of what happened, then, was played out in secrecy—behind closed government doors, at restricted military bases, and in the remote desert. Nevertheless, if Bob Cornuke and Larry Williams had been paying closer attention, if they had been reading the smaller stories in an eclectic collection of newspapers and magazines, talking to government officials, or meeting with defense contractors, they might have been able in the aftermath of the Gulf War to piece together what they had got caught up in when they had set out to climb to the top of Jabal al Lawz. But they had not. They knew none of this. They had their own priorities.

They had initially set off for an adventure in search of ancient history. They did not understand it was taking them to a world where the past was never past. History was religion, and religion determined politics: an inextricable circle of fate. But they were beginning to learn. Now that they were home, even as they tried to resume their previous existences, there were still surprises. With these new revelations they would begin to understand if not everything that had happened, then certainly enough. And their lives would be changed forever.

42

Site N-4: 1997

BEYOND the one-pump Al Kan gas station, close to where Cornuke and Williams had turned into the desert only to get lost and then mired in deep sand, a road had been built. Hard and smooth and wide enough for trucks, it led directly to Jabal al Lawz.

On the summit of the mountain, across from the blackened peak where Cornuke and Williams believed that God had descended to give Moses the Ten Commandments, two 24-foot towers—as high as four-story buildings—were being erected. Black and rectangular, they already appeared to rise straight up from the mountaintop like two colossal tablets. But this was unintentional, neither pop art nor parody. The towers were FPS-117 solid-state radar systems, each one 30,000 pounds of advanced sensor technology. At the cost of $30 million, Jabal al Lawz was being transformed into what the planners of Project Falcon designated as site N-4. The mountain of God had become part of the Saudi war machine.

When the Gulf War ended, the Project Falcon working group

moved quickly to obey the king. Prince Bandar, the genial, high-living Saudi ambassador in Washington, made an official protest. He complained that the kingdomwide air command and control system had been authorized by the U.S. Congress back in 1983. And he demanded that the U.S. Air Force, which was supervising the foreign military sales contract, hire a new contractor because of all the excessive delays caused by both computer software and site construction problems. The Boeing Corporation was soon "terminated for default" (and, in the largest claim ever filed by the U.S. Air Force in a contract dispute, sued for $605 million). The Hughes Aircraft Company of Fullerton, California, was selected to take over the job.

Six years and $5.7 billion later, the air combat control network was finally in place. Seventeen radar and communication sites were spread strategically throughout the kingdom. They were threat receivers; if there was an incoming missile or wave of enemy fighters, any of the 17 sensors could "zorch" the targets with more than 6 million watts of power. And even as the radars were lighting up the bogies, the sites' Digital VAX 4300 computers would also be relaying the information to sector command centers buried in deep, bombproof caves—subterranean fortresses loaded with the push-button technology of modern warfare—and to the Saudi Air Force's "Black Hole" command operations center in Riyadh. Within only 2.4 seconds, the computers in the Riyadh command post beneath Old Airport Road would calculate a program that would launch a welcoming volley of surface-to-air missiles.

A high electronic fence had, in effect, been erected around the kingdom. Any trespassers—missiles or bombers—would be destroyed. It was one of the most advanced air defense communication and control systems in the world. In its speed and computer tasking capabilities it was even more sophisticated than the North American Air Defense system. It was, as the trial tests demonstrated, a technological marvel. Saudi Arabia was virtually impregnable from an air attack. As a tribute to these defensive capabilities, the Saudi generals and the Hughes engineers called their multibillion-dollar creation "Peace Shield."

But this name was deliberately coy. The system was as much a sword as it was a shield. For despite what Congress had been told when it approved the original foreign military sales contract, Peace Shield was an offensive program. It could coordinate missiles and fighter attacks against enemies. It was the electronic brain for Project Falcon.

Major General John A. Corder, who was director of combat operations for Central Command Air Forces during the Gulf War and worked as a consultant on the system, was candid—to a degree. "Fundamentally, Peace Shield gives the Royal Saudi Air Force the beginning of an ability to conduct full airpower," he said. "They can go get the other guy back, or regain lost territory." Or for that matter, the general might have added, the Saudis do not even need to wait to get the other guy back. They do not have to regain lost territory. They can hit him first.

WHEN site N-4 was being built, a Filipino laborer mysteriously vanished. He had been assigned to one of the crews that had been clearing the summit for the huge radar arrays, but after a lunch break, he was reported missing. The Saudi security team began their search immediately. One fear was that he had fallen off the mountaintop. Another was that he was a spy. When he did not return to camp by the next morning, the Saudis decided it did not really matter. By now he was either dead or back in Israel. But that afternoon he returned, walking toward the summit like a man who had been through an ordeal. His movements were unsteady, and his eyes seemed to be fixed on some distant point. He was immediately examined, but he had no broken bones or even any cuts and bruises. When he was asked what had happened, he refused to answer. He seemed in shock.

Finally, after some prodding, he managed to tell a bit of what had occurred. The way one of the site supervisors, a retired American Air Force officer, remembered the story, the Filipino explained that he had wandered off to explore the mountain during his lunch break. His curiosity had led him to a cave. But when he entered the cave—and by this point in his narrative the Filipino's speech was not simply halting, he was in tears—it was as if he was trapped. Trapped? they challenged. There was a ghost, he said at last. This spirit kept him prisoner. It sang for him. It spoke to him. It haunted him. It was beautiful, and it was torture. When the spirit finally let go of him, he escaped.

The Filipino was sent back to Tabuk the next morning. There was no point, his supervisors decided, in keeping a mentally unbalanced worker at the site. Who knew what he would be seeing next on the mountaintop?

THE huge radars on the summit of Jabal al Lawz were aimed toward Israel. They looked out across the vast plain where the Israelites had camped, over the desert wilderness, and beyond to the Red Sea. Microwave links for the system were hidden in a secret military base outside Elim, an electronic intelligence fortress built adjacent to the caves that had been home to Jethro and his son-in-law Moses. The computers at the mountain were directly tied to an underground sector operations center just outside Tabuk. This command post was hidden in the King Abd al-Aziz Military City, one of the sprawling, modern-day desert forts that ring the kingdom. And in a remote center of this military city, buried deep below the sand in bunkers reinforced with concrete and steel, was an arsenal of the East Wind intercontinental ballistic missiles from China.

If the order were given to attack Israel, the destruction of the Jewish state would be coordinated from Jabal al Lawz. The mountain of Moses, where an angry, bellicose God had filled the sky with smoke and thunder and vowed the total destruction of Israel's enemies, had been transformed into an instrument of modern annihilation. With a terrible symmetry, a myth—if that indeed is all it is—had reached across the centuries. Mount Sinai was once again home to a warrior God.

If they were unfaithful, Moses had warned the Israelites, "The Lord will bring a nation against you from afar, from the end of the earth, which will swoop down like the eagle—a nation whose language you do not understand, a ruthless nation, that will show no regard and the young no mercy."

BUT perhaps not yet. Project Falcon was not complete. The missiles were in place. The command and control launch system was operational. However, the Saudi Higher Officers' Committee still had not been able to fulfill the king's order to arm the weapons with nuclear warheads. The $5 billion paid to Iraq was wasted. Saddam, even before he was a declared enemy, was too shrewd to share his nuclear weapons research with the kingdom. The purchase of the Chinese reactors had not been finalized; in fact, there had been no assurances that it ever would be. And in their increasing desperation, the Saudi officers in charge of the program turned foolish. Just before the start of the Gulf War they gave $15 million as a down payment to members of the Russian mafia for the purchase of $75 million worth of red mercury, which, the Saudis believed, was a substance that could be used to make a nuclear bomb. In reality, it had no fissionable potential at all. The $15 million was paid to con men. And it was only after the money was spent that the Saudis began to wonder if the sellers were not Russians but Israelis. Meanwhile, in the glass-walled complex at Al Sulayyil, teams of scientists and engineers continued their work. The Higher Officers' Committee assured the king that these researchers were making great progress. It would not be long before Project Falcon would be completely operational. It was, they believed, Allah's will.

BUT what about the treasure? Did the Saudis know that site N-4 was Mount Sinai? Did they realize that whatever was unearthed at Jabal al Lawz was potentially priceless, a portion of the gold of Exodus? This, too, was a royal secret. And even the few, purposefully guarded comments the kingdom was willing to make have been frequently revised.

After taking two weeks to consult with officials in Riyadh, a spokesman at the Saudi embassy in Washington stated that the kingdom had never authorized any excavation at Jabal al Lawz. When the point was argued, he insisted, "Categorically and without exception, not a single rock has been overturned."

Within days of this assurance, Dr. Abdullah Saeed Abu Ras, assistant deputy minister for antiquities and museum affairs, offered a different truth. "We would like to inform you," he wrote, "that our Ministry has conducted an extensive survey and excavation work at and around Jabal al Lawz. . . . The results of our survey and excavation research work strongly suggest that the site does not have any similarities to the Mount of Moses. . . . Therefore the Mount of Moses is naturally in the Sinai and not anywhere else."

Which might be true. But then again, the deputy minister's concluding paragraph stated: "It is the normal practice of our ministry to fence archaeological sites all over the country to safeguard them from intruders and trespassers, and hence the site of Jabal al Lawz is also fenced under this scheme and not due to any other reason."

He did not mention Peace Shield or Project Falcon. Or the $30 million the U.S. Air Force International Affairs Division acknowledged had been spent to transform the mountain into a military facility.

And the gold? Were Saudi officials being less than forthcoming about that, too? Fasold's frequency device had indicated there were large amounts of gold buried near the pillars at the base of the mountain. He had even seen a glittering piece of jewelry that had been dug up. Two years later, Williams saw the enormous pit that had been dug at precisely the spot where Fasold had determined the treasure was buried. Was the Al Saud family hiding another treasure in its vaults, one more immense than all its oil riches, one more valuable, more sparkling than all the crown jewels?

A national archaeological museum is presently under construction in Riyadh. Saudi Arabia is still struggling to pay off its $55 billion Gulf War debt. With the decline in oil prices, the kingdom has had to cut back on school construction. Medical services, once the pride of the government, have declined as unpaid hospital staff have staged work slowdowns. The state electric utility cannot meet the demand for connections and new homes remain dark. The Royal Defense Ministry has had to renegotiate its payment schedules on arms sales with five U.S. manufacturers. And yet the kingdom is purposefully spending more than a billion riyals—about $286 million—on a new museum. Although it will not be completed until the year 2000, Saudi officials have already boasted that its opening exhibition will attract international attention. "It will surprise the world," a member of the Saudi Ministry of Antiquities promised.

"THIS could only happen to the Jews. We find Mount Sinai—and it belongs to the Arabs."

This was the assessment, one part joke to an equal measure of exasperation, offered by an Israeli security official who had attended government meetings where Jabal al Lawz was discussed. The consensus at these sessions, he explained, was that even if it were possible to prove that Jabal al Lawz was the site where God had given His laws to the ancient Israelites, there was little the modern-day state of Israel could do about it—unless, of course, it was prepared to go to war.

Unfortunately, it was pointed out at one of the initial discussions, there was precedent not only for Saudi Arabia's control of the mountain but also for its ownership of any artifacts found at the site. In 1994, Israel had turned over to Egypt eight hundred cartons of antiquities its archaeologists had uncovered during the state's fifteen-year occupation of the Sinai Peninsula. At the time, the Israel Antiquities Authority had publicly said the country was committed to honoring the 1954 Hague Convention on returning archaeological finds to their country of origin.

Treaties, however, could if necessary be broken. It was the political consequences of any announcement that Jabal al Lawz was Mount Sinai that filled the Israeli government with dread. What sort of unthinkable concessions would the Saudis ask in return for allowing Jewish tourists and pilgrims to visit the site? In the past, secret preliminary discussions with representatives of the royal family had abruptly ended when the princes insisted on tying Saudi recognition of Israel's right to exist to the return of Jerusalem to the Arabs. Like the sacred Tomb of Patriarchs in Hebron, Jabal al Lawz would immediately become a fact of ancient history that would make a modern peace with the Arabs even more difficult. In Israel, history was fate.

It was decided that the state of Israel would not demand that its archaeologists and scientists be allowed access to determine if Jabal al Lawz could be Mount Sinai, at least not for the time being. Peace, if it ever came, would create new possibilities. Besides, it was passionately argued, the specific location of the mountain was not vital to Judaism. What continued to matter were the moral principles and laws that were articulated at Sinai. It was those ideas that transformed slaves into the Jewish people, that gave them the courage and the will to survive generations of Amalekites intent on destroying them, and that culminated in the founding of a nation in the promised land. If the state of Israel were to survive, it would be necessary to focus on what Mount Sinai had become.

And so, in the summer of 1996, a group of Israeli Air Force officers was sent to Fort Rucker in Alabama for special training. They were being taught to fly AH-64 Apache attack helicopters. The drill was to fly in fast, at 50 knots, and low, under radar, until an enemy fortification was in sight. While the pilots kept the birds hovering at about 100 feet, the front-seated gunners would make sure their optical equipment had zoomed in precisely on the targets. Then they would open fire. The first wave would be 2.75-inch rockets that would blanket the area. Next they would let loose with laser-guided Hellfire missiles. And if anything was still standing, they would open up with their 30-mm canons, each projectile armed with an explosive tip.

They were being trained to wipe out fixed radar installations like site N-4. If it became necessary, the Israeli Air Force was prepared to attack and destroy Mount Sinai.

43

BOB Cornuke returned to his hillside apartment in Colorado Springs and, full of an uneasy joy, moved back in with his wife. But he was a changed man. When Moses had come down from Mount Sinai, the Bible said, the experience had been so transforming that his face gave off beams of light. The prophet had to wear a veil. For Cornuke, too, the trip to the mountain—his entire adventure—was so overwhelming that it left him, he was certain, glowing with his own sort of radiance. Look what he had accomplished, he told himself. He had followed in the footsteps of the children of Israel to Mount Sinai. He had crossed the Red Sea, journeyed through the wilderness to camp at Elim, and had come to the mountain of God. Even more, he had climbed to its peak. He had stood where Moses had spoken with God. He had seen the altar of the golden calf, the boundary markers, the pillars of cut stone. He had proved that the Bible was not myth, that Moses was not a fictional character, that the story of the Exodus was not merely plausible—it was true, it had happened. How could his life ever be the same?

But one thing still troubled him: Why? Why had he been chosen for this special knowledge? What was he supposed to do with this gift?

He got the answer to those questions without warning late one afternoon as he was walking back to his apartment. It was just starting to snow, the sky was a deep slate gray, and as he turned the corner he saw his wife walking with another man. From the way they were with each other, Cornuke knew that they were a couple. His wife, he suddenly realized, loved someone else.

He was ruined. It was the hardest moment of his life. Worse, he could not seem to get over it. In the months that followed, it would not go away. He lived and relived it until it became all that he had. Each new day was filled with the same constant, inconsolable hurt. He was lost, and there was no way out.

But in the end there was. He believed. He knew there was a God. His trip to Jabal al Lawz, he began to understand, had been a preparation for this ordeal. It would be the most colossal sort of ingratitude, of arrogance, to ignore God's love. Who was he to murmur? To get caught up in obsessing over false idols? He would, with God's help, get through this.

And in time he did. It was a struggle, but he continued marching through his own wilderness until he arrived at a better place. He fell in love, and this time his marriage, he liked to tell people, was sweet with milk and honey. Grateful, he became a born-again Christian and took a job with an ecumenical religious foundation. And he was living contentedly in this promised land when, once again, Larry Williams reached out to him and turned everything upside down.

FOR Williams, there had been no peace. The triumph of his accomplishment had lost its initial exhilaration. That Jabal al Lawz was Mount Sinai he had little doubt. But what continued to gnaw at him, what he kept on trying to work out as he ran along the beach or sat in his study staring moodily out toward the vast blue Pacific, was another unsolved mystery. In the course of his great adventure, he had avoided or pretended not to notice the clues that, he now acknowledged, were as visible as the trail of footprints his Nikes made in the wet sand each morning during his daily run.

Oh, he congratulated himself, he had been inventive. When he needed a master villain, he had made Nikoli his Moriarty. After all, it was easy, almost logical, to believe that the commodities trader would have gone to the trouble of hiring Peter, the two women from the bar, even the thief who ransacked his hotel room. But when he added the events in the desert to the mystery, he realized this was a convenient simplification. The complicated causality of all that had happened in Saudi Arabia could not be traced back to a mischievous Turk out to make a buck. No, he decided, Nikoli was a false lead. The broker was genuinely ignorant of the larger intrigues that had manipulated their expedition. An explanation of what had happened in London, he came to believe, would not be revealed until he understood what had happened in the desert. Who had spied on them? Why were there soldiers at the mountain? Who had interrogated them? And what had he really wanted to know? Williams struggled with these questions over and over in his mind and he still did not have a clue.

It was Sherlock Holmes, Williams remembered, who advised that if you were stuck between the improbable and the impossible, simply rule out the impossible and you had your answer. But when Williams tried, even the improbable seemed impossible.

So he attempted to put all this aside and focus solely on the ancient mystery. He was secure in his conviction that the Bible's clues had led him to Mount Sinai, and he threw himself into the exercise of writing an account of what he had seen on the mountain. Very purposefully, he expurgated this report of all the lingering mysteries. He did not want to detract from what he and Cornuke had accomplished. Besides, he tried to convince himself, these other issues were irrelevant. Look what he had done! He was, he became fond of saying, another Schliemann but with his own Troy, another rich amateur who had made a spectacular archaeological discovery that would fill the professionals with envy. He had discovered the holiest place on earth.

But after Williams had finished writing his account, he was unsatisfied. He remained full of questions and suspicions, and in this brooding mood, he reached out to Cornuke for help. When Williams called his friend and told him what he had worked out and where this theory was taking him, Cornuke said he did not believe it. "Ridiculous," he said. Before a week had passed, however, Cornuke called back. He was not convinced, but now that he thought about it, he was, he had to admit, curious. Through friends he had become acquainted with U.S. Senator Bill Armstrong. "Why don't I run this by him? See if he can use his connections to get a lead on any of this?" Cornuke suggested.

"Please," Williams begged.

When Cornuke met with the senator in his office in Denver, the man listened attentively. He seemed to follow Cornuke's account of what they had discovered at Jabal al Lawz with genuine interest. But when Cornuke began talking about the soldiers at the mountain and his strange arrest, the senator seemed to lose interest. I'll have to get back to you on that, Cornuke remembered the senator telling him, and by the way he said it, Cornuke was convinced he would never hear from the man again.

But he was wrong. About a month later he got a call that Senator Armstrong wanted to see him. And when Cornuke arrived at his office, the senator shook his hand and suggested that they go for a ride. His mother, he explained, was sick and he was on his way to see her. When they were in the parking lot and sitting in the senator's blue Chevy, Armstrong turned to Cornuke and said he had followed up on their last conversation. What he had found out, he said, had persuaded him that perhaps it would be better that they speak where no one could be listening.

Suddenly, Cornuke was shaken, but he was not so uneasy that he could not remember precisely what the senator went on to say. "This is bigger than you realize," he was told. "It involves the national interest. . . . It's more important than you understand." The senator's advice to Cornuke as they drove in his car across town was succinct. "Just let it go. Drop it," he said.

Cornuke was eager, even content, to do just that. From his perspective, all the answers he needed could be found in the Bible. He had solved one mystery, and that was enough.

But Williams would not be deterred. The senator's comments were, he believed, another disconcerting clue. But where did it lead him? He still did not know who had reached out and decided to manipulate his life. Despite all his theorizing, he could not climb to the top of this mountain. And the frustration was taking its toll.

At last it was his turn to understand. It was the night of November 3, 1995, and like people all over the world, he was caught up in following the news from Israel. Prime Minister Yitzhak Rabin had been assassinated following a speech at a political rally in King's Square in Tel Aviv. Williams watched television report after report with an increasing sense of numbness. It remained incomprehensible, yet his attention was fixed by a morose, almost obsessive fascination.

Then all at once he saw a face he recognized. It was only for a second, and if Williams had blinked or turned his head, he undoubtedly would have missed him. But standing in the background of a cluster of Israelis, pressed up against the wall as if trying to hide, was the man who had interrogated him in the desert. He now wore a suit jacket and a white shirt with an open collar, but he had the same reasonable, intelligent, and completely unmistakable face. There was no doubt that he was the same man. And at that moment, Williams' suspicions started to head down a clear path. He did not understand everything that had happened to him, but it was a beginning.

In time, after months of prolonged reflection, he found himself turning repeatedly to the same chapter in the Bible for both solace and inspiration. It was the story of how Jacob had followed the cunning instructions from Rebekah, his mother, to trick Isaac, his blind father, into giving him a blessing. It was an ancient tale about deception and manipulation. And yet, Williams became convinced, it was not all that dissimilar to what had happened to them.

For in their ignorance, both he and Cornuke might as well have been as blind as Isaac. They had had no idea that from the very beginning—perhaps even from the day Cornuke had applied for his visa to enter Saudi Arabia—they had been targeted. From nearly the moment they had decided to go to Jabal al Lawz, they had become unknowing players on a world stage, unintentional actors in an international intrigue that was being scripted by a sly and manipulative Rebekah. They had been, he now realized, unwitting foot soldiers in the long-running battle of Jews against Arabs.

The way Williams worked it out, the entire mystery came down to this: the Israelis wanted to know what sort of military installation the Saudis were building at Jabal al Lawz, and he and Cornuke had been conscripted—without their consent, without even their knowledge—to help them find out. They had been spies, and they never even realized it.

Williams was as distrustful as ever of simple explanations, but when, with the advantage of his new insights, he reviewed all that had happened, a convincing logic emerged. He now was certain that Warren and Nikoli were as ignorant as he was of what had occurred. Neither of them was innocent, but in this instant, he felt they were not guilty. Peter, the ubiquitous driver, had said he was Lebanese, but it was more likely that he was an Israeli. He was there, like the bearded man on the motorbike, perhaps even the two hookers, and certainly Abu, the boatman, to learn if Williams and Cornuke were really who they said they were, adventurers off to Mount Sinai. And if they were, the agents' responsibility was to make sure the two men got there. That was why Peter helped him get their visas. But precisely how he managed that left Williams at a loss. It was a mystery that, he believed, only the Israelis could solve.

Unless Peter was, in fact, a Saudi agent. And if so, Williams was confronted with new contradictions. It was possible, he had to admit, that Peter had been assigned by the Saudi Intelligence Service to monitor their activities. And if he approached the puzzle from that perspective, then an entirely different scenario began to take shape. In this one, the Saudis were using them as bait, believing from the start that they were Israeli spies. Perhaps the Saudis had let them enter their kingdom so that an entire Zionist network of spies would be exposed.

Once he started thinking this way, Williams began to realize there were no certainties—anything was possible. It was a world filled with deceptions. Still, when he reviewed the events in the desert, he came to believe once more that it had been the Israelis who had been pulling the strings. After all, the interrogator in the hut was, he now knew, an Israeli, and he had been aware of their every move. Undoubtedly, the headlights shining into their camp each night were from Israeli vehicles. They had come to watch over them, to see that they were protected until they made it to the mountain. So, Williams decided, perhaps he should not be angry. Without the Israelis' help, they might not have made it to Jabal al Lawz.

But Williams also came to realize that nearly all he had was theories. If he wanted facts, he should have asked the man in the hut. Or Peter. Or Abu. But he never had, and there would be no answers. Except for one. Yes, he had said with genuine pride and wonder to Cornuke just moments before they raced back to the fence, it really was Mount Sinai. Like the blessing Jacob had received, that discovery could not be taken away from them, and in the end that was all that mattered.

IT was not long after that when Williams made up his mind to get rid of his Rolls. He bought a van, and when people at the club asked him why, he simply shrugged. What he did not feel like telling them was that he could no longer see the point of all that flash. He had gone off to the other side of the world looking for a fortune in ancient gold; and all he had returned with was a little rock as black as the darkest night that he had found on the top of a mountain. How could he explain to them that he believed this was treasure enough?

Afterword

In May 1997, nearly nine years after Cornuke and Williams returned from Jabal al Lawz, a new edition of the *HarperCollins Concise Atlas of the Bible* was published. It was the combined work of an international team of fifty eminent archaeologists, linguists, epigraphers, geographers, interpreters of ancient texts, geologists, and historians. Its editor was Dr. James B. Pritchard, a noted author, a recipient of the Gold Medal Award for Distinguished Archaeological Achievement from the Archaeological Institute of America, and until his retirement a professor of religious thought and curator of biblical archaeology at the University of Pennsylvania. It was Dr. Pritchard's intention that this new edition of the *Atlas* should be authoritative. In an interview about the forthcoming volume shortly before his death in January 1997, Dr. Pritchard said, "Geography is something we all have in common. We may not agree on who, what, when or why things happen, but we do have to agree on where."

In this new edition, a map tracing the route of the Exodus indicates that there are two "probable and possible" locations for Mount Sinai. One is at the traditional spot in the southern tip of the Sinai Peninsula near St. Catherine's Monastery. The other location is across the Gulf of Aqaba, in the northwestern corner of Saudi Arabia. It is the mountain known as Jabal al Lawz.

Author's Note

This is a true story.

It is largely Larry Williams' and Bob Cornuke's story. They are the sources for most of the events and most of the directly quoted dialogue. But it is also the story of the times in which they lived. And to tell that part of the story, I had to reach out to a variety of sources in government and in the public sector.

Also, while this is a work of nonfiction, I have taken certain small liberties. The names of a few minor characters have been changed and their descriptions have been altered. In order to tell the story more effectively, I have compressed the timing of certain events. These few concessions to the demands of the narrative, as well as specific attributions for each of the various aspects of this story, are clearly documented in the chapter-by-chapter notes on sources that follows.

Notes on Sources

As a young boy listening to the story of the Exodus being told at the Passover seder, I was captivated by the magic and adventure of the tale. A burning bush. Plagues. A sea that split in two. Manna from heaven. And a million people heading off into the desert with Pharaoh's chariots in pursuit. It did not matter—in fact, it never crossed my excited mind to wonder—if this was a true story. I was too enthralled.

In college and graduate school, it was not the miraculous but the worldliness in the drama of the Exodus that attracted me. Rereading the biblical chapters from this mind-set, I focused on a political story about the formation of a people: their escape from oppression and their journey—both a literal march and a moral transformation—to a promised land. Again, it did not matter if it had happened exactly as the Bible said it did. The Book of Exodus was one of the defining metaphors of Western thought: a model for action.

And now I have set out to tell a story that owes something to both of these personal experiences with the Bible. *The Gold of Exodus* has its beginnings in the supernatural, in the biblical tales of an ancient time when God visibly and directly intervened in the lives of mortals.

Yet this book is also a contemporary narrative of adventure and politics, a drama where a belief in the sacred had worldly consequences. Further, it is a reporter's account: a true story. Quite a balancing act, I admit. Therefore, I think it would be valuable—perhaps even necessary—to share with the reader how I shaped the story and what standards I used in putting together my book: how I arrived at the truth.

First, as much as I would like to, I don't think I can responsibly dodge the unarticulated question that runs through this book: Is the author insisting the Bible is true? Is this book written with the conviction that, to cite one extraordinary example, God descended from the Heavens to give Moses two stone tablets? Or is the author telling his story guided by another hardheaded attitude—that the Bible is merely literature? A fiction?

My own beliefs fall (conveniently, I realize) somewhere in the middle between such complete fundamentalism and total secularism. This book was written from a perspective that sees the Book of Exodus as a drama based on true and historically verifiable events. After the Jews left Egypt, *something* monumental happened at a mountain known as Mount Sinai. It was an event that transformed a nomadic tribe of former slaves into a nation, that is, into a unified people who now shared common laws. To my mind, the event was poetically, even mythically described in the Bible. But it was also real and transforming—and there was a Mount Sinai.

And I believe that Larry Williams and Bob Cornuke succeeded in finding the historic site described in biblical literature as the mountain of God. It was precisely where the Bible said it would be. The versions of the Book of Exodus that I used as references (and often quoted in the course of this book) were Dr. J. H. Hertz's English translation of *The Pentateuch* and *The New Oxford Annotated Bible,* edited by Herbert G. May and Bruce Metzger.

At the same time, *The Gold of Exodus* is also an adventure story. My goal was to create a dramatic narrative, a yarn, if you will, that is fact-based: It did happen. My primary sources for this aspect of the book were the memories of Larry Williams and Bob Cornuke. They were most cooperative witnesses, spending days sharing their biographies (and, in Williams' case, providing the quoted newspaper accounts of his political contests and SEC battles) and the specifics of their trips. And when the manuscript was finally finished, they kindly read through the pages and pointed out my factual errors (all were corrected) and offered their subjective comments (here I was less cooperative; there was some give-and-take discussion).

In the great majority of instances, Cornuke's and Williams' recollections were in agreement; however, there were a few times when I had to choose between conflicting versions of events (for example: Who was at the wheel after they were led at gunpoint from the hut and went off toward Tabuk?). In the end, I went with the version that to my mind made the most sense. Still, it would be a large vanity to assume I always was right. Also, when I write what was going on in either of the men's minds at a given moment (as, for example, in their nighttime climb to the summit of Jabal al Lawz, or when Williams' hotel room was ransacked), these are not imagined emotions. I have reported precisely what I was told (after, I admit, much probing). There was, however, one accommodation to the narrative. In order to give the reader a more accurate appreciation of the drama that Cornuke and Williams ultimately were caught up in, I condensed the chronology of their journey. For those readers wanting a more meandering account of their trips, I would suggest reading Larry Williams' informative and charmingly written *The Mountain of Moses,* privately published by Wynwood Press. Also like Williams in his account, I found it necessary not to reveal the true identities of some of their academic sources (e.g., the professor) and to use fact-based composites for a few of the minor characters (e.g., Nikoli and Warren). Actions and statements by these minor characters are, however, accurately depicted.

Additionally, I conducted supplementary interviews with Dave Fasold in the garage in southern California that serves as his makeshift office/command center, and I read with great enjoyment his witty account of his trip to Jabal al Lawz, which he published in several editions of his newsletter. Further, Ron Wyatt's videos and his newsletter (*Discovered!*) proved a valuable source of information, as, to a lesser extent, did our several telephone conversations.

On still a third level, this is also a book about international politics and the intelligence agencies that influenced and manipulated world events—as well as the lives of Cornuke and Williams. My research for this part of the story was facilitated by several occurrences. In my work as a reporter for *The New York Times* and in my book about the Walker spy case, I had made valuable contacts with agents and officials in both the U.S. and Israeli intelligence communities. Years ago, Israeli officials even went as far as to arrange a clandestine interview between Bashir Gemayel and myself in his fortress headquarters in Lebanon. This arrangement, of course, was as much in the Israelis' interest as it was in mine. They were eager to learn what the leader of their then still secret ally, the Christian Lebanese, would say to a member of the Western press; and I was out to get a scoop. My relationship with Israeli intelligence officials continued to be productive when I wrote this book; and, as always, I realized their cooperation was prompted by their own veiled agenda.

Another fortuitous event: In May of 1994, Mohammed Khilewi, the second in command at the Saudi mission to the United Nations, left his post and sought political asylum in the United States. He took with him a mountain of incriminating documents, including detailed accounts of the Saudi effort to get a nuclear weapons system. These documents were given extensive coverage in the British press (in July 1994, particularly in *The Sunday Times*). And, more important as far as research for this book was concerned, their publication helped create an atmosphere that encouraged individuals at several U.S. intelligence agencies to be forthcoming. But there was something else that also got people in the U.S. military and intelligence communities talking with surprising candor about Saudi Arabia's Project Falcon. In 1995, HRH General Khaled bin Sultan published his own account of the kingdom's forces during the Gulf War, *Desert Warrior* (New York: HarperCollins). Many knowledgeable people—that is, spooks and soldiers—thought this account was fanciful and self-serving. A lot more thought it was self-aggrandizing fantasy. They couldn't wait to set the record straight; and I was an attentive audience for their eyewitness stories. Of course, these conversations were conducted with one caveat: The intelligence operatives insisted that their identities be protected.

Much of what was happening at Jabal al Lawz was, however, on the record—if one was willing to dig. There was an English-speaking site manager—Col. (ret.) Jack Fisher—who granted interviews both at the site and by phone from Saudi Arabia. Joe Irvin, the Hughes Aircraft representative in the kingdom, was also helpful. Promotional pamphlets were eagerly provided by the manufacturers of much of the strategic equipment that was installed at the mountain ("Excellent Environmental Clutter Rejection, Enhanced Siting Adaptability" bragged Lockheed Martin in its brochure on the FPS-117 Solid-State Radar). Lieutenant Colonel Ron Espenshade, Deputy Under Secretary of the Air Force for International Affairs, Saudi Arabia Division, and Michael W. MacMurray, Assistant Secretary of Defense, Near Eastern and South Asian Affairs, kindly made available many of the unclassified U.S. government documents that played a vital role in the creation of Saudi Arabia's "Peace Shield" system. And there were informative articles in *Aviation Week & Space Technology* (5/29/95) and *Jane's Defence Weekly* (11/13/93) that further detailed the progress of the project.

By the time I and my research assistants finished conducting our interviews, we had compiled an inventory of 237 separate conversations. But this was nothing compared to the small mountain of books we eagerly (at least at first) went through. When this literary journey was completed, several titles stood out (in addition to those that have already been mentioned), which I would draw to the attention of anyone interested in doing his own supplemental reading. In no particular order of preference, they are:

Exodus and Revolution, Michael Walzer. New York: Basic Books, 1984.

Mystery on the Mountain, Theodor Reik. New York: Harper & Brothers, 1959.

Treasures from Bible Times, Alan Millard. Belleville, Michigan: Lion Publishing, 1985.

The Saudis, Sandra Mackey. New York: Penguin Books, 1990.

Saudi Arabia: The Coming Storm, Peter W. Wilson and Douglas F. Graham. Armonk, New York: M. E. Sharpe, 1994.

Territory of Lies, Wolf Blitzer. New York: Harper & Row, 1989.

Dangerous Liaison: The Inside Story of the U.S.-Israeli Covert Relationship, Andrew and Leslie Cockburn. New York: HarperPerennial, 1992.

Every Spy a Prince, Dan Raviv and Yossi Melman. Boston: Houghton Mifflin Co., 1990.

Veil: The Secret Wars of the CIA, Bob Woodward, New York: Simon & Schuster, 1987.

Anyone interested in the world of biblical archaeology would, I think, be fascinated by reading both of the journals edited by Hershel Shanks, *Bible Review* (*BR*) and *Biblical Archaeology Review* (*BAR*). The issues are consistently well written, informative, and, perhaps most impressive, manage to be both provocative as well as authoritative. And it was while I was rather absently browsing through the pages of *BAR* in the course of a plane ride to a wedding in Los Angeles in June 1994, that I first learned about Larry Williams and Bob Cornuke and their trip to Jabal al Lawz.

The specific sources for the information in each chapter of this book are as follows:

PROLOGUE

Interviews: Larry Williams (LW); Bob Cornuke (BC); Israeli intelligence sources.

Books: *The Mountain of Moses* (*MoM*).

CHAPTER ONE

Interviews: U.S. and Israeli intelligence sources; Lt. Col. Ron Espenshade (RE); Michael MacMurray (MM).

Books, documents, and publications: *The Saudis; Saudi Arabia: The Coming Storm; Desert Warrior;* Defense Security Assistance Agency transmittals; *Aviation Week & Space Technology; Sunday Times* (London); *Times* (London): a series of articles starting in July 1994; *Missiles of the World,* by Michael J. H. Taylor, *World Missile Forecast,* Defense Marketing Services; *Jane's Weapon Systems,* edited by Bernard Blake.

CHAPTER TWO

Patrick Teague is a pseudonym.

Interviews: U.S. military and intelligence sources; NPIC employees.

Books and publications: *The U.S. Intelligence Community,* Jeffrey Richelson; Defense Department's *Multispectral Users Guide; Desert Warrior; Dangerous Liaison.*

CHAPTER THREE

Interviews: U.S. and Israeli intelligence officials; Israeli Air Force officers.

Books: *Territory of Lies; Every Spy a Prince.*

CHAPTER FOUR

Interviews: LW; Dave Fasold (DF); Ron Wyatt (RW).

Publications and documents: *The Noahide Society's Ark-Update,* Fasold's newsletter; *Discovered!,* a publication of Wyatt Archaeological Research; Fasold's contract; *MoM.*

CHAPTER FIVE

Interviews: DF; RW; Jack Fisher (JF).

Publications: DF and RW newsletters.

CHAPTER SIX

Interview: LW.

Publication: *Treasure Hunter,* newsletter published by LW.

CHAPTER SEVEN

Interviews: LW; BC; DF.

Publications: *Forbes* magazine; *Wall Street Journal; Havre Daily News.*

CHAPTER EIGHT

Interviews: LW; BC; DF.

CHAPTER NINE

Interviews: BC; LW.

CHAPTER TEN

Interviews: BC; friends of Cornuke.

CHAPTER ELEVEN

Interviews: BC; LW.

CHAPTER TWELVE

Interviews: BC; LW; friends of Cornuke.

CHAPTER THIRTEEN

Interviews: BC; LW; Hershel Shanks; Prof. Frank Moore Cross; Prof. Kyle McCarter; Prof. R. Machinas; academic sources.

Books and publications: *Landscape and Memory,* Simon Schama; *Mount Sinai,* Joseph J. Hobbs; *MoM, The Mountain of God,* John D. Keyser; *BAR,* 7/85.

CHAPTER FOURTEEN

Interviews: BC; LW; academic sources.

Publications and letter: *BR,* 8/92; correspondence between Prof. Frank Moore Cross and researcher.

CHAPTER FIFTEEN

Interviews: BC; LW; academic sources.

Books and publications: The Book of Exodus; commentaries by Nachmanides, Ovadia of Sforno, Ohr Hachaim, Midrash Rabbah, Ibn Ezra, R. Hanina, Rashi, Tractate Sanhedrin, Tractate Berakoth; *Treasures from Bible Times.*

CHAPTER SIXTEEN

Interviews: U.S. intelligence sources.

Books: *Veil.*

CHAPTER SEVENTEEN

Interviews: BC; LW; Saudi embassy, Washington: Rebecca Haddad, Saeed Alahmed; Israeli intelligence sources; NSA sources; DF.

Books: *Every Spy a Prince; The Israeli Secret Service,* Richard Deacon.

CHAPTER EIGHTEEN

Interviews: U.S. and Israeli intelligence sources.

Books and articles: *Every Spy a Prince; Dangerous Liaison; Economist,* 9/24/88; *Sunday Times,* 11/16/88.

CHAPTER NINETEEN

Interviews: LW; BC; friends of LW.

Book: *MoM.*

CHAPTER TWENTY

Interviews: LW; BC; friends of LW.

CHAPTER TWENTY-ONE

Interviews: LW; BC.

CHAPTER TWENTY-TWO

Interviews: LW; BC.

Document: Letter, George Stephens to LW.

CHAPTER TWENTY-THREE

Interviews: LW; BC.

Books: Commentary edited by Dr. J. H. Hertz, *The Pentateuch; MoM; HarperCollins Concise Atlas of the Bible,* edited by James B. Pritchard.

CHAPTER TWENTY-FOUR

Interviews: U.S. and Israeli intelligence sources; LW; BC.

Books: *Every Spy a Prince; Dangerous Liaison; Operation Moses,* Tudor Parfitt; *MoM.*

CHAPTER TWENTY-FIVE

Interviews: LW; BC; Israeli intelligence sources.

Books: *HarperCollins Concise Atlas of the Bible; Mount Sinai.*

CHAPTER TWENTY-SIX

Interviews: LW; BC; LW's associates.

Book and document: *MoM*; copy of fax.

CHAPTER TWENTY-SEVEN

Interviews: U.S. and Israeli intelligence sources.

Books and publications: "Royal Mess," Leslie and Andrew Cockburn, *The New Yorker,* 11/28/94; *The Saudis;* "In Uneasy Time, Saudi

Prince Offers Hope of Stability," *New York Times,* 1/19/96; *Desert Warrior; Dangerous Liaison; Saudi Arabia: The Coming Storm.*

CHAPTER TWENTY-EIGHT

Interviews: LW; BC; DF; Israeli intelligence sources.

Books and article: *MoM; Every Spy a Prince;* "Israel, Unhappy with U.S., Orbits Its Own Satellite," Clyde Haberman, *New York Times,* 4/6/95.

CHAPTER TWENTY-NINE

Interviews: LW; BC.

Documents: Maps of Saudi Arabia.

CHAPTER THIRTY

Interviews: LW; BC; Peace Shield Managers (PSM).

Book: *MoM.*

CHAPTER THIRTY-ONE

Interviews: LW; BC; PSM.

Book: *MoM.*

CHAPTER THIRTY-TWO

Interviews: LW; BC.

Books and documents: *HarperCollins Concise Atlas of the Bible;* contemporary maps of Saudi Arabia; *MoM.*

CHAPTER THIRTY-THREE

Interviews: BC; LW; DF.

CHAPTER THIRTY-FOUR

Interviews: BC; LW; RW; DF; PSM; Prof. Kyle McCarter.

Book and publications: *MoM; Discovered!;* Noahide newsletter.

CHAPTER THIRTY-FIVE

Interviews: LW; BC; DF; RW.

CHAPTER THIRTY-SIX

Interviews: LW; BC; DF; RW.

Book: *Pentateuch* commentary, edited by Dr. J. H. Hertz.

CHAPTER THIRTY-SEVEN

Interviews: LW; BC; DF; RW; PSM.

Book: *MoM*.

CHAPTER THIRTY-EIGHT

Interviews: LW; BC; DF; RW; PSM.

Book and letter: *MoM;* Dr. Abdullah Saeed Abu Ras, Assistant Deputy Minister for Antiquities, Kingdom of Saudi Arabia, 8/29/95.

CHAPTER THIRTY-NINE

Interviews: Israeli intelligence sources; LW; BC.

CHAPTER FORTY

Interviews: LW; BC.

Book: *MoM*.

CHAPTER FORTY-ONE

Interviews: U.S. intelligence sources: Israeli officials.

Books: *Desert Warrior; Dangerous Liaison.*

CHAPTER FORTY-TWO

Interviews: PSM; JF; RE; MM; Craig Thorsted; Israeli intelligence sources; U.S. military sources.

Articles, documents, and book: "USA, Saudi Arabia Plan Crisis Co-operation," *Jane's Defence Weekly,* 11/13/93; "Peace Shield to Strengthen Saudi Arabia Defense Posture," *Aviation Week & Space Technology,* 5/29/95; Hughes Aircraft Co. press release, 6/11/95; *Desert Warrior;* "How an Insider Lifted the Veil on Saudi Plot for an 'Islamic Bomb,'" *Sunday Times,* 7/24/94; Dr. Abu Ras letter; "Archaeology Thriving in Saudi Arabia," Hamid Abu Duruk, *BAR,* 3/95; Cockburns, *The New Yorker,* 11/28/94; "Saudi Arabia Is Facing Debts and Defections," *Wall Street Journal,* 11/25/94; "Israel Returning Antiquities to

Egypt," *New York Times,* 11/29/94; *God, a Biography,* Jack Miles, New York: Alfred A. Knopf, 1995.

CHAPTER FORTY-THREE

Interviews: BC; LW; Bill Armstrong (In a telephone interview, former Senator Armstrong said: "I don't deny it. It's the sort of thing I might have done. But I don't recall it." He continued, "I just can't recall. But I'm not denying.").

Book: *Wrestling with Angels,* Naomi Rosenblatt and Joshua Horwitz.

AFTERWORD

Book, article, and documents: *HarperCollins Concise Atlas of the Bible*; biography, publicity interviews, and obituaries of Dr. Pritchard collected by the University of Pennsylvania and HarperCollins.

Acknowledgments

I wrote this book sequestered in a tiny room above a pizza parlor on the main street of a small Connecticut town. But, fortunately, I was never really on my own. At every stage—research, writing, and editing—I had help. From the moment (or so it seemed) I latched on to the idea of writing about Jabal al Lawz, Lynn Nesbit and Cullen Stanley were there to cheer me on with their wisdom, advice, and support. I kept turning to both of them for guidance on so many occasions as the idea became a book, and they never let me down.

At Simon & Schuster, this was my fourth book with Fred Hills and Burton Beals. It's a working relationship and a friendship that I have always valued. Leslie Ellen, also once again, played a key role in making sure the finished manuscript read well. And Hilary Black was always efficient and good-natured with her assistance.

Then, once the book was purchased by Castle Rock Entertainment, I found new supporters, friends, and very perceptive readers: Martin Shafer, Liz Glotzer, Jeffrey Levine, and Jim Fredericks. And I owe Russ Smith and John Malkovich; their intelligence was always appreciated. Also, Irene Webb and Bob Bookman played key roles in helping the book move forward toward becoming a movie; and, more important,

I relied on them daily, or so it seemed, for friendship and advice. As I did with Alan Hergott; he's the wisest man I know.

Of course, this book would not have been possible without the cooperation of Larry Williams and Bob Cornuke. From even our preliminary conversations, they were gentlemen. And their humor, thoughtfulness, and intelligence helped make the writing of this book a pleasure. I sincerely hope they are satisfied with the finished product. Also, I owe large debts to my indefatigable research assistants: K. Klass, Geoff Mattson, and the staff at S. Goldman-Otzar Hasefarim.

Then, I'd be remiss if I didn't acknowledge the support of my sister, Marcy, and my buddy Phil Werber. Sure, they both read the manuscript, but the truth is I counted on them for a lot more than that.

Also, Peter Guber offered advice, encouragement, and counsel. I value his friendship.

And at every stage of this process I truly believed I was uniquely qualified to write about a hunt for priceless treasure—because I've found mine. Jenny, Tony, Anna, and Dani—what a blessing.

About the Author

HOWARD BLUM is an award-winning former reporter for *The New York Times,* a Contributing Editor of *Vanity Fair,* and a best-selling author. His previous books include *Gangland* ("A block-buster," *Publishers Weekly*), *Out There* ("A significant journalistic coup," *Kirkus Reviews*), *I Pledge Allegiance . . . The Story of the Walker Spy Family* ("One of the best nonfiction works this year," *Philadelphia Daily News*), and *Wanted! The Search for Nazis in America* ("Such a fascinating story that one is glued to it, sharing its emotions," *The New York Times*). He lives in Connecticut with his wife and three children.

The Gold of Exodus will be produced as a major motion picture by Castle Rock Entertainment from a script by John Sayles.